Shauna Reid grew up in Australia. She enjoys travel, pub quizzes and watching men's tennis. As well as her 'Dietgirl' blog she also writes 'What's New Pussycat?', which has been featured in various newspaper, magazine, TV and radio publications, including the *Sydney Morning Herald*. Shauna is twelve and a half stone lighter than she used to be.

D0063413

THE AMAZING ADVENTURES OF DIETGIRL

Shauna Reid

CORGI BOOKS

TRANSWORLD PUBLISHERS
61–63 Uxbridge Road, London W5 5SA
A Random House Group Company
www.rbooks.co.uk

THE AMAZING ADVENTURES OF DIETGIRL
A CORGI BOOK: 9780552155786

First published in Great Britain in 2008 by Corgi
a division of Transworld Publishers

Addresses for Random House Group Ltd companies outside the UK
can be found at: www.randomhouse.co.uk
The Random House Group Ltd Reg. No. 954009

The Random House Group Limited supports The Forest Stewardship Council
(FSC), the leading international forest certification organization. All our titles
that are printed on Greenpeace approved FSC certified paper carry the FSC
logo. Our paper procurement policy can be found at
www.rbooks.co.uk/environment

Mixed Sources
Product group from well-managed
forests and other controlled sources
www.fsc.org   Cert no. TT-COC-2139
© 1996 Forest Stewardship Council

FSC

Typeset in 11/13pt Sabon by
Falcon Oast Graphic Art Ltd.

Printed in the UK by CPI Cox & Wyman, Reading, RG1 8EX.

2 4 6 8 10 9 7 5 3 1

For Ma, Rhi and Dr G

Introduction

I've got the biggest knickers in Australia.

I stood beneath the clothes line on New Year's Day, looking up at the washing I'd just pegged out. My sister's undies were lacy and impossibly tiny. Mine were made of sensible cotton and three times the width. They billowed in the sticky summer breeze, curved and enormous like the sails of the Sydney Opera House.

Just when did my smalls become so impossibly large?

They were Bonds Cottontails Full Briefs, size 26. I'd purchased them in a value pack of pastel shades – traditional white, baby blue and nasty beige. Now they were so stretched and faded they were almost transparent.

My mother and grandmother used to wear Cottontails and as a child I'd snigger at their gigantic frumpiness. But now not only have I embraced the family tradition, I'm in danger of outgrowing it.

For years I've been waiting for the perfect moment. The sign. The grand epiphany. Just *something* to finally get through to me. I was hoping to hear a voice from above, commanding me to put down the family-size bar of Cadbury's Dairy Milk and take back my life.

'Now is the time, Shauna,' the voice would say. 'Now is the time to go forth and lose your lard.'

But in the end it's just me under the clothes line, shocked and humiliated by the sight of my monster underpants. And I know I've really got to do something this time, because Cottontails Full Briefs don't come any bigger than a size 26.

DAY ZERO

15 January 2001

Half the population of Canberra was in the queue at Weight Watchers, spilling out through the door and down the footpath. We were a motley crew of plump-cheeked grannies, haggard mothers and besuited public servants, united in our determination and/or desperation to make 2001 the Year of Fighting the Flab.

I noted that I was the largest in the line. That's the first rule of Fat Club – when entering a room you have to see if there's someone bigger than yourself, because that could make you feel slightly better. But no such luck for me tonight, just as it always seems to be these days.

I craned my neck to get a look at the scale. It was one of those old-fashioned mechanical ones, metallic and clunky. It appeared to have a 22 stone (140kg, 308lb) maximum capacity. I tallied up all those bowls of Christmas pudding and leftover roast potatoes and had a sickly feeling I was heavier.

Too fat for the scale. I hadn't considered that possibility when I'd boldly declared I was finally going to Do Something About My Weight. I was going to be one of those sad cases you see on the news, so gigantic that they have to be taken down to a heavy vehicle weighing station to line up with cattle trucks and school buses.

I turned around and headed towards the door. But my sister Rhiannon, who had volunteered to tag along, grabbed my arm and thwarted my escape.

'Let's wait until after the meeting and get weighed when everyone else has gone.'

We sat up the back row as the meeting leader began her talk. Her name was Donna and she seemed lovely. She had to be lovely. I desperately wanted her to have all the answers.

They were still weighing the New Year's Resolutionists long after the meeting finished, giving me plenty of time to panic. Finally the room was completely empty save for Donna and her two assistants manning the scale. Even as Rhiannon stepped on, I still contemplated running away. Or waddling away, if you must be technical. But I knew if I ran I'd just wake up tomorrow feeling even worse than I do today.

Rhiannon was informed she had a measly stone to lose. She squeezed my hand and smiled. 'Your turn.'

'Hop on, darling!' said the weigh lady.

'I can't.' I could feel tears gathering. 'I think I'm too big.'

'Too big?' She looked confused. 'For the scale, you mean? It has quite a generous capacity!'

'I know.' I stared at my feet. 'But I think I'm bigger than that.'

She called Donna over and they whispered discreetly. They rummaged around in a cupboard and found an extra weight to hang on the scale, increasing its capacity to 26 stone. It took them ten minutes to find it, because they'd never needed it before. It was buried under a musty pile of discontinued cookbooks.

My face burned with shame as I climbed on. The scale rattled and groaned as Donna fiddled with the weights and tried to make it balance.

'You look like you're about to crack up!' She patted my arm. 'Don't worry. We're here to help you!'

The scale finally settled as I fought back sobs.

'I'm not going to tell you what the scale read,' said Donna as I stepped back down. 'I'll write it on your card but let's not worry about numbers or targets or anything like that for now. You made the first big step coming tonight. Let's just take it slowly from here.'

They were all looking at me with encouraging, sympathetic smiles. Why were they being so kind? I didn't deserve kindness. Anyone who needed the Special Scale didn't deserve kindness. I was so huge she didn't even want to tell me how much I weighed! I fled into a corner and hid amongst the pedometers and Point Free sweeties.

Donna came over and hugged me. The warmth of her gesture unravelled me, and I finally felt the enormity of what I had done to my body.

'You're going to be OK,' she said as I bawled uncontrollably. 'You're not alone.'

I couldn't speak, except to mumble 'sorry' over and over.

I cried in the car the whole way home.

'Donna is right,' Rhiannon said kindly. 'Tonight was

the toughest step. It can only get better from here, I promise.'

But I'd seen the number written on that card – 25 stone 1 pound (159.5kg, 351lb).

Twenty-five stone! And I'm 5′8″ tall, so I need to lose half my body weight just to be considered remotely healthy.

How could one woman weigh so much? Twenty-five stone is not just the equivalent of two people stapled together . . . it's practically the equivalent of two *fat* people stapled together!

Now it's almost midnight. The tears have dried and I'm cradling a cup of diet hot chocolate as I write this; the first entry in my brand new, top secret weblog. I am carrying so much shame and disgust that I've got to let it all out somehow.

I am going to call it *The Amazing Adventures of Dietgirl*. I like the idea of being an obese superhero, trussed up in Lycra and hiding behind a mask. There's a distinct shortage of fat superheroes out there, far slower than speeding bullets and unable to leap tall buildings in a single bound.

I also know it will take some sort of miraculous superhero effort if I'm going to banish over 13 stone. If there's one thing I have taken from today, it's that you have to be your own superhero. I don't want to feel as bad as I did tonight ever again. The only one who can rescue me from this big fat mess is me.

THE BACKGROUND

You may be wondering, how it is possible to weigh over 25 stone and wear size 26 knickers at the ripe old age of twenty-three?

I've been asking myself the same question, so I probably should explain how I managed to acquire such a depressing set of statistics.

I can't remember a time when I didn't feel fat. I don't know how or why it started, but the thoughts were always hovering below the surface.

The first moment of awareness came when I was five years old and starting a new school. My mother held my hand as we walked up the front path. Bees were droning in the bottlebrush shrubs in rhythm with my pounding heart and all I could think was, *'Everyone's going to hate me because I'm fat.'*

I grew up on a farm near a town called Cowra in the heart of rural New South Wales, with Mum, Rhiannon and my stepfather, and we always ate healthy home-cooked meals. There were fresh vegetables from our garden, fruit from our trees and tasty sheep and cows that had made the noble journey from our front paddock to the freezer. It was the sort of wholesome country lifestyle people get all misty-eyed about these days, but it never felt that good. Food was never just food in our household.

I was always a painfully insecure and nervous kid. My parents divorced when I was very young and their relationship was strained. Things were volatile between my mother and stepfather too, so I was always trapped in the middle of one conflict or another.

I spent my childhood with fear and dread constantly gnawing at my insides. It was like living at the foot of a volcano. There'd be long cold months where Rhiannon and I crept around the house, desperately trying not to disturb the ominous calm. Our bodies were always tense and alert to signs of trouble, any tiny changes in the atmosphere or the slightest tremble of the earth. I thought if I could just be a good child, quiet and obedient and perfect, then I'd be able to prevent the next eruption.

But something always set them off again. I'd be despondent for making a mistake, wanting to tear my hair out for being so foolish. It could be as simple as a sideways glance at the television during dinner instead of keeping our eyes on our plates, or not doing the dishes *the very instant* after our meal, or not sweeping the crumbs on the kitchen floor in *the right way*. These incidents would escalate and explode beyond all reason for days on end.

My mother was a Weight Watchers leader. You'd think with that sort of pedigree I'd have grown up to be a glowing picture of health – fighting fat is in my *blood*! But it mustn't have been a very dominant gene.

Every Monday night Rhiannon and I tagged along to Mum's Weight Watchers meeting. We were supposed to sit quietly in a corner and read our books, but this elaborate ritual intrigued me. Why did these women queue up like robots week after week? Why did they give money to the lady just to stand on a scale? And what mysterious power did that machine have to switch their moods to elation or despair with one shrill beep?

After the weigh-in they'd assemble in a circle of clunky metal chairs. Some would crow about losing a pound, some would tell how they'd fashioned a lasagne out of cottage cheese and tinned soup. Some tearfully confessed to scoffing their children's leftovers or the broken biscuits in the bottom of the tin. I began to understand that what you ate and what you weighed was a very big deal.

Sometimes after class Rhiannon and I pretended we were Weight Watching too. We'd take turns on the scale while Mum and her assistant Carol stacked the chairs.

'You've had a great week, pet!' I mimicked as Rhiannon jumped on.

'I switched to Weight Watchers margarine!'

Then we swapped places. I weighed in at five and a half stone (35kg, 77lb).

'Looks like a small gain, dearie.'

'Maybe it's That Time of the Month?' I said. And I had no idea what that meant.

Suddenly Carol appeared behind me and frowned at the scale. 'My *God*! She's big!' She spoke to my mother in outraged tones like I wasn't even there. 'She nearly weighs as much as I do!'

I was never a skinny child but I wasn't exactly fat either. Until that moment I'd hoped my greatest liability was my ginger hair. I did have round, rosy cheeks and rather chubby legs; but it was nothing that I wouldn't have grown out of when I hit puberty. And at nine years old I already towered over Carol, who was a dainty dame of just 4'10".

But I couldn't apply that logic at the time. I finally had confirmation of my darkest fears. I had been labelled. From that moment on her words clanged in my ears and began to take over my life. *She's big! She's big!*

It wasn't long after that incident that Mum put me on my first diet. One day my sister was given a sandwich for lunch and I got a plate of cottage cheese and vegetable crudités instead.

My stomach ached with shame and hunger as I gagged down the lumpy cheese. I'd learned from the Weight Watchers ladies that food was divided into good and bad. In the 'good' camp were vegetables, fruit and rice cakes. Chocolate, cakes and anything remotely sweet and pleasurable were 'bad'. So to be presented with a plate of Good meant there was something Bad about me. You didn't eat Good food because it was wholesome and healthy; you ate it because you didn't want to be fat. So at that moment I knew I'd found yet another way to disappoint.

The more I was forced to eat the Good foods the more the Bad stuff took on an irresistible, forbidden allure.

Throughout primary school I'd covet other people's lunchboxes. My best friend Katie was a rare creature whose mother packed her delicious sweet things for lunch but she seldom wanted to eat them. How could she not be interested in a Wagon Wheel or a Milky Way? Didn't her whole body ache to rip them open?

Eventually my hunger would triumph over my shame. 'Umm . . . are you going to eat that?'

'Nah, I don't want it. Do you?'

'Well, only if you're sure?'

One time Katie gave me some Nutella. It was one of those snack packs with a foil lid and a tiny plastic spoon. I peeled back the foil and the chocolate perfume punched me in the nose. The Nutella looked so smooth and calm in its little box, it seemed a shame to disturb it. But five minutes later it was gone, and I felt the tension in my body ease. I wedged my tongue into the little grooves in the bottom of the tray, making sure I didn't miss anything.

I was always trying to find ways to escape. I spent hours writing plays and 'novels' about faraway places. I read books by torchlight in the bottom of my wardrobe. I was a big fan of Enid Blyton and all her talk of treacle, chocolate cake and midnight feasts at boarding-schools.

I devoured Roald Dahl too. *Charlie and the Chocolate Factory* was an obvious favourite, but I loved *Fantastic Mr Fox* and his network of tunnels underneath the farmers' store sheds. I dreamed of digging my own secret tunnel into a cake factory, and there'd be nothing Mum could do about it.

When I ran out of books I'd read the fridge and freezer

pages of appliance catalogues. I'd stare longingly at the carefully styled shelves, trying to pick my Dream Fridge based on its contents. I loved the rows of condiments and posh bottled water, the celery lounging in the bottom drawer, the watermelon wedge smiling on a platter. And there were always elaborate sundaes in tall glasses. I wanted a family who had a fridge full of sundaes! And a freezer full of ice-cream, too. There was always ice-cream! We had half a cow and a stack of sugar-free stewed fruit in *our* boring freezer.

I began to notice how food was a weapon in my parents' never-ending war. My stepfather started complaining about Mum's Weight Watchers meetings, saying that they took up far too much of her time. At first she protested that she needed the support and accountability to maintain her weight, but eventually she caved in and quit. And then she gave up being leader of our Brownie pack, until all she had left was her teaching job. But that still seemed too much for my stepfather's liking, so he attacked in other ways. We would come home with the weekly grocery shopping and he'd tear through the bags, finding fault with every purchase. He criticized the way she dressed, the way she spent money, the 'lazy' way she dared to spend five minutes drinking a cup of tea when she got home from work.

When my mother started to regain weight, the onslaught was even more relentless. He presided over the contents of her dinner plate, passing judgement on every morsel. Of course he was naturally skinny, so this was an easy way to assert his superiority. I watched my mother trying to steel herself; at first she was angry and defiant, but as the years passed she seemed to get worn down. She'd eat perfectly in front of him, so as not to give him any ammunition, but then I noticed that she'd do the opposite when he wasn't around. One time I hid behind her bedroom door and watched her lift a pile of clothes out of her dresser and retrieve a bar of chocolate. She sat on the bed and put one square after another into her mouth, slowly and mechanically, as if she was in a dream.

The more my stepfather kept on at my mother about her weight, the more she began to do the same to me. Every summer started with a new diet. Maybe she was trying to stop me from turning out like her, or maybe she thought she could protect me from the same kind of suffering. But to me it just drummed in the message that I was deeply flawed, useless and out of control. I was afraid to eat so much as a lettuce leaf in front of my parents. I started to mimic Mum's secretive behaviour, stealing food and lugging it back to my wardrobe hideout. Stray biscuits, hunks of bread, a plastic-wrapped slice of cheese – I'd cram them into my mouth and feel ashamed, comforted and rebellious all at the same time.

The situation was awash with contradictions. Mum would give me salad one day then treat me to an ice-cream cone the next. We'd cook a healthy Weight Watchers recipe for dinner, but then I'd see her dig out a bag of crisps from a secret stash. Then some days Mum would send Rhiannon and me to the takeaway shop for hot chips, and we'd stuff them down as we drove home from school, winding down the windows to let out the greasy smell. We'd stop at a roadside bin to dispose of the wrappers so my stepfather wouldn't find out. I was confused, but revelled in the feeling that the three of us were united in a wonderful conspiracy.

I felt like a secret agent leading a double life. At school I strove to be outgoing and likeable and not give any hint of the madness at home. That was fairly easy to conceal, but there was nothing I could do to hide my body, so I tried to make up for it by being funny. I wasn't one for self-deprecating fat jokes; I couldn't understand why anyone should deliberately draw attention to their flaws. I aimed for general wit and wisecracks, hoping that people would remember me for my punch lines rather than my paunch.

I was an eager scholar too. My studies were an escape, and topping my classes made me feel there was something I could control. School was the only place I could get things right and that gave me a way to make my parents happy. Of course, I took great pains to be modest about my achievements, not wanting to be seen as *too* clever. I was desperate to please my teachers but couldn't risk alienating my peers.

I was amazed that I managed to accumulate so many friends when I got to high school. They'd invite me to their slumber parties and each time I'd have to beg my parents to let me go. I'd run from the car when Mum dropped me off, so scared that she'd change her mind.

Once through the door I was delirious with freedom. My friends laughed at the way I apologetically asked for a glass of water, for permission to sit on that chair, and would they mind terribly if I used the bathroom? But their lives were so foreign to me, so light and ordinary with no need to sleep with your head jammed underneath the pillows.

I'd panic when the food came out, frightened and excited by the array of crisps and pizza and cake. My friends' parents urged me to eat and remarked how strange it was that someone so young was so anxious about food. But I was already caught in the cycle of public dieting and secret eating. I was nine stone and 5'7" tall by the age of fourteen, which in hindsight was healthy, but my sprouting boobs and hips made me even more convinced I was hideous. Why couldn't my friends see that? I was fat. My family were always telling me, so it had to be true.

There are small moments that stand out, seemingly off-hand remarks that stuck under my skin and rotted away for years and years.

On a beach holiday when I was fourteen, my mother looked up from her book and said casually, 'You know, you have a lovely figure; if you could just make it a little smaller.'

Another time I was heading off to a party in a new dress. I felt almost beautiful, especially having lost 15 pounds doing Weight Watchers by Mail.

'What do you think?' I asked my parents.

'You'll be prettier when you lose a bit more weight,' said my stepfather.

I just nodded in agreement.

I stockpiled those idle comments and criticisms in my mind, magnifying and multiplying and turning them into fact. I'd lie in bed and dig my fingernails into my stomach, wanting to tear off my flesh.

It wasn't until I was 15 that my body really began to match my fat thoughts. Mum insisted I get an after-school job to help with my 'confidence issues'. Somehow standing behind the counter at KFC with a spotty face and a hot pink visor didn't seem to boost my self-esteem, it just felt as if I was displaying my loathsome body to a wider audience.

I still curse myself for not finding a job at the supermarket or chemist's. At least then I'd have been stuck behind a till and out of harm's way. But KFC was like waving a deep-fried red flag in front of a bull.

Fast food was a rare treat in our household. We had it maybe once or twice a year on holidays, if Mum hadn't already packed sensible sandwiches on brown bread. But now I had endless access to the Colonel's fine and oily wares. It started with a stray chip here and a Pepsi there, but soon I was eating a full meal during my breaks and then eating dinner when I got home.

They'd give us huge bags of leftovers too. I'd sit on the veranda after a shift, telling Mum I was going to give the dog a chicken nugget, but it was one for the dog and two for me. Or sometimes all for me, while the poor hound sniffed at my greasy shoes. Even as my trousers grew tight I felt brazen and defiant.

My minimum wage finally gave me the means to indulge in all those forbidden foods. By then I'd outgrown the bottom of my wardrobe, so I'd eat my chocolate bars under the covers in the middle of the night, my hands shaking with anticipation and fear. I'd smuggle the wrappers to school the next day, but sometimes I'd forget and stuff them under my mattress. Every now and then Mum would raid my room and lay her findings on the bed like bags of cocaine. She'd stare at me with grim disappointment as I pathetically proclaimed my innocence. All that was missing were sirens and a slobbering sniffer dog on a leash.

By my final year of high school things had completely deteriorated between my mother and stepfather. I studied obsessively, determined to ace my exams. My favourite subject was Modern History, especially the Russian Revolutions. A revolt was conflict I could understand. It had clear origins, crazy characters and confrontation. Nothing made sense at home, but I could shape Russia into neat little essays with logical arguments and a definite ending.

So I holed up in my room, forcing information into my brain and chocolate bars into my mouth. I wanted spectacular results to make my parents and teachers proud and prove to myself I could do something right. Most of all I wanted to earn my escape to university.

Two nights before my trial exams they had the worst argument I could remember. They were outside on the veranda, right beneath my window. I was reading about Stalin and the words swam on the page.

Around midnight Mum came into my room to find me still buried in the books. 'Are you all right?'

I burst into tears. 'I can't do this, Mum.'

'I know, darling.'

23

'I'm trying to block it out but it's hard.'

'I know. I'm sorry.' She was crying too. 'I'll think of something.'

We sat in silence for twenty minutes before she finally said, 'I'll take you to Angela's house.' Angela was one of her closest friends. 'You can stay there until your exams are done.'

'You promise?'

'Yes. Pack up your things and I'll take you into town in the morning.' She squeezed my hand and I wanted to believe her.

I threw all my textbooks and folders and notes into a laundry basket. I packed my school uniforms, hiding a few chocolate bars inside my socks. I could barely sleep, giddy at the prospect of getting away even for a few days.

The next morning the house was strangely quiet. Mum was drinking tea at the kitchen table.

'What time are we going to Angela's?' I whispered.

'We're not.'

'Mum, you *promised*.'

'Look, you don't have to worry, everything's fine now. Just forget about it, please.'

I shook my head and stormed back to my room. I would have slammed the door shut but we weren't allowed to shut our doors. I left the smallest chink of space open so technically I wasn't breaking the rule. I kicked over the laundry basket packed with my stuff and felt disgusted with myself for getting my hopes up. I wanted to scream but I remembered there was carrot cake hidden in my desk drawer, a whole family-size carrot cake with cream cheese icing that I'd bought from the in-store bakery at Woolworth's. I ripped open the plastic box and scooped out a handful, icing and all. I kept scooping and scooping until it was all gone and I was too sick to feel anything.

Something inside me shut down. I drifted through my days feeling numb and detached, as if my body was made out of lead. I'd stare into the distance in my classes, unable to focus, often forgetting where I was. I couldn't sleep and would binge in a trance. But still I pushed on with my studying, anxious not to disappoint.

When my final exams started my head felt like it was packed with cotton wool. I sat down in my Modern History exam, looked at my paper and none of the questions made sense. I'd been up studying until 3 a.m. I stared at the blank page and cried silently for two hours until it was over.

Somehow I still scored well in my other subjects and got into my course. Eventually the fog lifted, perhaps because I knew I was moving away. I chalked up that strange period to exam stress.

By then I'd been working at KFC for three years, and my uniform had gone up a size each year. Mercifully I went off to university just as the side seams split on my size 18 pair of the Colonel's black trousers and I'd reached the last notch on the Drive Thru belt.

In 1996 I started my journalism degree weighing in at 16 stone (101.8kg, 224lb).

I'd always known I loved to write more than anything in the world, so a journalism degree seemed to be a way to write and possibly get a job at the end of it. The only problem was, I turned out to be the world's most rubbish journalist. I could write, but I lacked the requisite passion for news. I hated interviews. I hated waddling into courtrooms or hassling people for quotes. I had an irrational fear of telephones, as though people could sense my fat over the line. My fellow students were brash, confident and opinionated but I just wanted to be invisible. I could barely fit through doors, let alone kick them down in pursuit of a good story.

So I had exactly zero of the qualities required to be a good journalist, but there was no way I could call up my mother and tell her I'd made a terrible mistake. I already felt guilty for all the money she'd spent getting me to university, and guilty for getting away from the farm when she and Rhiannon were still there.

I muddled my way through my degree and spent the three years with a sense of impending doom. The ambitious writer in me longed to write for the campus newspaper or try out for the student radio station, but the Fat Girl was more convincing: *Who'd want to listen to a blob like you?*

Instead I concentrated my efforts into accumulating a shocking amount of weight. My university was in Bathurst, a big town an hour away from home, so I embraced my new-found freedom and the wider selection of fast food outlets. I made a half-hearted attempt to diet for the first month, but then one night at the supermarket I wandered down the frozen aisle and picked up a tub of ice-cream. *I can buy this*, I thought. *I can take it home and eat it all.*

I'd never eaten ice-cream straight from the tub before. There was no one to tell me to *slow down* or that I'd *already had quite enough*. Gleefully, I shoved it into my mouth, loving how it made everything feel cool and calm inside my chest.

Soon I was revisiting every forbidden food from my childhood, in ever-increasing portions. I'd drive the three blocks to the supermarket and pace the aisles, delirious with the possibilities. I'd buy family-size bars of chocolate and demolish them in one sitting. I'd spend an evening toasting my way through a whole loaf of white bread. And then Ferrero brought out their Simpsons collectable Nutella glasses. I fully intended to stop at Homer – after all, how many glasses does a student need? But within two months he was joined by Bart, Krusty, Maggie and Lisa. I told everyone I scraped the Nutella into the bin, but I'd scoffed it all, straight from the jars until my throat hurt.

On my first day of classes I met Peita and Belinda, who became my closest friends throughout my degree. We'd drive laps of the Mount Panorama racing circuit, swap mix tapes, make sarcastic comments during *Days of Our Lives* and just laugh at the world. When we were together I could block out all my loathing and guilt and doubts about the future.

But I tried to confine our friendship to daylight hours. I was terrified of the ubiquitous university activities like bar nights and pub crawls. My body was not designed for dancing, flirting and snogging random strangers. I took up too much space on a dance floor. I hated just going to the bathroom, awkward in my elasticated jeans while everyone else clustered around the mirrors in skimpy out-fits. So I'd hide in smoky corners, feigning merriment and trying to make my drink last for three hours so I wouldn't have to get in everyone's way in the queue for the bar.

Food became my preferred companion. I kept a handy stock of excuses to avoid socializing, like urgent shifts at my part-time job or babysitting emergencies, and as soon as I was alone I'd eat. I'd do the rounds of the Drive Thrus and takeaway shops, picking up fries from here, a burger from there, a dessert from the other side of town. I was careful to spread my custom so I wouldn't be identified as a 'regular' anywhere. Sometimes I'd pull into a dark street and gorge in the car, trying to ignore how my stomach was closing in on the steering wheel. Or I'd come back home and keep my eyes glued to the television to distract myself from how much I was shoving away. I ate swiftly and urgently. Taste was less important than the texture – the fries jabbing the roof of my mouth, the salt stinging my lips, the grease filling up my insides. It was intimate, soothing and exhilarating all at once. It was an event.

But soon enough the trance would break and I'd register the oily wrappers and the crumbs clinging to my belly rolls. And then came the shame and disgust.

Once again I didn't choose my part-time jobs wisely. First there was the coffee shop, with endless cakes and biscuits and siphons of whipped cream that I longed to squirt directly down my throat. Then I saw a vacancy at the local fish and chip shop. Of course they gave me the job; I was a veteran of the deep-fat fryer. It was only two blocks from my house but I drove to every shift. My boss was generous with the freebies too, and on a student budget I pounced on all the hamburgers and chips and oily potato cakes, even though my trousers screamed at me to stop.

By the time I finished my degree at the end of 1998, I weighed 21 stone (133.6kg, 294lb) and was a size 22. For a while I convinced myself that I was just tall and curvaceous, but I'd lost all definition. My waist, hips and boobs blurred into one gelatinous heap of flesh.

Six months after graduation I was still in Bathurst and living alone. Peita and Belinda were now bona fide journalists but all I had was my lucrative fish and chip gig. I felt the fog closing in again. I'd spent the past three years burying my fears in food, becoming increasingly isolated and withdrawn. But now my friends had left there was no need to keep up the pretence. I was so ashamed of my size that I was afraid to go out in public, so I'd stay home and binge or sleep, only venturing out to work, supermarket or Drive Thru.

By then Mum had finally left the farm and was taking a strong interest in my job search. She was also reading a lot of self-help books, so she'd post me job advertisements with encouraging annotations: 'This sounds like you!' and 'Go for it, girl! Best of luck!'

But I felt smothered by the weight of her expectations. I'd done internships at newspapers and glossy magazines, squeezing into my size 22 K-Mart suit and nauseous with panic. I knew I didn't belong in that world. But what else would I do? I couldn't waste all the time and money she'd spent on my education.

I'd divide the advertisements into two piles, *Apply for These* and *If Mum Asks, Pretend I've Applied for These*. But I was forever forgetting which ones were which. She'd drop in to visit and ask how the Search was going and my brain felt tangled up with all the lies. I was exhausted from just trying to create the appearance of normality. I'd hide the dirty dishes inside the oven and pile all my unwashed, unfitting clothes into my car.

One time I got an interview in Sydney and had to ask Mum for money to buy a new suit because I'd outgrown the one she'd bought me just three months before. It wasn't until they asked to see my writing portfolio that I realized I couldn't remember the name of the magazine I was interviewing for. And I'd left my press clips on the bookshelf back in Bathurst. Afterwards I ate three Crunchie bars in quick succession, sobbing at the bus stop and showering my new suit with honeycomb.

I was overwhelmed by disgust and disappointment but my mind felt too soggy to stop it. I shut down completely, not answering the phone and closing the blinds so it looked like I wasn't at home. I spent my days sitting on the kitchen floor crying, or staring in the mirror and fighting the urge to smash the glass.

One night I was at the supermarket, looking for instant mashed potato and canned peas, because by then I couldn't even muster the energy to chew. I wandered the aisles for an hour, blinded by tears and panic because I'd forgotten what I'd come for. And then I looked down and realized I was wearing my pyjamas.

Finally it was Mum who reached out, in her own indirect way. In her latest bundle of job adverts she slipped in a photocopied magazine article titled, 'Are You Depressed?'

I sobbed as I read it, sitting on the kitchen floor in a shirt still crusty with last week's fish batter. She called me that evening and said, 'Shauna, are you OK?' and finally I broke down.

The doctor peered at me over the top of her glasses, and I wondered if she could see right through me. Mum insisted I seek medical attention, but I worried that no matter what I said the diagnosis would simply be, 'FAT!'

'Have you ever experienced feelings of hopelessness?'

'Yes.'

'Constant fatigue?'

'Yes.'

'Loss of appetite?'

'Ha!'

'Suicidal thoughts?'

'Never.' I started to laugh.

The doctor looked up from her checklist and frowned. I decided not to explain that while trapped in the depths of despair I could *never* kill myself, because I couldn't bear the thought of a mortician looking at my naked, obese corpse.

She agreed with Mum that I was clinically depressed. I should have been relieved to have a name for years of shitty feelings, but it seemed like a fancy excuse for my complete inability to get my act together.

But the antidepressants restored me to a fuzzy level of

31

functionality. Soon I was getting out of bed before 2 p.m. and I even opened the blinds. I saw a counsellor who probed away at childhood memories, but I was reluctant to talk. And somehow I managed to get through two months of sessions without once mentioning my weight.

Things started to come together. I finally admitted to Mum that journalism wasn't for me and in mid-1999 I moved to Canberra to begin a six-month diploma in digital publishing. I wasn't put off by the capital city's dull reputation; to me all the government buildings and clean roads felt controlled and orderly, like I desperately wanted to be. The course was a safe option too – it indulged my creative side but I was safely hidden behind a computer screen.

It was also sufficient to convince my mother, my counsellor and myself that things were moving in a positive direction. My studies went so well that I scored a great job before I finished the course: a web editor with an internet start-up company. Finally I was gainfully employed and financially independent. On the surface it looked like a complete transformation.

But I didn't stop eating.

Six months ago Rhiannon moved in with me. She'd spent a year in the USA and returned to Canberra to finish her degree. She came into my life like a cyclone, strong and confident with exotic tales of her life in New York and Chicago. She's two years younger than me but has always seemed to be made of stronger stuff.

'As soon as I graduate and earn some money I'm going

back overseas,' she declared. 'There's a whole other world out there, Shauna. There is life away from that farm.'

It shocked me to hear her mention the past. Despite growing up under the same roof we'd never talked about what was going on, mostly because we were always hiding away in our separate rooms behind almost-closed doors. We ate our meals and did our chores but otherwise avoided the main thoroughfares of the house.

On her first night back in Canberra we got McDonald's and shared a bottle of wine, sitting on the living room floor.

'Does this feel weird to you?' Rhiannon asked suddenly. 'Sitting here in this silence?'

'You mean this genuinely peaceful silence?'

She laughed. 'Yeah. That one.'

Finally after twenty years we were talking and comparing notes. Part of me had always wondered if I'd just imagined things were bad, if it was just my messed-up head interpreting events that way. But as we talked over that bottle of wine I was relieved and comforted to hear my memories being confirmed. Rhiannon made me feel I could stop pretending that I didn't feel bad about it. And the stories of her overseas adventures seemed to prove it was possible to move forward. For the first time I felt a tiny spark of hope that my life could be different.

Last month Rhiannon and I visited Mum in Cowra. I found an old photo album with thirteen years of my annual school pictures, carefully arranged in chronological order. As I flipped through the pages I was completely shocked to see a perfectly normal-looking kid looking back at me. Where were the hideous thighs I remembered? Where was the belly? I just looked like an ordinary, freckle-nosed, red-haired child.

It wasn't until the Year 11 photo that you could see the childhood chub turning into proper fat. But I'd thought of myself as repulsive since I was five years old. How did this happen? Why did Mum put me on all those diets? Why did they tell me I was fat when I wasn't? I'd spent my entire childhood letting my self-loathing dictate everything I said and did. If I hadn't carried that belief for all these years, would my body have turned into this massive, impossible mess?

It wasn't until that moment I felt the anger. I'd dulled my emotions with food for so long that I'd blocked out all the pain, but now I just wanted to point the finger. Perhaps I felt brave knowing Rhiannon was there to back me up.

Mum was in the kitchen starting dinner. I charged over to her, thrust the album into her chest and shouted, 'Why did you do this to me?'

Two decades of repressed fury came tumbling out. Every resentment, every memory. And then Rhiannon joined in with her own list of grievances. My stomach churned with guilt because I knew Mum wasn't the only one involved and she was hurting too. But we couldn't stop the avalanche.

We argued bitterly for hours, right through dinner. Harsh words flew as we chopped up the chicken and stir-fried the vegetables. There was a brief ceasefire when a saucepan of rice boiled over, but once that was cleaned up we began round two. We kept arguing as we ate, between bites or with mouths full. Rhiannon kept the battle raging even with her hands in a sink full of bubbles while I dried the dishes. Eventually it was all too much and everyone was crying. Mum stormed out on to the front veranda.

'Maybe we should go out there,' I said nervously.

'No! We're not backing down,' said Rhiannon.

'But it was hard for her too.'

'I know. But we can't carry this shit around for ever.'

'I guess.'

'This isn't about blame. She just needs to know how we feel.' Rhiannon yanked the plug from the sink. 'We'll drive back to Canberra tonight if we have to.'

After decades of doing everything to avoid conflict it was terrifying and thrilling to deliberately walk right into it. The guilt was overwhelming but I knew Rhiannon was right. I couldn't lock it away any longer.

But we didn't have to drive back to Canberra. Mum came inside and after twenty years we sat down and finally started to talk. In the end I knew she heard us. She simply said 'I'm sorry'. And that's all we'd ever wanted to hear.

*   *   *

Since I crawled out of the shadow of the past I've felt lighter, almost hopeful. But now the present has finally come into full focus. I'd convinced myself I've been happy these past two years, pulling out of the depression and getting a grown-up job and a nice flat and a car that works.

But now all the things I tried to block out are coming at me in little bursts of awareness. How I don't have a life outside work. How I buy a bigger size every time I go to the shops. How in summer my thighs rub together until they bleed. How no matter what fancy things my hairdresser does to my hair she can't disguise my chins. How I'm breathless just walking from the couch to the fridge. How I write emails to my friends instead of meeting them in person. How no matter what crazy angle I hold my camera there's no such thing as a flattering shot.

I looked in the mirror tonight and saw a stranger. I don't recognize this body. There's the same red hair I've always had, but it looks almost comical sitting on top of my big round head, like a cheap toupee. My eyes are just two little dots, lost in the vast sprawl of my cheeks. I look modular and disjointed, as though you could take me apart like a plastic Lego man. I don't look quite real. I wish I could crawl out of my skin and leave it behind.

In that moment under the clothesline, gazing up at my colossal knickers, I saw my life spinning away from me, out of control. I'm twenty-three years old and the highlight of my day is opening a fresh bar of chocolate. Instead of writing or travelling or partying I'm wondering if I can go to the McDonald's Drive Thru again without the staff recognizing me. At some point I convinced myself that this was how my life was meant to be, and I've let my weight smother all my ambitions and dreams. I'm not really living. I'm just idling, merely existing.

So that's why I've got to try and fix this, even though it feels impossible. I've got to see if there's anything on the other side.

YEAR ONE
2001

WEEK 1
16 January 2001
25st 1lb (159.5kg, 351lb)
13st 4lb to go (84.5kg, 186lb)

Day One dawned bright and full of hope. Sunshine blasted through the wooden blinds, bathing my bedroom in an optimistic glow.

Actually it pretty much looks like that every morning; it *is* the middle of summer after all. But maybe it was a dazzling sign that this Day One would be different from all the failed Day Ones that came before.

I've never been an optimist. I like to expect the worst; that way if something good happens it's a nice bonus. But this time I'm desperate to believe in sunshine and new beginnings, because surely there can't be anything worse than last night, sobbing on the scale in front of multiple witnesses.

As the great philosopher Yazz once said, the only way is up. Otherwise I'll die of a heart attack by twenty-five. Or I'll burst out of my trousers in a public place, which would be even worse.

Rhiannon was already up and pouring herself a bowl of muesli.

'Four POINTS with half a cup of semi-skimmed milk!' she announced with a grin.

'Bargain!'

The Weight Watchers POINTS system really irritates me. Why must the word POINTS always be in upper case? It sounds so loud and bossy. And the word POINT itself feels like an accusation, like a nagging schoolmarm poking you in the chest with her bony finger. *Why did you eat that cake, don't you know it's 120 POINTS? Spit out that pizza, it's 35 POINTS per slice!*

But Points are my currency now, the new language of my mealtimes; so I will have to shut up and obey.

I sat on the couch with my own bowl of muesli, looking at my Weight Watchers leaflets neatly fanned out on the coffee table. Diet paraphernalia always fills me with a great sense of purpose. Bring on the guidelines and graphs! Gimme the tools and rules! Lately my only rule has been 'Stuff your face with wild abandon then hate yourself afterwards', so I want to be told what to do. It gives me hope that I could become less hopeless.

I picked up the official Points tracker and stared at all the optimistic white spaces. There was a column for each day of the week, each divided into four boxes for Breakfast, Lunch, Dinner and Snacks. So . . . that's twenty-eight chances not to fuck this up.

I have to make this tracker *perfect*. I want to show it to Donna next Monday and have her tell me it's the best tracker she's ever seen. I want to be the Model Weight

Watcher! I can't bear to think about the horrific amount of weight I must lose, but I *can* focus on seven little days and this stupid Tracker.

I wrote *muesli and milk* in the Breakfast column in my best handwriting.

Rhiannon and I both had the day off work so we launched ourselves into Operation Lard Bust.

My usual half-hearted attempts at losing weight involve me buying a few apples and some rubbery low-fat cheese then hoping for the best. But this time we were on a serious mission. It involved precise planning and organization!

We made lists. We consulted cookbooks. We paced the kitchen like curmudgeonly generals in the Second World War.

I must admit Rhiannon is the brains behind the operation. She's the real superhero of this story; I'm more the bumbling sidekick. At twenty years old she's by far the most intelligent and mature person I know. She tackles problems with a calm and practical mind, whereas I throw my hands in the air and howl like a kicked puppy at the first sign of trouble.

I couldn't ask for a better ally in the fight against flab. The girl doesn't even need to lose any weight if you ask me, but she says her jeans are a bit snug and she wants to be healthier. I could bawl from sheer gratefulness. I feel so overwhelmed by my mountain of lard, but Rhiannon's support makes me want to try.

After we mapped out our meals we went shopping for all the wholesome ingredients. Then we tackled the pantry, tossing all the dodgy food straight into the bin.

My heart ached and my stomach growled at the memories. The near-empty box of Ritz crackers that I'd demolished while watching the tennis. The bag of chocolate chips that I'd been scoffing by the handful. The dozens of ketchup sachets from my endless sorties to the McDonald's Drive Thru.

'Goodbye, old friends,' I said solemnly. 'I'm going to miss you!'

'It's not for ever!' said Rhiannon. 'We just need to make healthier choices for now.'

'I know,' I sniffed. 'We're on a mission.'

Tonight we cooked mandarin chicken stir-fry from an old Weight Watchers cookbook I'd purchased on an aborted mission. I felt so smug and wholesome as we chopped up vegetables and weighed chicken breasts. The air filled with the aroma of sizzling garlic and ginger, which was a pleasant change from the usual French-fry fug. We huddled over the wok, plucking out stray mange-tout and carrot strips to sample the sauce.

'This is bloody beautiful!' said Rhiannon.

'I know!' My tongue was alarmed by bright and lively flavours. 'Maybe this healthy shit won't be so torturous after all!'

'Maybe! Shall we dish out the rice?'

'Half a cup each, right?'

I carefully measured out our allotted portions of sensible brown grains.

'Holy crap, is that it?'

'I know! I normally have four times that amount!'

'We're going to starve, Rhiannon. Starve, I tell you!'

But oddly enough I didn't starve. I felt pleasantly satisfied instead of my usual painfully stuffed.

So that was Day One, perfectly done. My Points tracker looked so tidy I almost kissed it.

WEEK 2
22 January 2001
24st 5.5lb (155.2kg, 341.5lb)
9.5lb lost (4.3kg) – 12st 8.5lb to go (80.2kg, 176.5lb)

The Triumph of Day One spurred me on to behave myself on Day Two. On Day Three I thought my body would explode with longing for a Mars Bar, but miraculously I settled for a chicken salad sandwich. Boosted by that small victory, Days Four to Seven were executed with robotic precision. Before I knew it, it was Monday again and we were back at Weight Watchers.

Why was I so nervous? I knew I'd been an obedient Weight Watching automaton all week long. I'd counted my Points and filled in my tracker to perfection. I'd eaten all manner of fruits and vegetables. I'd guzzled the recommended two daily litres of water. I hadn't driven through any Drive Thrus.

But I worried that it just wouldn't work. I've been fat for so many years – what if my body isn't capable of shrinking? What if the blubber plain refuses to budge? What if my fat cells have mutated into a strain of super-evil fat cells that laugh in the face of celery sticks and lean protein? What will I do then? Hack at my belly rolls with a chainsaw?

43

Once again we waited until after the meeting to get weighed.

Rhiannon hopped on first; she'd lost three pounds. Woohoo!

My heart hammered as they hung the special weight on the scale. *Oh please let this work. Please, please, pretty please.*

It took an eternity to balance. Finally Donna grinned at me. 'You're our biggest loser this week! 9.5 pounds off!'

Holy crap. It worked!

Rhiannon cheered. The weigh ladies went crazy. Donna stuck a gold star on my card and gave me a hug.

What a difference seven days makes. This time there were no tears on the way home, just me gurning at my gold star.

Veteran dieters call this the Honeymoon Phase, when you're flushed with enthusiasm and losing weight almost seems fun, in a perverse sort of way. I know I shouldn't celebrate too much, but I'm on my way, people! Just watch me do it again next week.

WEEK 3
27 January 2001
22st 12.5lb (145.7kg, 320.5lb)
1st 7lb lost (9.5kg, 30.5lb) – 11st 1.5lb to go (70.7kg, 155.5lb)

'Are you reading the scale properly?'

'Of course I'm reading the scale properly!' Donna laughed. 'I'm a professional!'

'But a stone and a half in a *week*?' I spluttered, 'How is that possible without sawing off a limb?'

She patiently explained that when you are extremely large, it's common to have crazy results in the first few weeks. She said it could be water loss, too. Personally I think my body is so frightened by all this salad and fruit that it's dropped a stone from shock. But Donna reassured me things should settle into a steady pattern soon, so I'll just count myself lucky.

I'm getting obsessed with Points. It's not enough just to count my own, now I'm snooping at my colleagues' lunches and mentally calculating the damage. At the supermarket yesterday I was peeking in people's shopping trolleys and crunching their numbers.

Just for fun tonight I worked out how many Points I scoffed the day before I joined Weight Watchers. This was my menu:

BREAKFAST: Bar of Cadbury's Dairy Milk

PRE-LUNCH: A cheese and bacon roll and a half-litre of chocolate milk while watching *Minority Report* at the cinema.

LUNCH: A donner kebab, extra large fries and Fanta at the Belconnen Mall food court.

POST-LUNCH: Chocolate croissant

DINNER: Big Mac, extra large fries and chocolate shake from the McDonald's Drive Thru.

POST-DINNER: Two bowls of home-made trifle

I know that sounds bad. But it was my Last Supper! On the eve of a new diet, it's traditional to gorge on all the sugary, fatty, salty delights that will soon be forbidden.

45

For who knows when they'll touch your lips again? Although with hindsight perhaps I should have stuck to a single meal, instead of making a whole day of it.

And the damage? Ninety points! I'm only allowed twenty-six per day. I ate enough for a family of four!

But the Last Supper is not just about stuffing your stomach. You have to fill your *mind* with food too. There are many dreary salad days ahead, but I've got plenty of full-fat memories to feast on.

WEEK 4
5 February 2001
22st 11.5lb (145.2kg, 319.5lb)
2st 3.5lb lost (14.3kg, 31.5lb) – 11st 0.5lb to go
(70.2kg, 154.5lb)

It was 40 degrees today! I'm sure the weight I lost this week was pure perspiration. I feel like a great sweaty hog, slowly rotating over the coals.

The Australian summer seems designed to torture the morbidly obese. While the majority of the population is rejoicing with their tiny shorts, bikinis and barbecues, us fatties must sweat and suffer on the sidelines . . . or just lie in dark, air-conditioned rooms and wait for the end.

I'm never more aware of the complete *wrongness* of my body than during a heat wave. The Fat Girl Logistics Department has to work overtime, figuring out how to manoeuvre my bulk through the day with minimal sweat and embarrassment.

The key is to keep your moves small and precise. I drove to work at 7.30 a.m and nabbed a space right

46

outside the building, thus minimizing (a) the distance I'd have to shuffle across the car park and (b) potential for witnesses to said shuffle.

The foyer was mercifully deserted too, so I could take the lift to the first floor instead of feeling obliged to huff my way up the stairs like normal people. The early start also gave me a good hour to catch my breath and blot my shiny face before the office got busy.

By ten o'clock the office was a furnace. My colleagues looked cool in their short sleeves and floaty frocks, but already my standard issue Fat Girl black trousers were glued to my thighs. Luckily I had no meetings today, so I could stay at my desk and not have to thunder along the corridors, getting even sweatier.

My job is dull and predictable but that's why I love it. I'm still working for the same internet start-up company as a content editor, but not long after they hired me I was subcontracted to a government department to look after a bunch of websites. I could do the job in my sleep, but I like the slow, predictable pace of the public service. I keep a low profile, tinkering away on pages and editing copy. I've been toiling away like a good worker bee for eighteen months and they keep extending my contract, so I must be doing all right. The Australian government is happy, my employers are happy and so am I.

At one o'clock my cubicle neighbour and good friend Emily asked did I fancy going out for lunch. But I'd cleverly prepared my excuse the night before.

'No thanks, mate,' I said cheerfully, 'I brought a big salad from home and I've got loads of work to do, so I'll have to give it a miss today.'

I just couldn't face the walk to the shopping centre in the middle of the day, trying to keep up with Emily's swift and slender strides. I feared she would actually *hear* my thighs smashing together like a pair of flabby cymbals.

So I sat by the window with my salad and glared down at all the lunchtime joggers. They were making themselves sweaty *on purpose*, rather than it being an unfortunate consequence of simple, everyday movement. Do you think I'll ever be able to do that? I have my doubts, considering the things that currently leave me red-faced and panting:

- Walking up the stairs in our flat
- Making the bed
- Tying my shoelaces
- Bending down to fetch vegetables from the fridge
- Dislodging myself from behind the steering wheel to get out of the car

The one good thing about this weather? I'm sticking to my stinking Points. I've barely got the energy to sip a glass of water, let alone waddle to the fridge.

WEEK 5
13 February 2001
22st 7.5lb (143.4kg, 315.5lb)
2st 7.5lb lost (16.1kg, 35.5lb) – 10st 10.5lb to go
(68.4kg, 150.5lb)

Another week of obedient Weight Watching and another gold star on my card. I've now lost two and a half stone!

'That still sounds like an awful lot of lard,' I said to Donna.

'Shauna, you're doing great,' she smiled. 'Stop worrying and just keep going!'

But I have to worry! If I don't worry, I might allow myself to feel smug and successful, and then I might think it's OK to scoff a couple of Mars Bars, and we all know what happens then. I'll finally burst out of my trousers and have to order a mumu from a mail order catalogue. So you see, fear is my friend.

Another thing I keep hearing is, *Just take it one day at a time*. That's impossible! My mind is always racing ahead in a panic. I may have strung together a few healthy weeks and lost a few pounds, but what if it's all too good to be true? I worry my old bad habits are lurking behind a tree, waiting to pounce and take over again.

It also makes me nervous that I'm enjoying my food. We've been cooking fresh, veggie-laden meals and so far I'm not missing the burgers and shakes at all. My inner masochist believes I'm not entitled to lose any weight unless there's suffering and deprivation involved. If my stomach was rumbling and my taste buds were shrivelled up from lack of stimulation, maybe *then* I'd deserve to drop a few pounds. But to eat a huge plate of food and actually enjoy it . . . surely that's not going to work?

Yet there's a tiny, happy part of me knows that it *is* working. If I admitted that out loud I'd get run over by a bus for being so self-congratulatory, so I'll just whisper it here instead.

WEEK 6
19 February 2001
22st 6lb (142.7kg, 314lb)
2st 9lb lost (16.8kg, 37lb) – 10st 9lb to go (67.7kg, 149lb)

Another pound gone! I know it's early days but I can't help fantasizing about my less flabby future. So today I bring you a list:

Things To Do When I'm Skinny!
1. Go swimming.
2. Walk up to a guy that catches my eye and say hello.
3. Wear dainty, strappy little shoes (with my chunky legs they currently make me look like a drag queen).
4. Run!
5. Buy some sexy leather trousers. Mrowr!
6. Have a full body massage (like I'd let anyone look at me naked right now!)

WEEK 7
26 February 2001
22st 4lb (141.8kg, 312lb)
2st 11lb lost (17.7kg, 39lb) – 10st 7lb to go (66.8kg, 147lb)

Sometimes, just for a tiny moment, I forget that I'm fat. I'll run a hand through my hair and notice how soft it feels. Or I'll admire the curve of my eyebrow as I slap on some mascara. I'll smile to myself and think, *You're not half bad!*

Then other days I'll be out shopping and catch a glimpse of a fat woman in a mirror. I can't help staring at the stomach rolls clinging to her shirt and the thick sausages of her forearms. I marvel at how her eyes have almost disappeared into the chubbiness of her cheeks.

And then I finally realize, *Shit. That's me!*

It happened again this morning when I went for a walk. Deliberately! I decided it was high time I did some proper exercise.

I was rather proud to be lumbering down the street. 'Look at us go!' I cheered. 'We're out and about. We're doing it, baby!'

I didn't even get to the end of the block before I had to stop. As I clutched my knees and wheezed, I caught my reflection in a car window. My face was a violent shade of Call the Ambulance red. My chest heaved like a monstrous jelly.

I felt sick. Who was I kidding? It was impossible. I'm never going to change this body.

For the most part, every pound I lose feels like a little triumph. It's another bit of fuel on this fire of hope building inside me – a cautious, fledgling hope that I could actually do this, that I could really be slim and healthy. I count the stars on my Weight Watchers booklet and it feels as if all the effort is adding up to something.

Yet as soon as I look in the mirror it seems pointless, because the pounds I've lost are just a drop in a very fat ocean. My confidence comes undone and I'm back to feeling hopeless and disgusted again. Everyone keeps saying,

'Be kind to yourself' and 'Focus on the positives!' But surely there needs to be a balance between optimism and reality.

3 March 2001
22st 2.5lb (141.1kg, 310.5lb)
2st 12.5lb lost (18.4kg, 40.5lb) – 10st 6lb to go (66.1kg, 145.5lb)

Oh dear. As you may have gathered, this lard-busting caper is turning out be an emotional rollercoaster. But I'm happy to report that the dark clouds of PMS have now departed. And losing another pound tonight certainly helped my mood!

It intrigues me that the weight continues to come off. How is it possible? Why haven't I given up and returned to my cake-chomping ways? Why is it different this time? And most scary of all – why am I so convinced that it's going to be for good?

Here are my preliminary theories:

1. I want it bad

My last attempt at getting skinny was back in Bathurst, just after I finished university. Mum was troubled by my rapid expansion and subtly suggested I join Weight Watchers by posting me a 'No Joining Fee!' coupon and a cheque for ten meetings with her latest batch of job advertisements.

So I went along and discovered I weighed 21 stone.

Instead of being shocked into action, I hit the Drive Thru and cried into my fries.

For the next ten weeks I dutifully showed up to the scale but my heart wasn't in it. I was also extremely depressed by then and could barely cope with getting out of bed, let alone tracking my food, planning meals or filling the house with healthy foods. Nor did I have any goals. All I had was a vague desire for my fat to go away.

But this time my mind is in a better place. I want to succeed with every flabby cell of my body. Unlike my previous attempts, this time I've figured out exactly what success looks like, so I know what I'm aiming for. I want to reach my ideal goal weight of 11 stone 11 pounds. I want to get there by my twenty-fifth birthday next November. I want to be healthy. I want to wear foxy clothes. I don't want to feel like I'll die after climbing a short flight of stairs.

2. I am Weight Watchers' bitch

When my car breaks I go to a mechanic. When my teeth hurt I call the dentist. When I want to lose weight I slink off to Weight Watchers. It's not that I am a mindless slave to the global conglomerate; I just know it's a safe and reliable option.

I've never been one for crash diets. With half my body weight to lose it could be tempting to go crazy with cabbage soup or grapefruit, but I know too much about vitamins and good fats and whole grains to ever fall for that. Perhaps that's why I neglected my weight for so long, because deep down I knew there were no miracle cures . . . just hard work and sensible eating. Boring!

53

So now I'm back in the fold and remembering all the things I chose to forget about portion sizes and good nutrition. I love the reassurance and ritual of the Monday night weigh-ins – putting on my official weigh-in outfit, slipping into my lightest shoes, going to the toilet a dozen times in case I can pee out another ounce. I love the metallic clang of the old-fashioned scale as it registers a loss.

And I must admit I'm a fool for the gold stars and Donna's praise. She makes me feel it's OK to be fragile and afraid. Ever since my Week One meltdown, the Weight Watchers girls always give me a grin and a thumbs-up when they see I've made it through another week. I'm like an oversized schoolgirl, eager to please the teacher and glowing at the slightest compliment.

3. I've made peace with the past
My bitterness and resentment have faded since last year's confrontation with Mum. When you get a little older you can look back at the past with a certain maturity and forgiveness. I've finally taken responsibility for my role in this lardy mess – five years of appalling eating habits – and realized that I'm an adult and it's entirely up to me what happens to my body from now on. I'm the captain of the tubby ship!

4. I have witnesses
I've always been a secret dieter. I'd do anything to avoid the dreaded phrase, 'Are you allowed to eat that?' Best of all, if I failed spectacularly nobody would ever have to know.

Funnily enough, these covert operations never worked. It meant I was relying entirely on myself for motivation and support, and all too easily I'd convince myself to give up and head for the fridge. This time I've let people in on my secret – Rhiannon, Mum and obviously the Weight Watchers gang. I always thought sharing my problems would mean judgement and disapproval, but instead it's brought wonderful support and much-needed accountability.

5. I am not alone
I am by far the fattest person I know. I out-fat my family, friends and every lardy lady at Weight Watchers. Whilst I have a lot of support, I don't know anyone who has actually experienced such a ridiculously large weight problem. But thanks to this journal I've found some lovely and equally lumpy souls online! Now I don't feel quite so freaky and alone. Instead of suppressing my fat-related angst, I'm writing my way through it. I've always felt more comfortable expressing my thoughts in text, so blogging has all the confessional allure of an old-fashioned diary, with the added benefit of a sympathetic audience. It's like anonymous group therapy!

6. I'm changing my wicked ways
Rhiannon and I have rearranged our eating habits so it's just easier to take the healthier option than not. We've wholeheartedly embraced our weekly routine of meal planning and grocery shopping. Gone are the days of arriving home from work, flinging open the pantry doors and wondering why the contents don't quite add up to a

meal. Now we know exactly what's for dinner so there's no excuse for takeaway pizza. We also cook extra for leftovers so I don't succumb to greasy food court lunches. Yes, we have truly become lean, mean dieting machines.

7. I don't have a life

As my body grew bigger, my world became smaller. Over the years I systematically removed anything remotely fun and exciting from my life, until I'd created a reclusive existence limited to home, work, the supermarket, and that's about it. I haven't had any hobbies aside from . . . eating a lot of crap.

But the positive side of being so anti-social is I've got very little to distract me from the task. I can conduct my everyday life on autopilot, leaving my mind free to obsess about Points and menu plans. I don't *want* a life right now, to be honest. I don't want to have to think about anything else but blasting away my pile of blubber. A weight problem this huge demands nothing less than 100 per cent focus and commitment.

I used to fantasize about being abducted to a Secret Fat Camp. I longed to vanish from society for a solid year and be bullied into shape by a crack team of shrinks, chefs and military men, then once slim and reformed I'd be released back on to the streets. But back here in reality, living like a recluse is my next best option.

Can you believe it's been almost two months since I started on this adventure? I lost another two pounds on Monday night, so now I've lost three stone overall.

They tell you at Weight Watchers to use everyday objects to visualize your weight loss, so today at the supermarket I stared at the margarine display and did the sums: 3 stone is about 19 kilograms. A tub of margarine is half a kilo, therefore I've lost 38 tubs of margarine.

The numbers sound impressive but I still don't look any different. Certainly not like someone's hacked 38 tubs of margarine from my body. How bloody long will it take to get some visible results?

Rhiannon is out on the town tonight so I've been left unsupervised for the first time since this adventure began.

I don't quite know what to do with myself. Being alone used to be my cue to engage in serious feasting. A clandestine run to the supermarket or Drive Thru, or if that was too strenuous I'd just dig out a chocolate bar from my secret store. But now I've declared my bingeing days are over, what am I going to do instead? It's not much fun, just me and my brain and a boring bottle of water. Without the distraction of food the reality of my pathetic hermit life is biting me in the arse.

Over the past five years I've elevated avoiding social situations into an art form. I've weaselled my way out of parties, weddings and funerals. I even ran away from my university graduation ball. Just like Cinderella, except in an ugly size 24 polyester shirt and sensible black trousers.

I'll never forget that shirt – shiny gold with a hideous floral print, the nearest thing to formal wear in the plus-size section at Myer. I did my slow, glittery shuffle on the dance floor, feeling like a loser beside my tiny girlfriends in their gorgeous frocks but doing my best impression of Having a Great Time. When they decided to move on to a club I knew I had to escape. Fat chick in a nightclub? No way.

So I lied.

'I'm just going home to change into my dancing shoes,' I said. 'Meet you all there!'

I waddled off into the night. Luckily I lived just down the street so it was a plausible excuse. As soon as I got home I locked the doors and drew the blinds. For a whole hour I stared in the mirror, quietly trembling with rage and disgust. I looked at my carefully applied eyeliner, the dangly earrings and the remnants of lipstick. Such a noble attempt to pretty myself up, but fat dressed up in sparkly fabric is still just fat.

My hair crackled with static electricity as I whipped off that horrible shirt. I put on my pyjamas, fetched my trusty jar of Nutella and ate it by the spoonful while watching a rerun of 21 Jump Street.

Tonight I feel just as pathetic and lonely as I did back then. I hate to admit it but everything I do in life – more specifically, what I *don't* do – is dictated by how I feel about my weight. I'm afraid of the world beyond my house. I can't go to a meeting at work or fill the car with petrol or walk past a bunch of schoolkids without panicking that they're all staring at me and writing me off as incapable and/or stupid because of my size.

And if I'm terrified of these tiny everyday interactions, how am I ever going to have any meaningful relationships? Dare I mention romance? It's been so long since I've been kissed. Or even had my hand held. Sometimes I hunger for someone to simply look my way and smile. But with all this fat surrounding me I'm completely sexless and invisible. It's funny how the more space you take up, the more you blend into the wallpaper.

Now I've started this weight loss caper, I feel better about myself every day. But for the most part I can't imagine a life for myself beyond this couch. And even if the blubber does come off, will anyone like what's underneath? I'm still going to be plain old me, just slightly smaller. Will losing weight make me more confident or will I still be socially inept? Right now if no one wants me, I can chalk it up to morbid obesity. But what if I get smaller and no one wants me even then?

I don't know why I even think about these things. It's not something I'll need to consider for a long while yet. I'm still a whale.

WEEK 10
19 March 2001
22st (140kg, 308lb)
3st 1lb lost (19.5kg, 43lb) – 10st 3lb to go (65kg, 143lb)

After my disastrous walking session last month I had to

come up with a new exercise strategy. I call it the Vampire Method (patent pending). You simply slink out of the house once the sun goes down or just before it rises. Instead of avoiding garlic and crucifixes, you're avoiding warm temperatures and people!

The world is cool and peaceful at 5.30 a.m. It's completely silent but for the steady wheeze of my unfit lungs. Under the cover of semi-darkness I don't fret about my belly rolls or my cottage cheese thighs. I just amble along and think about my weight loss goals, what to cook for dinner, or who is the most handsome doctor on *ER*.

At first I could only walk to the end of the street before giving up, but a week later I made it around the whole block. Then I added another, and another. After four weeks I'm up to four whole blocks. Move over, Michael Johnson!

Today I cleaned out my desk at work. I've had my job for eighteen months now, and my inability to close the drawers without kicking them indicated it was time for a tidy up. Inside I found a friendly reminder of my former fatty life. The bottom of each drawer was covered with millions of tiny brown crumbs. Chocolate crumbs!

It's funny how ten weeks ago I was so baffled to discover I weighed over 25 stone when all this time I had a Cadbury's factory sitting in my desk.

I was very dedicated to my stash. I bought a plastic tub just for the purpose, and each day I'd arrive early to work with a new batch of goodies. I'd break the chocolate into squares so I could gorge without the tell-tale rustling of foil wrappers.

If I felt particularly energetic I'd go to the supermarket at lunchtime and hit the Pick-and-Mix sweeties. We were never allowed near the Pick-and-Mix as kids; 'Overpriced rubbish!' Mum declared. So I got an extra thrill from buying forbidden candy – caramel kisses, coconut drops, chocolate frogs, chocolate almonds, chocolate cherries, mini Easter eggs – the sickly sweet taste of rebellion. Back at work I'd quietly empty the bag into the tub and dig in throughout the afternoon.

Chocolate became a habit, like answering the phone or blowing my nose – a regular part of my workplace routine. I barely even tasted it after a while. It was just an unconscious habit; something to occupy my jaws.

I always thought I was discreet too, but it turns out I was as subtle as my enormous arse. I recently confessed to Emily that I was doing Weight Watchers, and she said with a grin, 'Does this mean you'll have to give up your choccie stash?'

Do you know it's been ten weeks since I've had any chocolate? I went cold turkey because I don't trust myself to be left alone with the stuff right now. When the cocoa calls my name I'll have a diet chocolate mousse or a sachet of diet hot chocolate instead.

Lately it feels like I am waking up from a five-year bender, discovering all the crazy things I did while under the influence. Except instead of being surrounded by a pool of my own vomit, it's old chocolate wrappers and one extremely large body.

It scares me how my life revolved around food. As I ate my breakfast I'd be pondering what to have for lunch. What fatty concoction should I choose from the food court today? And even as I scoffed my lunch, my thoughts would wander to my afternoon snack. Chocolate bar or crisps? Or why not both? And what's for dinner? And let's not forget dessert, and perhaps a late supper in front of the box.

I know that was only ten weeks ago but already I couldn't imagine going back to that life. Every time I lose another pound it feels as if I'm another pound closer to escaping that miserable 25-stone girl crying on the scale in her giant knickers. I have to keep moving away from her. I have to convince myself that the brief thrill of a chocolate bar doesn't compare to the thrill of taking control of my life.

WEEK 11
27 March 2001
21st 10lb (138.2kg, 304lb)
3st 5lb lost (21.3kg, 47lb) – 9st 13lb to go (63.2kg, 139lb)

'Hello?'
'Shauna! It's the Mothership calling!'
Oh dear. She's using the third person now?
The whole Mothership thing began last year when Rhiannon and I were doing our usual frantic cleaning spree in anticipation of her latest friendly visit/inspection.
'Quick!' I screamed as I scrubbed the bathtub. 'There's only ten minutes until the landing of the Mothership!' She got wind of the nickname and decided she quite liked the sound of it.

'So how are you, dearest? How's the Weight Watching going? Of course I'm more concerned with how you are *personally*, than I am about your *weight*. No pressure, you understand?'

Ever since our explosive argument she's been determined to be the new and improved Mothership. She's completely supportive of my lard-busting efforts even though she still battles with her own weight. Our relationship has changed dramatically. It feels as if we're equals now and we can talk and listen without judgement. We're more open and honest, as if trying to make up for all those years of emotional distance. I feel I'm getting to know her at last. She's warm, funny and ever so slightly annoying with her self-help books and new age jargon, and I relish our newfound closeness.

'Ma, I'm fine. And I don't mind you asking about the Weight Watching.'

'Well, if you're sure.'

'I'm sure. I lost another four pounds this week, which means ... drumroll please! – I don't need that extra weight on the scale any more!'

'Wow!'

'So I'm no longer super-fat. Next week I can stroll in and jump on the scale like a "normal" fat person!'

'Shauna,' she clucked, 'you shouldn't put yourself down like that.'

'I'm not! It's just a big milestone for me.'

'Well I'm very proud of you.' She cleared her throat. 'Listen, I have to tell you something very important. I just finished this book that Oprah recommended.'

'Oh ... great.'

'Shush, you! It was all about controlling parents and how they have such high expectations of their children. And how this is so very traumatic for the child! So I had to call you and say I'm sorry for all the pressure I put on you over the years.'

'Pressure?' I laughed, 'You?'

'I just want you to know I don't have those harmful expectations any more. All I want is for you to be happy and to do what you want to do, whatever you're passionate about.'

'OK.'

'So don't go thinking I'm disappointed about the aborted journalism career. And if you don't do the computers for the rest of your life I don't mind about that either! You'll have no crazy expectations from me any more.'

'Oh cool. So now I can fully focus on all the expectations I have of myself!'

'I'm trying to be serious!'

'I know.'

'Good. Well, I'm glad we had this conversation.'

WEEK 12
6 April 2001
21st 8lb (137.3kg, 302lb)
3st 7lb lost (22.2kg, 49lb) – 9st 11lb to go (62.3kg, 137lb)

After the dazzling success of the Vampire Method walking regime, this week I went back to the gym.

Rhiannon and I joined up six months ago in a fit of good intentions but my efforts were short-lived. I had an induction with a friendly girl called Angela, but I don't think she quite knew what to do with me. She weighed me (22 stone, the scale maximum) and tried to do my measurements, but her tape measure couldn't reach around my hefty hips. Then she tried to take my blood pressure, but my arm was too big for the cuff.

So we moved on to the fitness assessment. Rhiannon had told me about the rigorous moves they'd put her through, but I was spared by virtue of the fact that I was already pink and puffed just from stepping on and off the scale. Instead Angela got me to walk on the treadmill. I barely managed five minutes at a mighty 2.5 miles per hour.

There was space on my programme chart for two dozen different weights and cardio moves but she could only write one pathetic instruction: *Treadmill, 2.5m.p.h., 20 minutes.*

'Wow, what an athlete!' I said with a pained smile.

'Hey, don't worry,' Angela said kindly. 'We all have to start somewhere. We'll be filling this chart with all sorts of exercises before you know it! Give this six weeks then come and see me again.'

'OK,' I lied.

Rhiannon cleverly suggested we make our comeback an hour before closing so the gym would be quiet and less intimidating. She knows me too well.

Surprisingly, my chart was still in the filing cabinet. I thought they'd have removed it by now, maybe shoving it into a box labelled LARDY LOSERS WHO COULDN'T HACK THE PACE. But there it was, with the same smiley face that Angela had drawn all those months ago.

The cardio theatre was deserted but for a lone brunette on a treadmill. I froze in the doorway, mesmerized and terrified by her pert buttocks and swishing ponytail. What if she saw me? An arse like mine is hard to miss. What if she screamed at me to be gone from her sacred temple of fitness?

'She's not looking at you!' said Rhiannon. 'She's engrossed in her run.'

'I can't go in there. Look at her boobs, they don't even move!'

'They're either fake or she's got a fantastic sports bra.'

'What do you think she's thinking as she runs along like that? *God, I'm so fucking sexy, I can barely stand it!* That's what I'd be thinking if I looked like her. I wouldn't be able to take my eyes off myself!'

But for the foreseeable future I'll be keeping well away from the mirrors. It was demoralizing enough just listening to the ragged beat of my flabby heart without actually looking at myself. Rhiannon jogged while I did my 2.5-mile per hour plod. The treadmill groaned every time I put my foot down. I could feel my flesh ripple and rattle all the way from my chin down to my toes. After spending so many years trying to keep my body as still as possible to avoid attracting unnecessary attention, it felt so unnatural to make it move deliberately!

But I persisted until the end of the twenty minutes. The highlight was filling in my chart. I wrote the date and put a neat tick beside Angela's instruction, then drew another smiley face. I can't say I'll keep doing this for the love of exercise, but I reckon I could do it for the love of a good chart.

WEEK 13
9 April 2001
21st 8lb (137.3kg, 302lb)
3st 7lb lost (22.2kg, 49lb) – 9st 11lb to go (62.3kg, 137lb)

'You know, if you'd peed before you got here,' said Donna, 'you would have had a loss.'

'But I *did* pee before I got here!' I sulked. 'Five times!'

The scales didn't move this week and I'm not happy at all. It's far too early in the game to be stalling!

It's been a shitty week all round. I started a new job, sort of. My government contract ended so now I'm back at my company's head office. I hate being the new kid, more specifically the new *fat* kid. I almost felt svelte on Monday morning when I put on my new size 24 shirt, but then I arrived at the office and found I outweighed my new colleagues by at least ten stone.

I miss the public service already. Sure, I was the fattest lady there too, but everyone has their quirks in the public service. Perhaps it's thanks to Equal Opportunities legislation. There were fat people, thin people, annoying people, old people, incompetent people, bossy people and people with no fashion sense. There were people who were all those things at once. So I slotted in nicely to that mix. It was a wonderfully predictable and non-threatening environment.

In contrast, my first impression of the private sector is that everyone is poised, perfectly groomed and incredibly busy. I guess you have to look professional when every hour is billable. There'll be no time for morning teas, *Big Brother* gossip and bunking off early on a Friday.

I've spent my first week hiding at my desk feeling fat and inferior, my automatic reaction to being placed in any new situation. I hate meeting new people. I fear that no matter what I say or do, the only first impression I can leave is . . . fat!

My computer died yesterday, and it took me two hours to work up the nerve to call the help desk. Somehow I'd hoped I could heal it with my penetrating stare. I hated the thought of the IT guy coming up from his dungeon and seeing me: 'Aha! Stupid fat chick's broken her computer.' And I would feel compelled to say, 'It was like that when I got here! I didn't sit on it or anything!'

In the end I phoned right before I left for the day, and mercifully the IT pixies fixed it overnight.

I know I'm being pathetic; I just hate change. Change is scary and it gets in the way of my weight loss mission. And after eighteen months I was settled in the public service. I'd managed to endear myself to my colleagues with hard work and sparkling wit, showing them that there was more to me than my blubber. But now I've got to start all over again!

I'm also petrified of my new job and worry I'm incapable of doing it. My boss seems to think I'll be fine because she's already given me about 127 tasks and made me leader of the Content team. Me, a leader? I've only ever led myself. To the fridge.

Even so, Rhiannon and I went out for lunch on Saturday to celebrate this grand promotion. It was the first time I'd taken my fat out in public since the Weight Watching began so I fretted over the menu. I ordered a healthy-sounding grilled teriyaki chicken burger, but it arrived with an unexpected side order of chips.

How can anyone resist chips? So fresh, salty and sizzling! They were delicious, but with every mouthful I was terrified that those lost pounds would instantly return. Which is rather sad. Am I going to be afraid of a handful of fried potatoes all of my life?

Scared of new jobs, new people, new challenges and . . . chips. Could I be any more pathetic?

WEEK 17
7 May 2001
21st (133.6kg, 294lb)
4st 1lb lost (25.9kg, 57lb) – 9st 3lb to go (58.6kg, 129lb)

I'm alive! I'm coping! Work got in the way of writing for the past four weeks but not in the way of lard busting. I've lost another half-stone and suddenly everything is changing!

1. I can breathe
I used to wake myself up during the night because my breathing was so loud and fractured. But now there's less

flesh around my neck and chest so the wheezing has stopped!

2. I'm officially a size 24
My size 26 jeans have been looking a bit dumpy lately, so I dug out an old size 24 pair from my wardrobe museum. Can you believe they fit perfectly? I hadn't worn them since 1999, so you could say I've lost two years of blubber.

3. I found my vagina
It's been hiding for years, concealed by the sprawling tsunami of flesh that is my stomach. But this morning I stepped out of the shower and was startled by a bright red thing in the mirror. My pubic hair! So I *am* female after all, not just a lumpy mountain of flesh!

4. My heart will go on
On Monday I had a fitness assessment with Fitness Chick Angela. She took my resting heart rate and it was down to 78 beats per minute. When she tested it last year it was 100 bpm. How was I not dead? No wonder I got puffed just washing the dishes. But now, thanks to the treadmill and the Vampire Method, I've scraped into the healthy heartbeat range.

'You're doing brilliantly,' said Angela, drawing another smiley face on my chart. 'Despite hiding from me for seven months!'

'I know,' I said sheepishly.

'Ooh and you've lost a stone too!' she squealed as I hopped on the scale.

'Wow!' I tried to look surprised. 'A whole stone!'

I couldn't bring myself to tell her I'd technically lost four, since I'd gained three since our last meeting. Why ruin a beautiful moment? She was showering me with hugs and kind words and I was glowing with Good Little Fat Girl pride. I'm paying a handsome monthly fee for that kind of external validation! The more people that tell me I'm doing well, the more I might start to believe it myself.

WEEK 21
4 June 2001
20st 6lb (130kg, 286lb)
4st 9lb lost (29.5kg, 65lb) – 8st 9lb to go (55kg, 121lb)

I've discovered the joys of Microsoft Excel. My brand spanking new weight loss spreadsheet has a dazzling array of columns streaking across the screen – *Date, Week, Weight, Pounds Lost, Pounds to Go, Percentage of Goal Achieved, Percentage of Start Weight Lost.* I just plug in my weight each week and it spits out all the data! Not only in stones but pounds and kilograms too! Did you know that as of Week 21 I've lost 29.5 kilograms, 18.5 per cent of my starting weight and now have 121 pounds to go? These statistics give me the same cheap thrills I used to get from a jumbo bag of marshmallows!

I'm obsessive in analogue too. There's a year planner in the back of my work diary in which I record my results each week. I love staring at the figures after a hard day's web editing. I calculate my average monthly loss, then draw little graphs of how long it's taking me to lose a 10-pound block. Then I calculate weekly averages, and based on those averages I can forecast how many weeks of good behaviour it will take to reach my goal weight.

All this cold hard data is strangely comforting. If I don't like my weigh-in result, I can manipulate the data and spit out a statistic that will make me feel better.

WEEK 23
18 June 2001
20st 4.5lb (129.3kg, 284.5lb)
4st 10.5lb lost (30.2kg, 66.5lb) – 8st 7.5lb to go
(54.3kg, 119.5lb)

There are many different instruments of torture at the gym and I passionately loathe them all – the exercise bike, stepper and elliptical trainer, pedalling and plodding my way to nowhere. They say you're supposed to do cardio three times a week: does this mean I'm to be completely bloody *bored* three times a week for the rest of my life?

The rowing machine, however, is quite a charmer. Our gym has two at opposite ends of the cardio suite, so Rhiannon and I take one each and pretend we're college lads out on an English river.

'Hallo, old chum!' she yells over the techno music.

'I say, lovely day for a row!' I shout back.

The rowing motion is strangely hypnotic and makes my shoulders burn. Sometimes I feel almost *sporty*. Last night I got carried away completely, trying to beat my best time for 500 metres.

'Eat my dust, old chap!'

'Not fair!' said Rhiannon, 'I've got a slow boat!'

After tonight's gruelling workout we soaked our aching muscles in the spa. I finally summoned the nerve to get into the damn thing. I'd been using my lack of swimsuit as an excuse, but Rhiannon said, 'Just stick on a T-shirt and knickers and live a little!'

The spa is set on a platform in the middle of the changing rooms, flanked by plastic plants and wood panelling for that porno set ambience. From this secluded position, I watched the patrons come and go. I was awed by how they casually peeled off their sweaty workout clothes and strolled to the showers without a trace of self-consciousness. I always turn up dressed and ready to go, and then either go home stinky or change my clothes in the shower room. I don't expose so much as a lily-white toe!

I couldn't resist peeking at other chicks' boobs in a critical, comparative, scientific kind of way. Being of the heterosexual persuasion, I don't get to see naked breasts very often. It was incredibly enlightening. Who knew there were so many varieties? I'm so accustomed to my own gelatinous girls that I never appreciated that there are also little ones, pointy ones, bouncy ones and ones with wacky nipples. Such diversity; but all had their own charm.

It made me think about how much time I spend fretting about my body. This bit is too big, that bit is too blobby, that bit is too ugly, that bit's just plain wrong. Being so paranoid and critical is exhausting. Who's to say what's normal anyway? Why can't I appreciate what I've got?

I now realize what I desperately want out of this lard-busting caper, more than a size 14 dress or a number on the scale. I'm aching to be comfortable in my own skin, with all its quirks and flaws, just like the women at the gym seem so comfortable in theirs. I want to be happy just being me.

But I'm not quite sure how you're meant to get there.

WEEK 26
9 July 2001
19st 12.5lb (126.6kg, 278.5lb)
5st 2.5lb lost (32.9kg, 72.5lb) – 8st 1.5lb to go (51.6kg, 113.5lb)

'Oh my. Goodness me. Crikey!'

The Mothership stood on the front veranda of her house, clutching her heart theatrically as I climbed out of the car.

'Ma, don't be a drama queen!'

'I'm not! I haven't seen you for two months!'

After twenty-five years in education, Mum is incapable of switching off her teacher voice. It boomed across the street, as if she was reading a story to her kindergarten class.

'I mean, *wow*. You're shrinking! Rhiannon, isn't she shrinking?'

'Yes!' Rhiannon grinned and rolled her eyes. 'She's shrinking.'

Mum thrust a giant bunch of dahlias into my chest. 'These are for reaching your Five Stone milestone.'

'Aww Ma, you big cheese!'

'I'm very proud of you. I'm very proud of both of you!' She patted our heads as if we were oversized Labradors. 'Now, who's going to make the Mother a cup of tea?'

I hate going back to Cowra; it feels like returning to the scene of the crime. I cringed as we drove past my old haunts – the KFC, the Chinese takeaway; the cinema where I worked one summer and had unlimited access to free popcorn.

I hate Coles supermarket most of all, which unfortunately was our destination today. It's the beating heart of this rural metropolis, the modern equivalent of a town square; which makes it extremely dangerous. There's always a 95 per cent chance I'll run into someone in the aisles, which is hell since I've doubled in size since I left town six years ago.

'Now this is just a quick trip to Coles,' Mum promised. 'I only need a few things!'

But there's no such thing as a Quick Trip to Coles. We'll go in for a loaf of bread and Mum will inevitably be distracted by what she calls the Chuck-Out Bin, the place where reduced-price near-death cheese and yoghurts lurk. To her an expiry date is not a recommendation but a challenge.

That's my cue to hide my hefty arse behind a display of cornflakes or a tower of oranges and quietly panic. Who will ambush me today? What nosy questions will they ask? How will they react to my bulk? Please hurry up, Mum. What if I see one of my old teachers and they

75

discover their dedicated student turned out to be such a crushing disappointment?

It was particularly traumatic during my post-university jobless bum phase. The questions were always the same. 'So I hear you've finished your degree! What have you been up to?'

You mean, aside from becoming hideously obese? Well, I rise at noon but leave the blinds down so no one thinks I'm home, and then it's ice-cream and *Days of Our Lives* for breakfast. And then I curl up in a nest of rejection letters and cry great self-indulgent sobs, and then it's nap time until *Macgyver* comes on.

'Oh, not much,' I'd eventually say.

'So have you got a MAN yet?'

'Oh, not yet.'

'Well, dear, it will happen when you least expect it!' Cue sympathetic pat on the shoulder. 'And same goes for your job situation, I'm sure!'

And then I'd descend into gloom for days, picturing them rushing home to tell their families, 'That Shauna, she peaked way too early.'

You'd think I'd feel less neurotic now that I've got a good job and I'm losing weight, but I don't particularly.

'Ma, I think I'll just wait in the car while you two go in.'

'But you can't—'

'I'm twenty-three now! I'm old enough to wait in the car by myself!'

'Well all right,' she relented. 'But don't touch anything.'

I think I'll keep a low profile in Cowra until I get down to a size 18, which was my approximate lardiness when I finished high school. It will be as if that whole pesky morbid obesity thing never happened.

Next stop on the itinerary was my grandparents' house. Nanny and Poppy are two of my most favourite people in the world. They lived on a farm much the same as ours, with crops, tractors, cowpats to step in – but things couldn't have been more different inside the house. They had cake! Ice-cream! Mashed potatoes! Harmonious relationships!

Like all good farmers my grandparents worked hard, but there was always time for a cup of tea. I used to sit at the kitchen bench, eyes wide as Nanny dragged out the biscuit tins and sliced up a home-made cake. I'd wriggle in my seat, overwhelmed by choice and wondering how much I could eat before Mum would say, 'No more for you, young lady.'

I thought Nanny and Poppy's house was a veritable palace of fat and sugar, but they actually had a moderate approach. Nanny cooked hearty meals in sensible portions, always with lots of vegetables. Dessert and cakes were reserved for special occasions or a treat for the grandkiddies. Food was just *food* with Nanny and Poppy. It didn't mean anything. They didn't use it as a weapon or a punishment. Mealtimes were beautifully ordinary, with no tense silences or bitter arguments; no one making pointed comments about your thighs one minute then demanding you finish your lamb chop the next.

Rhiannon and I still reminisce about that one glorious time when Mum and my stepdad went out of town so we got to stay with Nanny and Poppy for ten whole days. It was just another school week, but with Poppy driving us to the bus stop and Nanny filling our lunchboxes with white bread and home-made lamingtons it was like being transported to a magical parallel universe. On the second day Rhiannon said in awed tones, 'Isn't it weird to look forward to going home after school?'

As we seem programmed to do, Rhiannon and I quickly established a routine. We loved eating breakfast with Nanny and Poppy, chatting about the day ahead over cups of cocoa. In the evenings we did our homework at the kitchen table, soothed by the sound of Nanny bustling round the house and Poppy cracking jokes at the television. There were no arguments, no mind games, no unease, no need to hide away in our bedrooms. Everything was safe and predictable; so perfectly mundane.

I felt guilty for enjoying myself so much but I didn't want it to end. On the last night I buried my nose in the soft scent of the flannel sheets, trying to memorize the feeling.

Rhiannon whispered across the room as we fell asleep, 'This has been the most perfect week of my life.'

'Mine too.'

'Maybe there'll be a flash flood or something,' she said, half joking, half hopeful, 'and we'll be stuck here for ever.'

When they finally picked us up we looked at each other and shrugged as if to say, oh well. It was fun while it lasted.

I hadn't told Nanny about Operation Lard Bust and had sworn the Mothership to secrecy. I wanted to see how long it would take for someone to notice I was a loser without me having to *tell* them I was a loser. Somehow it's more valid that way, you see.

So it was rather satisfying to see Nanny do a double-take when I waltzed into the house today. 'Well look here!' she crowed. 'Somebody's lost some weight!'

'Woohoo!' I hugged her tight. She is barely five feet tall so I tried not to crush her.

'You're looking well,' she said.

'Thank you! So you won't be offended if I steer clear of your caramel shortbread for a while?'

As usual Poppy was sitting in his armchair in the living room. Mum, Rhiannon and I chatted to him while Nanny went to make tea.

Circumstances have changed since those days on the farm. Five years ago they sold up and retired to Cowra. Just before they moved, Poppy was diagnosed with Parkinson's disease. Every time we see him he has faded a little more. He can barely walk, his vision is weak and he can't really speak any more. He was always tall, tanned and rugged from years of working in the sun, but now he's so pale and fragile.

Poppy has always been my hero. I admired his hard work and fierce intelligence, but most of all I loved his sharp wit. He was always firing a pithy one-liner or cooking up a practical joke. That's what makes Parkinson's so cruel: the disease is slowly destroying his body but his mind is still intact. He's perfectly aware of what's going on around him but doesn't have the means to communicate. He was always so strong and capable, but now sometimes people patronize him or shout because they think he's deaf or demented. He's painfully aware that Nanny has to feed, clothe and bathe him like a child. He can no longer arrange his face into a frown, but you can tell how frustrated he is at being trapped in his body. It's incredibly heartbreaking for Nanny and Mum too.

Every time I see Poppy I can't help feeling guilty. For years I was trapped in my body too, but it was entirely my own doing. Poppy hasn't got a choice. I feel ashamed for abusing a perfectly healthy, young body with food. So many things can go wrong that are completely out of your control, so it seems painfully indulgent to have harmed myself deliberately.

I can't change the past, but I'm even more determined now not to screw up my future.

WEEK 27
16 July 2001
19st 10lb (125.5kg, 276lb)
5st 5lb lost (34kg, 75lb) – 7st 13lb to go (50.5kg, 111lb)

Dare I admit that I'm feeling rather happy lately? I blame all the gold stars at Weight Watchers, the smiley faces on my gym chart and the sudden roominess of my size 24 trousers.

After this week's 2.5-pound loss, I've got less than eight stone to go. I know that's still a couple of supermodels glued together, but it sounds far less daunting than six months ago when I had 13 stone to lose.

I'm determined to blast that blubber in time for my twenty-fifth birthday. That's fifteen and a half months away. Do you think I can do it? My trusty spreadsheet reckons it's possible. I desperately want to be skinny for the second half of my twenties. I'll have a big party and invite all you lovely *Dietgirl* readers. I'll wear a slinky size 14 dress and we'll all get sloshed on champagne!

I can't wait for the day when I'm finished with this lard busting so I can get on with my life. I'm sure it must sound like I have no hobbies aside from crunching carrot sticks and worrying about my thighs. And I can admit that sometimes, particularly when I'm staring at my weight loss spreadsheet at 3 a.m., that I'm a tad obsessive.

It's easy to see myself as nothing more than a lobotomized lump of lard – especially when colleagues avoid my gaze in the corridors or salesladies blank me in shops. It used to be a relief to be invisible. But the more weight I lose and the more my confidence inches higher, the more I think, *Hey, don't look right through me! I'm a person too. I've got hopes and dreams and hobbies and urges just like you!*

I need to remember there's more to me than my fat. So what can I tell you? My favourite movie is *Roman Holiday*. I have red hair. I love Radiohead. My car is twenty years old and needs a wash. I love mangoes and men's tennis. I'm quite happy being single, but wouldn't mind a bloke some skinny day. I hate Coca-Cola. I wish I could sing. I have brown eyes. I want to go to Russia and see Lenin in his tomb. I don't hold my pencil properly. I've just failed to finish *In Cold Blood* by Truman Capote for the fifth time. I'm rubbish at housework. I hate shopping.

Hmmm. I doubt that makes me sound particularly exciting, but will you come to my party next year anyway?

Fitness Chick Angela has left me! She's gone overseas. Fair enough if she fancies some adventure, but who's going to marvel at my wondrous feats of weight loss now?

I've been assigned Fitness Chick Kristy who seems lovely, but she's not as gushing and exuberant as Angela. Plus she wasn't there at the beginning when I was completely hopeless and lardy. She's come in all these months down the track when I'm . . . you know, *slightly less* hopeless and lardy. So she'll never fully appreciate how far I've come. After all, I'm only in this weight loss caper to dazzle people with my superhero transformation from couch potato to svelte sexpot!

I weighed in a stone lighter than my last assessment, which helped me forget I'd gained a pound at Weight Watchers on Monday.

'Well done,' Kristy said in her mild-mannered way.

I'm sure Angela would have wept, or at least given me a high-five. Oh well. If I can't impress other people, I'll just have to work harder on impressing myself.

WEEK 29
2 August 2001
19st 8.5lb (124.8kg, 274.5lb)
5st 6.5lb lost (34.7kg, 76.5lb) – 7st 11.5lb to go
(49.8kg, 109.5lb)

Last night I spent an hour writhing around on a giant rubber ball.

I told Fitness Chick Kristy I was bored with the cardio machines so she suggested I take her Fit Ball class, a low impact workout on a stability ball.

'Suitable for all shapes and sizes?'

'Yes.'

'Even my shape and size?'

'Yes!'

'I had a bad experience,' I muttered darkly, 'so I just had to check.'

Last year Fitness Chick Angela had recommended I try BodyBalance, allegedly a 'gentle and relaxing' hybrid of yoga, Pilates and tai chi. So I squeezed into my size 26 tracksuit and brought Rhiannon along for moral support.

When they say 'suitable for all fitness levels' I guess they don't classify 'welded to the couch' as a level of fitness. I was far too big to do the moves; my body refused to bend or stretch. At one point we did a Pilates roll-down manoeuvre, in which you sit on the floor with your hands hugged around your knees. You gradually unfurl your spine to the floor, vertebra by vertebra, then gently peel back up.

I managed to roll down but I got stuck. I rocked and grunted and flapped my arms and legs but I just couldn't roll back up! I made the mistake of looking in the mirror and got the shock of my life. I looked like a dying cockroach twitching on a kitchen floor. A giant, red-faced, dying cockroach.

When did I get so hideous? Where did all those chins and tummy rolls come from? And whatever happened to my neck?

Somehow I made it to the end of the class but afterwards I fled to the car and sobbed. Rhiannon tried to comfort me but I was speechless with rage and disgust. I wanted to scratch off my skin and rip my hair out. I couldn't shake that horrid image of me sprawled out on the floor, completely devoid of dignity. How could that be me? How did I let it happen?

You'd think an experience like that would have spurred me into action. But instead I vowed never to return to the gym and got busy gathering up a few more stones.

But that was almost a year ago and I'm a lot bolder these days. Thankfully the Fit Ball demographic looked much less intimidating – there were plenty of baggy T-shirts and even a few dimpled thighs.

Kristy gave me a little wave and a smile as we all sat down on our balls.

'OK ladies,' she said. 'Let's get ready to bounce!'

Bounce? Now that's a verb you don't want to hear at my size. My body bounces just walking across the street, so why would I want to make it bounce on purpose?

Turns out there are a million different things you can do on a rubber ball. We bounced up and down; we rolled side to side. We kicked our legs in all directions, waved our hands around in the air, tossed the ball above our heads, lunged, squatted then bounced around some more.

Kristy told us to use our abdominal muscles for balance, but no amount of gut-clenching stopped me falling off a dozen times. By the time I managed to get a rhythm going the rest of the class had moved on to something else. Or I'd see Rhiannon's arms flailing like a deranged puppet and fall off again in a fit of giggles.

The class was the perfect example of my Jekyll and Hyde extremes. One minute I was snorting with laughter and amazed that exercise could actually be fun, the next I was gloomily counting my fat rolls and comparing myself to my classmates. Despite all the pounds I've lost, I was still twice the size of the biggest woman. And only half as coordinated!

As the hour wore on, my spirit slumped along with my posture. *Why did you come here?* my brain churned bitterly. *This is just as crap as that BodyBalance class. You're even rounder than that ball!*

This whole love/hate relationship with my body is exhausting. How do you tame that negative voice? How do you learn to like yourself? I'd settle for mere tolerance, just enough to make me believe I'm worth all this effort.

But I can't run away this time. I'll go back to the class next week. I'll keep on going and I'll get better at it. These days, I'm not the kind of girl who gives up.

STOP PRESS!
LOCAL WOMAN DISCOVERS BOOBS ARE
BIGGER THAN GUT

A young Australian woman was astounded to find today that her breasts actually stick out further than her stomach.

The woman, who would only be identified as 'Dietgirl', discovered this phenomenon when checking out her own reflection in a shop window.

'It was in the post office,' said Miss Dietgirl. 'I got the shock of my life when I caught a glimpse in the glass and there they were! Just sitting up like that, as if they were their own entity.'

Miss Dietgirl says previously there was no distinction between her breasts and the 'colossal spare tyres' of her hips and waist.

'It's been at least five years since there was some discernible shape about me,' she said. 'The stomach was always protruding further than the boobs. I am finally starting to feel like less of a shapeless blob and more like a normal, albeit chunky, woman. I can't tell you how happy I am.'

Cynical sources inside her head have refuted her claims, saying that Miss Dietgirl was wearing a new bra that hoisted up her bosoms, thus creating the illusion that they were 'unnaturally perky and upright'.

'She also was probably sucking her tummy in,' they added.

In other breaking news, Rhiannon reached her Weight Watchers goal weight tonight! I was so proud. Not to mention flamingly jealous. Imagine how cool that would feel – to actually be *finished*.

WEEK 32
20 August 2001
19st 0.5lb (121.1kg, 266.5lb)
6st 0.5lb lost (38.4kg, 84.5lb) – 7st 3.5lb to go (46.1kg, 101.5lb)

I've always been one of those people-pleasing, passive fat chicks. You could say, 'Shauna, why don't you go swim in that vat of sharks?' and even though my brain would tell me it was a bad idea, I would nevertheless take up your suggestion. Why? If you're smaller than me, then you're automatically smarter too. But lately I'm wondering if the skinny people really do know best.

Take the Fitness Chicks at the gym. While I'm grateful for their support, they seem more concerned with weight loss than fitness. You can hardly blame them when I am twice the size of their other clients. But although I'm obese, there's an increasingly energetic girl lurking beneath the blubber who wants more of a challenge!

A few months ago I'd asked Fitness Chick Angela to add weight training to my programme. I'd seen women in the gym lifting weights and admired their muscles. But she insisted it was a bad idea, because weights would make me ever bulkier. With so much weight to lose I could end up disillusioned. 'Muscle weighs more than fat,' she explained.

'No worries,' I shrugged. I was happy to play the Clueless Fat Chick, because she was skinny therefore far better qualified than me. So I carried on with my endless cardio.

I've been more courageous with Fitness Chick Kristy. First she made cardio fun with her Fit Ball class, and then last week I convinced her to give me a weights programme! It seemed a bit of a token effort though, just a few upper body exercises. She gave me a quick demonstration but didn't say anything about form, or what muscles I should be working, or what should be hurting. She just gave me a gloomy warning: 'Muscle might push out the fat more.'

Now I see where I've been going wrong. I can't expect the Fitness Chicks to have all the answers when they only see me for fifteen minutes every six weeks. They may be skinnier than me, but how can they know what's best for my body? How can they know what I'm capable of? I'm the one that hangs out with this body all day long, seeing how it's shrunk and adapted over the past eight months. It's time I took my brain off ice and started thinking for myself. If I'm bored with my exercise routine then it's *my* responsibility to change things.

I've been reading about women's weight training on the

internet. Far from making you a bulky freak, it turns out that lifting weights can help burn the blubber! According to the extremely popular 'Krista's Women's Weightlifting Page', pumping iron is actually ideal for us fatties. The moves are simple and, unlike with cardio, you often see results quickly. Building muscle can boost your metabolism and strengthen your bones. It could even help tone my hideous upper arms!

I was tempted to abandon my current regime and dive into Krista's 12 Week Beginners' Programme, but I've got to break my habit of blindly following the advice of others. I'm going to take it slow, sift through all this new knowledge and make it work for me.

So first of all, my sporty friend Cassie has volunteered to come to the gym and show Rhiannon and me how to use the weights properly and help us design a programme. Then, in the ongoing fight against cardio boredom, I've lined up some new activities – swimming and BodyCombat classes. I just hope they make swimsuits in a size 24.

WEEK 34
3 September 2001
18st 13lb (120.5kg, 265lb)
6st 2lb lost (39kg, 86lb) – 7st 2lb to go (45.5kg, 100lb)

I gained a pound and a half tonight.

I didn't get upset. Instead I stood haughtily on the scale and made a brief statement of justification about how my 'rigorous new weights regime' must be affecting my performance on the scale.

'I've heard that happens,' Donna said kindly. 'But I'm sure it will help your weight loss in the long term!'

'Yeah.'

'You'll get there eventually! Did I tell you about that guy who climbed Everest, and he said, "If I'd looked at the whole mountain I'd never have climbed it. I just had to take it step by step."'

'Exactly!' I sniffed, stepping down from the scale.

But I was thoroughly disgusted at myself for being such a whining twit. Why did I feel the need to justify that tiny gain? Especially when I lost three pounds *last* week.

Week after week I see the same faces at Weight Watchers, making the same excuses. 'It's that Time of the Month!' they'll laugh. Or, 'That cake was calling my name!' Or 'I just didn't have time to exercise!'

But I'm not making excuses. After all these months, I'm still eating the healthy food. I'm lifting heavy objects and pounding the pavement. I'm dedicated! I'm pushing my lardy arse to new frontiers! I was overcome by the urge to scream at all those ladies in the queue, 'I am not like you people!' but I was running late for the gym.

WEEK 37
24 September 2001
18st 8.5lb (118.4kg, 260.5lb)
6st 6.5lb lost (41.1kg, 90.5lb) – 6st 11.5lb to go
(43.4kg, 95.5lb)

Spring has sprung here in the southern hemisphere and I've not a stitch to wear. Last year's clothes are either too big or the fabric in the crotch has worn through, thanks to my mighty thighs. So tonight Rhiannon and I hit the shops.

We went to the Big is Beautiful section at Myer. They've buried it on the basement floor, so Big is Bloody Inconvenient. You have to trek past the levels of perfumes, pretty shoes and flimsy frocks before you finally descend into polyester hell. I bet the security guards are watching the CCTV and laughing, 'Giddy up, fatty! Down you go! Keep going!'

I just wanted to get it over as soon as possible, so I grabbed everything dark in a size 26 and trudged to changing rooms.

'What are you doing?' Rhiannon rapped on the door a moment later. 'You're not a 26 any more! Here, try this on!'

It was a V-neck top in a light lime green, size 22. And it fitted!

I am still completely lumpy and could really do with a better fitting bra, but it was an improvement. I was amazed how the colour lit up my face and made me look feminine and . . . *alive*. Perhaps the gigantic Goth look doesn't work for me after all?

Despite that small triumph, the overall shopping experience was no less traumatic than two sizes ago. All the clothes are still designed for the colour blind and/or those who don't mind being highly flammable. Why are clothing designers so reluctant to cash in on the Fat Dollar? I earn a decent salary; I'd pay for some well-cut clothes in natural fibres. But instead I'm stuck with what look like the remnants of curtains and trampoline mats.

Furthermore, I should never go shopping with

Rhiannon. I swear every garment looks perfect on her.

'Does this look OK?' she asked with genuine concern as she tried on her fifteenth flawless outfit.

'Brilliant!' I had to sound cheery, since the poor girl had just endured two hours in the fat shops.

It's so demoralizing, sitting outside the changing rooms in some poncey skinny boutique, surrounded by shopping bags from all the other poncey skinny boutiques that had clothes Rhiannon looked perfect in. I've lost ninety pounds but I'm still at least ninety light years away from fitting into anything from a normal shop.

I looked around at all the skinny people plucking skinny clothes off the racks and the skinny salesladies trying to pretend I wasn't sullying their line of vision. I snatched up all the bags, fled outside to the donut shop and just stared at the donuts until Rhiannon was done.

WEEK 39
8 October 2001
18st 10lb (119.1kg, 262lb)
6st 5lb lost (40.4kg, 89lb)– 6st 13lb to go (44.1kg, 97lb)

Operation Swimming Pool is go! After six dry years, today I got back in the water.

Swimming has always been the personification of suffering and humiliation to me. It's all my fat girl fears and insecurities tied up in a neat little Lycra package.

It's hard to avoid the water, growing up in Australia. Kids + scorching summers = pools. My problems really began in primary school, where it seemed we did nothing but swim. We had swimming lessons every Monday during February and March, then every day for the last two school weeks of December. So I'd start building up my anxiety around October each year.

I remember the feeling of dread as the school bus headed for the pool, the smell of zinc cream making me heave. It wasn't that I was afraid of the water; I just had no confidence. Ever since that 'She's fat!' episode at Weight Watchers I'd believed I was lardy and loathsome, so I hated putting my body into a swimsuit.

My heart would race every minute of our lessons, wondering what they'd make us do next. I didn't want to jump into the pool because I thought I'd make a bigger splash than my friends. I didn't want to stand on the starting blocks because it felt like the eyes of everyone in the pool – even those fifty metres away in the shallow end, even those *underwater* – had zoomed in on my freakishness. I was pretty paranoid for a ten-year-old.

All that fear and self-consciousness made me a rubbish swimmer. I couldn't dive for shit, for instance. Half a dozen different teachers tried to teach me but I couldn't make my body relax; I belly-flopped every time. The most mortifying 'method' was when I had to stand on the block and my teacher would wrap his hands around my ankles then sort of fling me in, forcing my body into the correct hands-first, feet-last position. Almost fifteen years later I still can't stand by the edge of a pool without feeling there's a big pair of hands clamped around my ankles.

And then there was that time when another teacher made me jump off the big diving board. I didn't *wanna*

93

jump off the big diving board! It wasn't because I was scared of heights. I just didn't want to elevate my body and make it even easier for people to stare at my fat legs.

But she made me climb that ladder and I stood trembling at the end of the board as the whole class chanted, 'Jump! Jump!' I stared down into the blue abyss for so long that the pool manager, watching the action from the kiosk, called out over the booming PA system, 'C'mon, Shauna! If you jump off your mum will buy you a packet of crisps!'

Cue raucous laughter from the crowd.

I distinctly remember glaring down at them and thinking, *Oh great. Now if I jump off everyone's going to think I only did it FOR THE CRISPS because I'm such a fatty!*

In the end I jumped. I don't remember if I got the crisps, but I've never trod the diving board since.

The worst part of that story is that my swimming teacher just happened to be the Mothership! She taught at my school at the time. Periodically, I remind her of this incident and the resulting emotional scars, but she insists she was only trying to be encouraging. I have to say that fifteen years later I am finally letting go and can almost see why everyone else thinks it was so bloody funny.

After that came puberty, which made me even more paranoid about my body. Ever since, I've zealously avoided swimming pools, beaches, rivers and puddles.

So because of my traumatic swimming history I was nauseous with fear when we arrived at the pool on Sunday evening. But we'd used the Vampire Method – who the hell goes swimming on a Sunday night? Only a few dedicated lap swimmers and old ladies in flowery bathing suits. The crowd was sufficiently small and unthreatening for me to dare unveil my dimpled flesh.

I slinked up to the pool edge in my dowdy new swim-suit, trying to ignore the fact that the octogenarians had better skin tone than me. I tossed away my towel and slipped into the blue.

I seemed to have forgotten how to swim. I made a thrashing attempt at the front crawl but ended up taking in mouthfuls of chlorine. How the hell do you breathe underwater? After all those years of lessons, I've held on to the trauma but forgotten all the instructions!

But I was happy enough to just paddle around. Oh, how I'd missed the water. I could have wept from the pure joy of its soothing coolness after so many years. I felt luxurious and serene. For years I've told myself that fat chicks have no place in the pool, but on Sunday night in the dark with the old ladies, I was happy. It didn't matter that beneath the surface lurked a size 22 body, because the world could see only my chubby cheeks and a megawatt grin.

WEEK 41
22 October 2001
18st 5.5lb (117.5kg, 258.5lb)
6st 9.5lb lost (42kg, 92.5lb) – 6st 8.5lb to go (42.5kg, 93.5lb)

This morning I washed my hair and styled it to perfection. I put on a new pair of size 22 knickers straight from the plastic wrapping. I wore clothes that were actually ironed instead of plucked from the bedroom floor. I put on lipstick. I spritzed on perfume.

Hot date? Not quite. My mate Jenny has just arrived back in Australia after living in London for eighteen months. Last time she saw me I was still three stone shy of my ultimate heftiest, but a lardy sight nonetheless. So I've been anticipating her return not just because I've missed her like mad, but because I desperately want to find out if she'll notice anything different.

As she pulled up outside my house, I arranged myself in the doorway like a game show hostess. I sucked in my stomach and pulled my shoulders back, trying to look as elongated as possible.

'Holy *shit*, Shaun!'

Jenny slammed her car door shut. We ran towards each other, arms open wide like in the movies. Except she ran at normal speed and I was in slow motion, as that is my natural pace.

'You're back!'

'You've shrunk!'

'Really?'

'Well duh! You've clearly lost a shitload of weight!'

I'd missed Jenny and her trademark bluntness.

'Not many people have noticed, you see,' I said coyly.

'How could they not notice?'

'Oh, you!'

It was so good to catch up with Jen. I'm in awe of how much her overseas adventures have changed her. She's now so cheerful, confident and bubbling over with exciting tales of countries visited, weird food eaten, handbags lost and romance found.

'She just glowed,' I told Rhiannon later. 'She just seemed so happy within herself and enthusiastic about life!'

'We should do that too.'

'Do what?'

'Go live in Britain and have adventures.'

I snorted. 'Maybe you could, but not me.'

Rhiannon raised an eyebrow. 'Why the hell not?'

'Because . . . you've travelled before. That's your caper. It's not the sort of thing I'd do.'

'It *used* to be not the sort of thing you'd do,' she said. 'You're different now.'

I squirmed. 'Not different enough yet.'

'C'mon . . . Paris, London, Rome! And what about all those places you studied in History class? You've always talked about seeing Red Square some day!'

'Yeah, but you know me – all talk, no action!'

'I'm serious, Shauna! We can get the Working Holiday visa like Jen. I'll even let you pick which city we live in.'

'I'm still too f—'

'You're not too fat, you goose! Look, why not just have a little think about it, for now.'

'Sure!' I said, without a trace of conviction.

30 October 2001
18st 2lb (115.5kg, 254lb)
6st 13lb lost (44kg, 97lb) – 6st 5lb to go (40.5kg, 89lb)

Holy statistical milestone, Batman! I've passed the halfway mark in my epic adventure. I've now achieved precisely 52 per cent of my goal!

That's about the highlight of the week, since Operation Swimming Pool has turned into a complete disaster.

I was so excited after last time: I'd be able to cross something off my 'Things To Do When I'm Skinny' list before I was remotely skinny! I even bought goggles and a swimming cap. But I guess the enthusiasm was purely circumstantial. Foolishly I forgot the Vampire Method, put on my swimsuit and headed to the pool on Saturday afternoon.

My heart turned to shit the instant we got out of the car. The place was mobbed with taut teens in bikinis and screaming toddlers circling the car park like seagulls.

'I can't do this!' I blurted.

Rhiannon instantly smelt a Fat Girl Freak Out. 'Don't worry, mate. We'll just get straight in the water like last time, it'll be fun.'

'There's too many people. I can't do it. I can't do it.'

I froze beside the car; 18 stone of pure panic trussed in pink beach towel. My face burned and my breath came in short, painful bursts. I couldn't go into that pool with all those gorgeous skinny people. Not with this body.

'You go ahead,' I said. 'I'll come and pick you up later.'

'I'm not going without you.'

'I'm sorry,' I started to cry, my sobs making my wobbly body wobble even harder. 'I'm sorry.'

I bawled all the way home, just like that first night at Weight Watchers. I may be almost seven stone lighter, but all that shame and revulsion is still there. It almost felt worse, because at least on the scale you can cover your flabby bits with clothes.

Some days I'm positive and proud to have come this far. But some days my confidence and resolve feel flimsier than those string bikinis, ready to come undone at the slightest hint of a breeze.

WEEK 43
5 November 2001
18st 4lb (116.4kg, 256lb)
6st 11lb lost (43.1kg, 95lb) – 6st 7lb to go (41.4kg, 91lb)

Last week I turned 24. My gift to myself was a restaurant meal with friends, finished with half a slice of orange and poppy seed cake. My gift from the scale was a two-pound gain.

'Two pounds?' I squeaked indignantly to Donna. 'I didn't even have the garlic bread!'

Hopefully this time next year I'll be at my goal weight and too drunk at my party to care about the stupid scale numbers.

I've finally struck gold on the exercise front. Operation Swimming Pool may have been a stinking failure but I've fallen in love with two new classes!

First up was BodyCombat on Saturday morning, a

martial arts inspired workout. Oh my Lord. Fit Ball is a casual bounce in the park compared to this. I was dripping with sweat just from the warm-up. But safely hidden in the back row, I was determined to carry on and not have a Fat Girl Freak Out.

I muddled along at my own less than stellar pace, doing my best approximation of kicking and punching. I felt ridiculous at first, but when the instructor told us all to yell and scream and pretend to be wounding mortal enemies I really got into it. Pretend violence and thumping techno music, what a winning combination! Finally after fifty minutes we flopped to the floor for the abdominal workout and cool-down. My face was so red that the instructor asked if I was OK. I grinned and gave a feeble thumbs-up.

The next day I woke up in delicious agony, my back and shoulders screaming from all the hooks and uppercuts. But there was no time to moan because on Monday night we were off to BodyPump.

This was a whole new world of pain! Using a barbell, we worked one body part per song – squats for legs, then chest, back and hamstrings, triceps, biceps, lunges (legs again) and shoulders, finishing with abs and stretching. Although I only had a tiny one-kilo weight on each end of the bar, it was far more intense than the weight machines we'd been using for the past month. My limbs were jelly and the next day I could barely sit down on the loo.

The class instructors are so inspiring. Out on the gym floor my concentration always wanders – I read magazines, scratch my butt or get absorbed in an episode of *Neighbours*. But there's no hiding in the class and the instructors keep you working for a whole hour. By the time I collapsed into the cool-down stretches, I knew I'd found my Holy Grail of fitness. I've already been back twice. No more Vampire Method for me!

I'm excited about exercise for the first time in my life. The classes marry my fanatical love of music with my profound laziness. All I have to do is show up and a nubile wench will cheer and scream and tell me exactly what to do. It's fun and efficient. Best of all, I can lurk at the back of the class unnoticed and let the skinny girls hog the mirrors.

It's taken many months of trial and error, but I think I've finally figured out what exercise is going to work best for me. I always told myself those classes were reserved for hardcore gym bunnies so I couldn't join in until I got skinny. I'm so glad I got the nerve to step inside and prove my Fat Girl beliefs wrong. I may be big, slow and uncoordinated, but I have every right to be there.

Week 46
26 November 2001
18st 1lb (115kg, 253lb)
7st lost (44.5kg, 98lb) – 6st 4lb to go (40kg, 88lb)

Hooray! Another pound off and only eighty-eight to go. Eighty-eight! Two fat ladies!

So when the powers that be start telling everyone to prepare for 'redeployment', what the hell does that mean in this dot-bomb crazy world? It sounds like I'll be stuffed into a cannon with a laptop tucked under my arm and blasted off into the ether, then wherever I land, I'm to dust myself off and get straight back to work.

Whatever it means, the winds of change are a-blowing at work. The department workload has dwindled over the past few months, so it hasn't come as much of a surprise. But I worry because I have no idea what they'll do with me, or where I'd go if I left the company. I've been so caught up in my fat-blasting efforts this year that I've just worked like a zombie and not thought too critically about it. I've been a professional cut and paster for the past two years, so I'm not exactly brimming over with marketable skills. I do have that journalism degree but no experience (or interest) to accompany it. Oh shit. Who the bloody hell would employ me?

WEEK 47
3 December 2001
18st 1lb again! (115kg, 253lb)
7st lost (44.5kg, 98lb) – 6st 4lb to go (40kg, 88lb)

It's December and I feel good. Normally I dread this time of year, the start of the Sweaty Skin and Chafing Thigh season. But this year, two sizes and seven stone smaller, I'm slightly better equipped to handle the heat.

I'm officially hooked on BodyPump and BodyCombat. I did three classes this week! I can feel the benefits already – my quads feel firmer and my biceps are growing. They're all disguised by a giant layer of blubber, but it's a start, right?

Exercise gives me a genuine sense of purpose and achievement. I'm euphoric every time I put a heavier weight on my barbell, or do a lunge without falling over, or make it through a whole BodyCombat track without needing to stick my head out the window and gulp for air. Each tiny change spurs me on. And it's such a healthy approach too – I'm focusing on getting fitter and stronger, rather than obsessing about Points and numbers.

Witness the sad case I have become: our Monday night BodyPump class is at 6.30, which means we have to Weigh and Run at our six o'clock Weight Watchers meeting then zoom across town to the gym. We arrived last night to find there were no barbells left, despite the fact that we'd reserved a place for the class a week ago! They'd either over-booked or a pair of evil bitches had sneaked into the class.

Rhiannon and I were outraged. We stomped off to the car and ranted all the way home. But I had to laugh. Who'd have thought that I – breathless from a walk to the fridge ten months ago – would wind up hysterical because I couldn't exercise?

I was already in a rotten mood having maintained my weight at Weight Watchers. I was positive I was due a big loss because I'd been feeling so smug and slinky! Damn those misleading exercise endorphins. Sometimes I feel like running away from Weight Watchers. The scale is not my friend. At least the exercise makes me feel I'm getting somewhere. Maybe I should just swap my scale obsession for an exercise obsession.

Tonight our house was full of girls. There was the gorgeous Rhiannon, the gorgeous Jenny and Emily, two of Emily's equally gorgeous friends, and lardy old me. The purpose of the gathering was to consume a lot of alcohol, dress up foxily, then take on the Canberra night life.

I had a handy excuse not to drink, because I'm doped up on antihistamines thanks to my hay fever. I had to blow my dripping red nose after every song in Body Combat this morning.

It's strange watching people get drunk. The gradual loosening of tongues; the unravelling of inhibitions. The more they talked, the more I wished the couch would swallow me up. I had nothing to contribute to their anecdotes of blokes at the bar and ill-advised flings. Instead I laughed too loud and nodded a lot, trying to hide my stomach behind a cushion and hoping no one would notice I wasn't contributing to the conversation.

After a few hours they clambered into high heels and put on their lipstick.

'Shauna dear,' Emily said, 'why haven't you changed yet?'

'I think I'm going to stay in,' I said casually. 'My hay fever is rotten today.'

'You have to come out!' Rhiannon was tipsy but she could still detect a Fat Girl Freak Out. 'You can't stay here!'

'But my Rudolph nose! I just don't feel up to it.'

There was a slurred chorus of 'Aww!'

Luckily the taxi arrived and I took the role of Mother Hen. 'Chop chop, girls! Meter's running!'

'Next time, Shaun!' said Jenny.

'Of course!' I smiled and shoved them out the door.

I just couldn't do the Fat Girl on the Town routine tonight. For starters, I have nothing to wear. I may have dropped a few sizes but I still look enormous, especially when standing next to my slender comrades. And I've tried drinking to numb my insecurities, but no amount of alcohol can make me feel good. This large body sobers up far too quickly. I'd wind up sitting on the sidelines with my fake smile pasted on, fake laughing and waving to my friends with their slinky tops and entourage of male admirers. Then there'd be that inevitable moment when Jenny or Emily beckoned me on to the dance floor, and after ten minutes of protest I'd waddle my way into their circle and do a graceless boogie in my Big Is Beautiful trousers.

As soon as the girls left I burst into tears and I've barely paused for two hours. If my face weren't so red I'd go to McDonald's for a couple of soothing sundaes. I feel so fucking ugly and hopeless. And undesirable. It's been years since I felt that someone was attracted to me. I forget what it feels like.

I'm angry because part of me so badly wants to be out there enjoying myself. I want to act like my twenty-four years, instead of holing up in the house like a sociopath. I want to dress up and dance and go wild. But even if I could find something to wear, my vodka-induced confidence would only last thirty minutes before the awareness returned and I'd be looking for the nearest exit.

I hate feeling like this. I thought I liked being me these days. But that only seems to be true under cover of darkness, or in the safety of the back row of BodyPump class. Am I ever going to like myself all the time, in every place?

WEEK 49
17 December 2001
18st AGAIN! (114.5kg, 252lb)
7st 1lb lost (45kg, 99lb) – 6st 3lb to go (39.5kg, 87lb)

'So,' said the Mothership, 'what's new?'

'I already told you . . . nothing.'

'Are you sure?'

We were sitting in the foyer of Parliament House, waiting for Rhiannon's graduation ceremony to start. She actually graduated last year but was coming back to receive the Dean's Award.

'It's so hot today,' Mum went on. 'I hope she's wearing a good deodorant, especially under that heavy gown. Do you think she's got a good deodorant on?'

'Let's pray that she does.'

'Can you imagine how many of our tax dollars it took to pay for all this marble?' She pointed to the foyer floor. 'Aren't you glad you're not the one who has to polish it?'

'Mmm.'

'What's wrong with you?'

'Nothing, just pre-menstrual grumpiness. I feel like a blob today.'

106

'Well, you're quite an attractive blob.'

'Um. Thanks.'

'See, don't you just love me? This is why you bring me places.'

Then five minutes of blissful silence.

'So what's new?'

'Nothing!'

'Well there has to be something!'

'There isn't!'

'Well. All right. Hey, I see you are wearing a skirt today.'

'Excellent observation.'

'It's nice to see you wearing a skirt.'

'It's nice to be wearing one!'

Today is the first time I've displayed my calves since my high school uniform. For six years I've hidden my pale, trunk-like pins in long trousers, even in the height of summer. But on a surprisingly successful shopping trip last week, Rhiannon persuaded me to try on a skirt, just below the knee in a loud purple. I grumbled and bitched, saying my ankles were 'too thick' for such a thing, but she made me try it on. It looked great. And it was a size 20!

It's been five years since I could get into a size 20. I've lost five years of fat! And my legs don't look too bad either. They're still chunky but they're starting to develop a hint of shape, thanks to all those squats and lunges. I almost cried in the changing rooms. Me in a skirt!

So here I was at the graduation, feeling feminine and trendy for the first time in years, if slightly self-conscious about wearing something other than a shapeless sack.

Could people see my cellulite? Were they counting the flab rolls on my back?

'The important question is,' said Mum, interrupting my thoughts, 'are you wearing a petticoat?'

'What?'

She brought out her purse-lipped, over-enunciated schoolteacher voice: 'Are. You. Wear-ing. A. Petticoat?'

'Do you take me for some sort of a crusty old spinster?'

'You should wear a petticoat if you're going to wear a skirt,' she sniffed, 'You may as well be naked without one.'

Mercifully the ceremony began, and when Rhiannon received her award we were misty-eyed with pride. While she handed back her robes and cap, I sneaked off to Weight Watchers for a quick weigh-in before we all went out for dinner.

'Look at you!' cried Donna as I sashayed to the scale.

'Ahh!' I waved off her compliment.

'Will you stay for the meeting and talk to everyone about your achievements?'

'Why? I'm nowhere near my goal!'

'How many times must I tell you, it's all about the journey! You're an inspiration.'

I squirmed. 'I have to run. I'm meeting my mum and Rhiannon for dinner.'

'Two minutes, please?'

After all she'd done for me this year, holding my hand and wiping away my snotty tears, how could I possibly say no?

'Ladies, I want to introduce you to Shauna. She's been with us since January and she is amazing.'

My face burned. Amazing?

'How much have you lost now, Shauna?'

'Seven stone!'

There were gasps and stares. Some ladies frowned at me critically, perhaps trying to picture me with those extra stones.

'I just want you all to see what you can achieve with hard work and determination. What do you say, Shauna?'

'Oh yes!' I was such a fraud. 'Hard work. Determination. Just keep counting those Points!'

I gave Donna a hug and rushed out the door. How long had it been since I stayed for a meeting? How long had it been since I'd filled in a Points tracker or eaten a Weight Watchers chocolate mousse? I can't help feeling I'm outgrowing Weight Watchers. I feel like a rebellious, ungrateful teenager in my lipstick and new frock, sneaking out the bedroom window in search of new adventures.

WEEK 51

31 December 2001

18st (114.5kg, 252lb) (back here again!)

7st 1lb lost (45kg, 99lb) – 6st 3lb to go (39.5kg, 87lb)

I survived my first Christmas as a dedicated fat-fighter! Temptation abounded in the form of pavlova and ham, but I stuck to salads and fruit. My only concession was Nanny's caramel pie. Shortbread crust, oozy caramel innards and an artery-clogging layer of whipped cream – it's an annual treat that I refuse to give up!

I weighed in tonight and there was a belated Christmas

Miracle – a minuscule half-pound gain over the festive period! Which was the same half-pound I'd lost on Christmas Eve. The Lord giveth and he taketh away.

In other news, I've chopped off my hair. After my pity party earlier in the month, I decided it was time to start taking some pride in my appearance. My new graduation outfit reminded me that looking good helps me feel good.

My hairdresser Michelle smiled at me in the mirror. 'So Shauna, what shall we do today? Just the usual trim?'

'No! I feel old and frumpy. I want to look young and hot. Do you think that's possible?'

An hour later there was a puddle of ginger on the floor. I emerged with a short, funky cut and blond highlights. I love it! I've never had people rave over my hairdo before, telling me it's flattering and demanding to know who did it. It's an excellent way to distract them from my thighs.

I'm about to clock up one year of lard-busting adventures. Somehow I've managed to lose seven stone, tame my chocolate addiction and coax my arse off the couch. I'm still a hefty lass at 18 stone but I've got a new hairdo and I've got hope. Onward and downward!

YEAR TWO
2002

WEEK 52
7 January 2002
17st 13.5lb (114.3kg, 251.5lb)
7st 1.5lb lost (45.2kg, 99.5lb) – 6st 2.5lb to go (39.3kg, 86.5lb)

The instructor came up to me after BodyPump tonight and told me I had Good Form.

'I've been watching you hiding at the back,' she said. 'You're doing great. Your squats are superb, too. Keep up the good work!'

I blushed and stammered as though I'd been touched by a rock star. I thought such a muscle-bound goddess would only speak to the nubile hipsters in the front row. But she noticed me! Me, twice the size of the average participant. Me, without rippling body or coordinated outfit. She looked beyond the red face and tummy rolls and saw the athlete within. Happy New Year, indeed!

28 January 2002
17st 12lb (113.6kg, 250lb)
7st 3lb lost (45.9kg, 101lb) – 6st 1lb to go (38.6kg,
85lb)

I've flown the coop. I've left Weight Watchers!

I've been fantasizing about leaving for months but never felt ready to actually do it.

I can't help feeling ungrateful, especially since Donna and crew looked after me like a helpless baby bird for a whole year. I squawked and flapped and demanded constant nurturing, but just like Rhiannon they were patient and understanding. Who knows how different the past fifty-five weeks could have been without their support? I might have wound up with a heart attack, face down in a four-litre tub of ice-cream.

So I must credit Weight Watchers with reminding me how to eat healthily. They gave me the rules, structure and accountability that I desperately craved. I wanted a system to believe in, because I didn't believe in myself.

But now I do believe in me, and I do believe I've had enough of the system too. I'm tired of standing in the queue, listening to other ladies justifying their gains before they've even got on the scale. I'm tired of the weekly fee, the Points, the magazine and the crappy cereal bars.

To be honest, the gym is the biggest reason I'm fleeing the nest. Not only do I get more satisfaction from getting fitter than from getting on the scale, but the Weight Watchers meeting really is a rude clash with my Body Pump class. Why stand in a queue when I could be securing my favourite spot in the back row? Why listen to some old dame asking how many Points are in a Fisherman's Friend when I could be burning blubber?

I weighed in tonight at 17 stone 12 pounds. I grinned because my mental spreadsheet told me I'd finally cracked the magical 100 pounds lost mark. It seemed poetic somehow, so neat and tidy; the perfect milestone to wind up this chapter of my lard-busting adventure.

So how does one break up with Weight Watchers? Do you go for a long, tearful goodbye or just walk out the door and never look back?

Donna was surrounded by a horde of New Years Resolutionists, helping them fill out the membership forms. I smiled and waved, mouthing goodbye.

'Off to your weights class?' she called out.

'Oh yes. Gotta make some muscles!'

'Have fun!' She smiled and turned back to her brood.

Maybe I should have thanked her again, for her kind words and encouragement; for helping me through the shittiest moment of my life. I know I'll always be grateful for that. But there were dozens of new recruits that needed her.

So I'm going to do this on my own now. I want to keep learning how to think for myself. There's a tiny gnaw of doubt that it's too soon, that all the exercise endorphins are pumping me with false confidence. But I've got to try.

I bought some new knickers the other day. Still the same horrible Bonds Cottontails, as worn by nuns and spinsters; but these ones are a size 20. They're hardly dainty compared to Rhiannon's but they still look much smaller when hanging on the line next to my ancient size 26s. Weight Watchers helped me shrink my smalls, but I did a lot of the work myself. When I come to buy the next size down, I want to take all the credit.

7 February 2002
17st 10.5lb (113kg, 248.5lb)
7st 4.5lb lost (46.5kg, 102.5lb) – 5st 13.5lb to go (38kg, 83.5lb)

I rocked up for my BodyPump class tonight to find the gym was CLOSED.

Not only was it closed; there was yellow tape and a burly security guard blocking the entrance. According to the carefully worded note on the window, there's been a 'misunderstanding' between the building owners and the gym management.

It costs $700 for a yearly membership and there must be at least 700 bazillion members, so what's their excuse?

Naturally I panicked. What if they don't pay up? What if they're siphoning my fees to feed drug habits or buy luxury cars? What will I do without the gym? What about my growing muscles? Will they just deflate overnight? Will all the fat come back?

My body was twitching to get inside. I needed my fix. I wanted to jump on the scale too, to make sure the two pounds I'd lost on Monday were still lost. I almost *cried*! Can you believe how things have changed around here? I wanted to cry because I couldn't exercise.

We've been assured the gym will be open tomorrow. It bloody better be.

Apologies for such a long period of silence; I've been too busy worrying about the future. I had a total of one billable hour on my timesheet last week. Which means I did bugger all for thirty-nine hours. This was a remarkable improvement on the previous two weeks in which I had zero billable hours.

My working day consists of sitting at my desk nursing a sinking feeling, wondering what attempts at redeployment will occur today. This involves a lot of rejection. My boss Jill's phone will ring and it will be the Resource Manager.

'Does Shauna have the skills to do X, Y and Z?'

'Regretfully no!' says Jill.

Today I accompanied her to a meeting with someone in another department.

'Can Shauna do A, B or C?' they asked.

'No, Shauna is a content editor.'

'I see.'

Now I know how people who used to screw things together in factories felt when they invented robots to screw things together in factories. Goddamn technology. Only two years ago everyone was crying out for people to edit content for websites. Now our clients have the software to produce a web page as easily as a cup of tea. They don't need me to make things bold and hyperlinked any more. They've finally discovered how ridiculously simple it is, so why should they pay me to do it for them? This year the content work has completely dried up, and the role of professional cut and paster is all but obsolete.

I spend a lot of time asking Jill can I help her with anything. She laughed on Friday and said, 'You're really worried about this lack of work thing, aren't you?'

Well I guess the novelty of surfing the net for eight hours a day has worn off. Things are getting grim. I bought the *Canberra Times* tonight and moped all over the Positions Vacant. What do I do now? Why didn't I see this coming?

My friends have suggested I retrain and become a programmer, but I'm really not interested in high-level geekery. I'm interested in the words on the screen, not the technical crap that put them there. I don't know where to go from here. I feel so bloody unemployable.

But I'll keep looking, or otherwise join a convent. The job security is good – I'm not likely to be replaced by a robot – plus a nun's habit is very slimming.

WEEK 64
2 April 2002

In the past fortnight I've signed up with four recruitment agencies and applied for eight different jobs from the paper. I'm trying not to panic, but I would just like to say that this whole *thanks but no thanks you're too inexperienced not confident enough too overqualified not as good as that guy over there too tall too short too browneyed too two-legged for this position* caper is extremely demoralizing.

Today Jill and I went down to the greasy little shop behind our building to catch some lunchtime sun. I had a greasy chicken wrap that I regretted before I'd even taken a bite; she had a salad roll.

'So boss, heard any more news?'

'Bloody hell, I said no onions. Now my breath will be feral all afternoon.'

'Anything?'

'Nothing concrete yet. But perhaps it's safe to say that our jobs are unsafe.'

'Oh. Great.' Why did I buy that stupid wrap? I kid myself it's healthy because of the salad and wholemeal lavash bread, but what about the cheese, barbecue sauce and oily rotisserie chicken?

'But don't worry, it'll get sorted. You're a smart girl. Whatever happens, you'll land on your feet.'

'Yeah.'

'Honestly,' she smiled. 'You don't have to look so scared.'

But I am scared. My mind is cloudy with fear. I hate the uncertainty. I hate my lack of control over the situation. That's why I like dieting, in a perverse way. The outcome is entirely up to me. If something turns to crap, I can put it right again. I am in control.

Or am I? The scale hasn't moved for weeks. Maybe my Weight Watchers withdrawal was too hasty. After all, there I was eating a greasy chicken wrap that would make a Points calculator explode.

I had my annual performance review today and it was a disaster.

The official review was fine – apparently I've been a pretty good worker bee. The Boss said I am bright and reliable, but my lack of confidence and initiative is holding me back. That was when my stomach started to churn with dread.

Jill put down the review papers and told me she wanted to address me on a personal level. Apparently she is very worried about me. I have this 'attitude' lately and I am all 'quiet and withdrawn'. I put on my headphones and stare at the screen and if she speaks to me I give her 'a look' that suggests she shouldn't have interrupted me.

On and on she went. I kept staring at my hands and realized I needed to do something about my nails. They were getting longer than the red polish I'd put on last week. She said I seemed to be drifting away and not wanting to engage in conversation. Blah blah blah. She said I was clearly unhappy and perhaps I needed a change.

'What do you think of all this? Do you agree with me?'

I just stared at the table, until the grains in the wood swirled beneath my eyes like river currents. I wondered if they'd swallow me up if I just kept staring.

'A change might do me good,' I said quietly.

'Shauna, you've got a face that just can't lie. Anyone can see that all is not well.'

My body betrayed me and I started to cry like an idiot. 'I just can't get it together,' I sobbed, 'I hate being me lately.'

It all tumbled out – how it feels like I'm going nowhere; how everything has become a blur. I felt ashamed and fat and stupid but I couldn't stop the words.

I didn't go to work yesterday, I just couldn't get out of bed. I almost called in sick again today until I remembered my review at the last moment. I don't know what's happening to me. Ever since things started going bad at work, everything else has started to slide and I can't seem to stop it. I'm trying to convince myself it's just a bad patch but it seems to be getting worse. It's like being on the verge of drowning and not knowing if you want to struggle or just let go.

'You don't have to feel down, you know,' I heard Jill go on as I counted the lines on my knuckles. 'You can make a conscious decision whether to feel down or not. You just have to ask yourself, "Am I going to feel like crap or am I going to get over it?"'

I nodded but wanted to punch her.

Jill is a take-charge type. I guess that's why she's the boss. When I said I needed a change, I meant I should get the fuck out of this company and find a new job or perhaps finally join that convent. But she was thinking of a change within the confines of the company. Perhaps my redeployment had been planned for months, or perhaps I was so miserable she didn't want to see me sulking beneath my headphones for one more day. Either way, with a quick call to the Resource Manager, she had found me a new job within ten minutes.

'Amanda needs a project assistant and thinks you'll be perfect!' she smiled triumphantly. 'It will be a great experience for you!'

121

'I don't know anything about being a project assistant,' I said feebly.

'You're smart, Shauna, you'll do great.' Jill squeezed my shoulder. 'We'll go around and talk to Amanda in a moment.'

'OK.'

'You start tomorrow.'

'Oh.'

I felt as if I was watching myself from above, that everything was spinning out of control and I was powerless to stop it. I'm trying to think like a good corporate lackey and see it as a career opportunity. Surely it had to be better than surfing the net all day, waiting in vain for some editing work to roll in? At least it's something to do while I keep looking for work elsewhere.

But I have no faith in my ability to find something else. What happened to all my confidence and bravado from the end of last year? I felt I could conquer the world. But lately I want the world to fuck off.

WEEK 71
22 May 2002

Imagine my surprise when I discovered yesterday there was such a thing as a staple remover. For years I've painstakingly plucked them out with my fingernails. But now I know there's this little contraption with fearsome teeth that rips the staple out for you. Amazing. I found myself stapling random pieces of paper together, just so I'd have some staples to remove.

So despite protesting to Jill that I didn't know anything about being a project assistant, I seem to be managing. Turns out Project Assistant just means doing all the crappy jobs no one else wants to do. Aside from the staple removing, there is the data entry, the photocopying, and the sticking of barcode stickers on to computers.

I had nine paper jams yesterday afternoon. The photocopier sees me coming and cackles to itself, *Aha, look at this amateur*. That machine has far too many orifices for paper to hide in.

As I dismantled and declogged, I thought of paper jams and how there's so many types of paper jam. Like the pulpy kind you spread on your toast. It keeps you regular. Or when there's a whole bunch of notebooks and Post-Its™ driving home from work and the roads get all congested. Or when the ream of A4 calls up his old high school buddy the legal pad and they get together with drums and guitars in their garage. Paper jam.

OK, I am going insane. As pleasant as my new boss Amanda has been over the past month, I fear I'm losing the plot. I thought it was bad having nothing to do in the Content department, but being completely swamped by repetitive and mundane tasks is far worse. I spent six solid hours typing asset numbers into Excel today, and it was nowhere near as fun as my weight loss spreadsheet.

Most nights I get home late, eyes burning from staring at serial numbers all day, and fall asleep in front of the telly instead of going to the gym. The size 20 jeans I bought from a catalogue back in February are painfully tight and I'm too scared to get on the scale.

It started innocently enough with that one chicken

wrap two months ago, from the little shop behind our building. The first time I ordered it, I asked for no cheese and no sauce. But the next time I had cheese and sauce. Then the next time I washed it down with a bottle of chocolate milk. And the time after that I got a hamburger with the lot with my chocolate milk. Today I got the burger, the chocolate milk and a four-finger KitKat.

What is happening to me? Why can't I stop? I don't even like KitKats.

WEEK 73
3 June 2002

CANBERRA, AAP – Local woman Miss Dietgirl was coaxed down from the capital's tallest building today after receiving the seventeenth rejection letter in her fruitless quest for a new job.

'This one really gutted me,' said the distraught Braddon resident. 'I've been looking since February and this time I dared to dream. Thirty-five applicants and I actually managed to get an interview. I prepared like crazy and thought I had it in the bag.'

After receiving her rejection letter, Miss Dietgirl went to Telstra Tower where she stood on the viewing deck and bellowed 'Goodbye cruel world!' to anyone who would listen, dangling her toes over the edge.

The woman's deranged cries were heard by two Japanese tourists, who alerted Tower staff. After three hours of intense negotiation and use of mega-phones, Miss Dietgirl was lured from her perch on Canberra's tallest building with the promise of chocolate and an agreement that Channel 10 would reduce its screenings of *Everybody Loves Raymond* by 75 per cent.

Representatives from the interview panel were hesitant to comment on why Miss Dietgirl was not offered the position, a web developer role in a government department.

'We cannot divulge this information as it is classified. However, Miss Dietgirl's claims that we coldly rejected her because she is untalented, un-attractive and incapable are not wholly unfounded.'

Meanwhile, the secretarial world rejoiced at the news that they would not be losing one of their brightest new talents.

'She is really coming along with that Excel,' said an anonymous source. 'And today she learned how to change the toner cartridge on the printer and only got a small amount of ink on her clothes. We all gathered round and clapped politely.'

WEEK 78
8 July 2002

When I christened this journal 'The Amazing Adventures of Dietgirl' it was part sarcasm and part optimism. 'Yeah, like losing half my body weight is going to be *so* amazing,' I thought. 'Then again . . . maybe it will be?'

Seventy-eight weeks later it's not Amazing. I'm not having Adventures and I'm certainly not on a Diet. So all we have left is, 'The Girl'. I'm no weight loss superhero. It was tempting to torch this whole journal and run away, rather than slink back here after five weeks' silence and admit to you all that I'm a stinking failure.

But I just need to tell somebody.

It was *déjà vu* at the doctor's surgery today. It was a different town, a different doctor and three years later, but I was back down in that impossible black hole.

'I've tried pretending everything is OK,' I explained, 'But I just feel lost. I wake up every day and that suffocating panic is still there. It's like someone threw an invisible net over me. I'm writhing and clawing but I can't find a way out.'

She nodded but I was paranoid and felt she didn't believe me. Depression has become almost fashionable over the past few years; I didn't want her thinking I was just hopping on the bandwagon.

'OK. Have you tried talking to your family and friends?'

'Yes,' I lied.

I haven't told a soul. It was embarrassing enough having to confess I'd been demoted to Photocopy Girl, moving even further away from that expensive degree. I'm determined not to let them know I'm back down here again.

'Look, I've been here before,' I rushed on. 'I had some problems three years ago, I took antidepressants. I've been OK for ages but somehow it's happening again. I'm trying to pull myself out of it but it feels completely hopeless.'

'How's your diet?' she asked politely. 'Are you eating well?'

'Most of the time.' I squirmed. Part of me has enjoyed bingeing again. I'd missed the secret, urgent ritual of cramming myself with food until I'm finally numb. And nauseous.

But then yesterday I remembered the consequences. I was typing serial numbers when I suddenly felt cool air on my stomach. My jeans had spontaneously unzipped themselves. I'd felt so skinny when I bought them back in February but now they couldn't contain the advance of my midriff. I tugged my top down and sat with a folder in my lap for the rest of the day.

'What about exercise?'

'I haven't been to the gym in months.'

'Well,' she smiled gently, 'even if you could manage a daily walk. Eating well and looking after your body can really help keep you feel balanced.'

You know, normally I would have loved to find a doctor like this. Someone who wasn't content to just throw me a prescription and shove me out of her office. But today I just wanted the fucking pills.

'I'm not one of those quick fix people,' I said, trying not to sound desperate. 'I didn't want to come here. But I just need a boost so I can get out of bed, so I can get up and try to fix things.'

'OK.' She reached for her prescription pad.

I started to cry from sheer relief.

I feel guilty about picking up that prescription. Depression doesn't sit well with me. No matter how many people tell me it's an illness, it feels like a failure of my character. I can't help thinking of my grandfather, slowly dying in his armchair. I come from a long line of resilient farmers just like him. There's no time for emotional shit when there's sheep to be shorn and crops to be sown. Depression seems so indulgent. Surely medication should be reserved for genuinely ill people, not just some fat chick who's lost her way. Surely if I just snapped out of it and stopped eating so much crap and found a new job everything would be fine.

I hate admitting I'm down here again. I hate admitting that I have failed to solve this on my own. But right now I can't see a future beyond hamburgers, unzipped jeans and barcode stickers. I need to find some self-respect again. I know that doesn't come in a pill, but I hope the pill will help clear my head for the search.

WEEK 80
22 July 2002

Rhiannon and I met Jenny for laksa at Asian Noodle House. Such an innocuous thing to do, but I was anxious. After two weeks of antidepressants I'm past the initial delirium and have settled into feeling quietly functional. Boosted by a fresh haircut and a clean set of clothes, today I felt ready to try engaging with the humans again.

As always, I was awkward with the chopsticks. *Just take it easy*, I told myself. I stabbed the squishy tofu and slowly reeled in the noodles. But somehow I lost control of the vehicle. The chopstick flew across to the next table and landed on someone's shoe with a plasticky clink at the same time as I schlooped up the noodles. Dots of spicy liquid pelted my T-shirt like tiny gunfire. It's the curse of the fat chick. You reach a certain point of fatness and you don't really have breasts, it's more of a flesh trough from chin to stomach, always ready to collect food stains.

'Jeez, you wouldn't want to have laksa on a first date, would you?' said Jenny as we all snorted with laughter. 'It's not the most becoming dish.'

I smiled as I dabbed at my chest with a tissue. I had no idea how many Points were in a laksa but I didn't really care. I know I'll be ready to get back to my lard busting soon. Even in my most bleak, bingeing moments I had no intention of giving up for ever. But right now I have to focus on little things like getting out of bed and opening the curtains.

Perhaps it was the dried chillies but I felt ready to sob at any moment. I was so overwhelmed by emotion, just to be out of isolation and surrounded by their presence. I talked and laughed and sprayed more dinner on my shirt, trying to remember what normal feels like. I couldn't bring myself to tell Rhiannon or Jenny about the depression, but at least I wasn't hiding from them any more.

I'm starting to see why things fell apart. I was so obsessed with my weight loss last year that I shut out everything else. When work went down the tubes I didn't have the resources to handle it. I switched my obsession to job hunting instead, and let everything else slip. I know I've got to find a way of doing things without the extremes.

But for now I feel a little better. As soon as I admitted that I wasn't coping, I started to cope again. I'm not so angry now. I'm trying to be forgiving and not let my moods be defined by my job woes and giant knickers. I don't need to hide. I will get through this.

WEEK 82
5 August 2002

My new boss Amanda is gorgeous. She has beautiful almond eyes, a creamy complexion and a delicate frame. I feel like a hulking lumberjack standing beside her. But today she announced she's on a diet.

'Why would *you* be on a diet?'

'My jeans are so tight I can barely breathe,' she said. 'I'm all belly. Soon I'll have to lie down on the bed and haul up the zip with a coat-hanger.'

'I see.' I thought of my self-unzipping jeans, now tossed in the back of my wardrobe. *You think you've got a fat belly? I'll show you a fat belly, baby.*

'I've joined SureSlim,' she went on. 'Have you heard of it?'

'No?' I honestly thought I'd heard of every diet.

'My friend did it and she lost three stone in eight weeks. It's amazing!'

'Eight weeks?' Now she had my attention. 'How?!'

'Well, they give you an individualized diet that's designed to boost your metabolism,' she explained in authoritative tones. 'They customize it based on your blood test results.'

'I don't like the sound of *bleeding* to lose weight.'

She laughed. 'They only need a little syringe-full.'

'So what do you eat?'

'You get three meals a day. You're not allowed to eat in between meals.'

'Not at all? What kind of barbaric system is this?'

'It makes your metabolism more efficient. I have yoghurt and fruit for breakfast, then protein and salad for lunch and dinner.'

'Sounds . . . thrilling.'

'You can only eat certain veggies, mostly green ones. You have to weigh them first.'

'No way!'

'But you don't have to weigh cucumber, lettuce and celery. They're unlimited.'

'That's generous.'

'But only at mealtimes,' she added.

'Well no wonder your friend lost so much weight, she must have been starving.'

'Oh no!' Amanda gasped defensively. 'It's nutritionally balanced. Lots of lean protein, and you get all your essential fats from the seeds.'

'Seeds?'

'Linseeds, sunflower, sesame and pumpkin seeds. A tablespoon of each per day.'

'Are they awful?'

'Yes!' she confessed. 'I feel like a budgie. But I want to get back into my jeans.'

'Tell me about it,' I sighed, eyeing the Dairy Milk wrapper on my desk. After a month on the loony pills I've been feeling rather good, bouncing out of bed and

attacking my job search with renewed vigour. But I'm still gaining weight. I need to do something before I'm right back where I started.

'They have free information sessions every Tuesday. You could check it out.'

'Sounds interesting,' I said. 'But it doesn't really sound like my cup of tea.'

WEEK 82.5
9 August 2002

Today I gave a pint of blood and a one-off payment of $700 to SureSlim.

OK. I know I'm a sucker. But I'm a desperate sucker. Try and understand, people.

I went along to the information session with no intention of signing up. They had a short video and a Powerpoint presentation, full of scientific jargon and graphs to make it all sound very important. I remained sceptical, but then they told us about the individual weigh-ins. Apparently it's just you and the SureSlim lady in a discreet cubicle. No Weight Watchers queues, no hissing at the weigh-lady to *please* not say your weight out loud, no more overhearing everyone's boring tales of fluid retention. Just me and one person devoted to my weight loss needs. That sounded good.

And finally the killer punch – a slide-show of Before and After photos. Mary Bloggs lost two stone in five weeks. Five stone in four months. Seven stone in six months. Page after page of slob morphing into slender.

My heart swelled with longing. I want this to be me. I want to be a loser again. I want to be a success story. I don't care what I have to do.

So I signed up and sent my bank account into the red. I know I would have spent all that money on chocolate eventually.

WEEK 83
12 August 2002
20st 6lb (130kg, 286lb)
2st 9.5lb GAINED! (17kg, 37.5lb)
4st 9lb lost (29.5 kg, 65lb) – 8st 9lb to go (55kg, 121lb)

The SureSlim scales are digital and can assess your fatness to two decimal places. If I'd known that, I'd have removed my watch and shaved off my eyebrows today.

20 stone 6 pounds.

These past few months of gloomy gorging has set me back nearly *40 pounds*. I've regained nearly half of what I lost last year! I blinked back tears in the little cubicle, completely stunned and almost impressed by how I'd managed to screw up in such a swift and spectacular fashion.

My consultant was babbling on about my so-called Customized Eating Plan. It was exactly the same as Amanda's but with bigger portions since I'm twice her size. My yoghurt ration is 200 grams whereas she gets 90 grams. Except they don't call them portions at SureSlim. They say *grammages*.

'It's important to eat all your grammages,' said my

consultant. 'There's your protein grammages and your veggie grammages.'

That's not even a proper word! I snorted inwardly. But I kept silent, because I had paid her $700 and given a pint of blood for her to have the answers.

'And in addition, you get four crispbreads per day or one slice of Mountain Bread, which is like a flatbread.'

'Is that all the carbs I get?'

'Well, there's carbs in your veggies as well,' she explained.

'Oh yes. Tasty.'

If I didn't feel so crap about my massive regain, perhaps I would have argued that there was no way this programme was sustainable. But right now I'd do anything. And I have to admit it: I need my hand held again. I have a reassuring list of rules and instructions and I will obey them. I'm just going to let someone tell me what to do until I feel strong enough to figure it out for myself.

WEEK 83.5
16 August 2002

I'm on Day Four and feel I can officially declare that I hate SureSlim.

I hate the natural yoghurt. I hate the dull green vegetables. I hate the lack of carbohydrates. I hate the stinking birdseed and most of all I hate myself for thinking this was a good idea.

They told me I might experience some headaches and irritability on Day Three as my system adjusted to a new way of eating. I swear I felt the precise moment the last granule of sugar dissolved from my body. The withdrawals were my punishment for all those months off the wagon. Last night I was so fucking desperate for a piece of bread I actually threw myself on the floor and pounded the carpet.

'Tell me, what is so wrong with a piece of bread?' I cried to Rhiannon.

'There's nothing wrong with a piece of bread,' she replied patiently. 'But you told me not to let you eat any bread if this happened.'

'Well, clearly I was an idiot.'

'Just think about the seven hundred bucks.'

'Fuck this! I'm going to bed.'

It was only 7.30 p.m. At least I was safe under the covers. I almost asked Rhiannon to lock my door so I wouldn't raid the fridge in my sleep.

WEEK 84
19 August 2002
19st 9lb (125kg, 275lb)
5st 6lb lost (34.5 kg, 76lb) – 7st 12lb to go (50kg, 110lb)

I'm a loser again!

I weighed in at SureSlim today. Eleven pounds gone! I made the lady weigh me three times just to make sure it was true.

I can't believe I made it through the week without kicking any puppies. I've been having nightmares about

135

linseed and my poo has turned an alarming shade of green from all those vegetables but . . . 11 pounds!

I was worried sick that it wouldn't work. I thought my body was defective, that I was destined to never be any smaller. But 11 pounds have disappeared and I can't wait to crack on this week and make it happen again and again.

I'd forgotten how good it feels to be good to your body.

WEEK 85
26 August 2002
19st 7.5lb (124.3kg, 273.5lb)
5st 7.5lb lost (35.2kg, 77.5lb) – 7st 10.5lb to go
(49.3kg, 108.5lb)

Someone in the UK did a study and found that there's been a dramatic increase in the number of soppy pop songs being played at funerals instead of traditional hymns. On Friday I was at a funeral that featured the number 2 tune on the list, 'My Heart Will Go On'.

Usually I hate that song but on Friday in a tiny church in Grenfell, with the sunlight filtering through the stained glass, it was suddenly the most soul-wrenching tune ever invented.

Mum's cousin Rick had passed away from a heart attack. He was only forty-eight. I barely remembered him from all those family reunions, so I thought I'd breeze through the day untouched. But that song ripped me up. Something about you being here, so there's nothing to fear. What the hell are you on about, Celine? He's not here.

As her mournful voice rose higher my throat felt like cement and I was glad I'd bought tissues. *When I die*, I said silently to no one in particular, *I want you to play 'Pyramid Song' by Radiohead. That song makes me cry, but at least it's not Celine. If that's too depressing, then please play 'Bootylicious'.*

The wake was back in the old church hall. Her Majesty smirked down at us from a faded portrait above the stage. All those little things you only see in country towns seemed so comforting now. Egg sandwiches and sponge cakes made by the ladies of the church committee. Rumbling urns of tea and coffee; pale green cups and saucers.

I hovered around Mum and Rhiannon. I didn't want to be far from them at that moment. I gazed at the glorious buffet for a full ten minutes before I finally buckled and had a cheese and tomato sandwich. Sweet, forbidden carbs.

My Aunty Marg came over for a chat. Rick was her nephew; she's one of Poppy's four sisters. I've always adored my great-aunts, so tall and warm with peaches-and-cream complexions. We joked around and talked about how sad it is that people only seem to catch up at funerals. Mum, Rhi, Aunty Marg and I all stood there for a minute holding hands. In another context I would have felt ridiculous, but right then it felt like the perfect thing to do.

'We'll have to head off,' said Mum. 'We need to visit Poppy before we head back to Canberra.' Poppy's deteriorated even further in the last couple of months. No one's saying it but we all feel the need to see him as much as possible while we still can.

137

Aunty Marg nodded. Her expression clouded and she clutched my arm. 'It's the hardest thing in the world to see my big brother like that. When I lean down to kiss him goodbye and he squeezes my hand, I swear I can hear my heart breaking.'

I hugged her tight for the longest time.

Suddenly she grabbed my hands and looked right at me. We're a family of jokers. We're not ones to get philosophical or serious. But she squeezed my hands and said, 'Shauna, you have dreams, right?'

'I think so.'

'Well you have to make plans. You have to make your plans then go out and make them happen.'

I squeezed back and nodded.

'Look at what's happened to us all lately,' her voice cracked with emotion. 'You don't know what's around the corner. Promise me you'll make some plans.'

I haven't stopped thinking about that since.

WEEK 86
2 September 2002
19st 4lb (122.7kg, 270lb)
5st 11lb lost (36.8kg, 81lb) – 7st 7lb to go (47.7kg, 105lb)

After two more weeks of SureSlimming I've lost another five pounds. I think it's safe to say I'm BACK, baby!

Right now I'm full of that insufferable smugness that comes when you find your dieting groove. The wheels are back in motion, you're in control and it seems impossible that you could ever feel any other way. This time I'm not naïve enough to believe it will just carry on indefinitely, but I'm going to cling to the feeling for as long as I can.

Now that I'm over the sugar withdrawal, I'm enjoying the simplicity of my SureSlim diet. Almost everything I eat is fresh and wholesome. Yoghurt, fruit and seeds for breakfast. Chicken and salads for lunch. Stir fries or lean meat and veggies for dinner. The most processed I get now is a can of tuna or a crispbread. When I was doing Weight Watchers, I was so obsessed with keeping my Points count low that for me nutrition was often a secondary concern. Lord knows how many dodgy chemicals were lurking in all those Sugar-free Fat-free Taste-free yoghurts.

I also don't mind going cold turkey on the junk food. Last year I was for ever plotting ways to fit a sundae into my Points allowance, but now I'm content with my three meals a day with no fancy stuff.

That said, I know I can't do this for ever. A life without bread is not a life worth living! And the diet is impossible if you want any sort of social life, as not everyone serves up big bowls of birdseed and lettuce for dinner. For now I'm sticking to it as much as possible so I can blast off this regain, but in the long term I'll need to borrow the best bits of the plan and come up with something more sustainable.

So right now it feels like I'm heading down a healthy road. And already when I zip up my jeans, they're staying zipped again.

9 September 2002
19st (120.9kg, 266lb)
6st 1lb lost (38.6kg, 85lb) – 7st 3lb to go (45.9kg, 101lb)

I dreamed of how I'd find my perfect job. After searching for so long, I thought there'd have to be some sort of dramatic moment. I'd spy the advert in the newspaper and I'd hear a sudden chorus of angels. 'Yes!' I'd cry, raising my hands to the heavens. 'This is the one!'

I'd write a stunning application, spend a ridiculous sum on a new suit then dazzle 'em in the interview. They would drop to their knees and beg me to work for them.

But in the end it was quite an anticlimax. Yesterday morning one of my recruitment agencies called about a job with a company downtown – a twelve-month contract with a view to permanency. Ho hum. I sneakily knocked out an application while pretending to type up meeting minutes. Two hours later the agency called back – the client wanted an interview.

Here we go again, I thought. This morning I told Amanda that I was meeting a friend for lunch then changed into my suit in the car. It started to rain as I scurried into the building, so my hair was glued to my temples like limp spaghetti. But as soon as they started talking about the job I realized, *Holy shit! This IS me!*

For once in my life I had all the answers. Yes, I can write copy. Yes, I can edit and make websites and take photographs. In fact, I'd love to do it! I felt poised and confident. I'd just got back to work when my mobile rang with the job offer.

For some reason I was feeling plucky and haggled to get a higher hourly rate. They didn't need to know I've been stapling for a living, I could pretend I was a hot commodity. And it worked!

I can't tell you how much I enjoyed typing out my resignation letter and signing it with a flourish. I finish next Wednesday. Freedom at last!

And the new job is around the corner from the SureSlim office. Could it be fate?

WEEK 88
16 September 2002
18st 7.5lb (118kg, 259.5lb)
6st 7.5lb lost (41.5kg, 91.5lb) – 6st 10.5lb to go (43kg, 94.5lb)

I'm a mountaineer!

Well, sort of.

My Edmund Hillary kick started a few weeks ago when my best mate from university moved here to Canberra. I can't believe my luck lately. New job, new diet, and now Peita is living in my town and working at Parliament House.

She called up and asked if Rhiannon and I fancied going for a walk. How very strange! I've met friends for movies or cake but never for exercise. This would normally be my cue to devise an excuse – the Mothership is coming to visit, I have an unspeakable rash; my house is on fire.

141

But I had to be bold. The new Shauna is not a hermit!

Mount Ainslie is plonked in the middle of the city behind the War Memorial. I'd never really noticed it before until I was standing at the foot of it. Apparently it was an easy two-kilometre trail to the top, but it might as well have been Everest. Fifty metres up I slumped against a gum tree and begged for water. While Rhiannon and Peita chatted and admired the scenery, I wheezed and wondered if rescue choppers would be able to penetrate the rocky terrain to collect my corpse.

It took an hour to reach the top. Small children, wiry grannies and arthritic dogs all overtook me along the way. I could very well be the unfittest person in the world.

The next morning my leg and butt muscles were so stiff I had to roll out of bed and crawl along the floor to the bathroom. It was ten times worse than the agony after that first Body Pump class.

But we trekked up again today. This time we were ten minutes faster and I only stopped nine times. I even found enough oxygen to briefly take in the view. I thought my hamstrings would snap and ping me off the side of the hill, but I made it! I leaned over the fence and bellowed down to all the public servants, 'KING OF THE WORLD!'

It's a truly killer workout. And I like the metaphorical significance of climbing a mountain – overcoming obstacles, striving towards a goal and all that. Even though it's only really a hill.

Week 88.5
20 September 2002

They're a friendly lot at my new job. When my boss Sue took me around for introductions, every colleague had a welcoming smile. On Tuesday I was hunting through the fridge for my salad when someone came in for a cuppa and started talking. I looked around, even checked in the freezer compartment, but they were actually talking to *me*!

As the week went on, I found my feet. So this is what it's like to use your brain at work! I spent the last three years on autopilot with all that HTML and photocopying; but now I get to write and talk and come up with ideas. I can't believe my luck.

Best of all, I'm busy. I didn't have time to think about KitKats or hamburgers or my general state of fatness. Sue had to remind me it was lunchtime, and I went out to the park with my salad and felt utterly content.

I'm wary of saying I love my new job, because as you know I'm paranoid and if I dare to say I am happy it will all turn to shit. So let me rephrase. This week was great. There was no crying in the loos, no photocopying, no staple removing, no data entry.

But I actually kind of miss the staple removing.

Week 89
25 September 2002

Poppy is in Orange Base Hospital. He's extremely weak after an operation on Monday.

The smell and brightness of the place is suffocating. My aunt and uncle were there too and we hadn't caught up since Christmas, so we talked too loud and too cheerfully in order to drown out the sound of Poppy's broken breathing.

Later on when the others had gone, Mum and Rhiannon and I couldn't take our eyes off him. His lips seem to have retreated back into his face, only moving now and then to curl up in pain. He looks swallowed up by the big wheelchair they've put him in. He has to wear huge aviator sunglasses because the light hurts his eyes. He used to wear those glasses while he drove the tractor; now they look so far out of context I almost smile.

We talked to Nanny about work and Mount Ainslie and any old shit. We were there for hours and hours and his body was perfectly still. His muscles have deteriorated so much that his face is smooth with hardly a wrinkle.

There was a long minute where we all held our breath. Slowly he raised his hand and pointed to Rhiannon, beckoning her closer. He put his hand over hers and when she squeezed it, he made a tiny, sad sound.

Then he pointed to me. My sister and I changed places. His hand was like crêpe paper. He hooked his fingers round my thumb like newborn babies do. I gripped a little tighter, wishing I could pour my strength into his body somehow. His hand trembled but he squeezed back.

And then it was time to go; we had a long drive back to Canberra. We didn't want to say goodbye. We all kissed him then hugged Nanny so tight. She'd never hugged back so hard before.

I don't know what's going to happen next or how long

this will continue. No one wants to speculate or think about it. There was a heavier feeling this time. We left the ward but turned back to hug and kiss them again.

Out in the car park Mum started to cry. It ripped me apart to see her look so vulnerable. Rhiannon and I squeezed her between us and searched for the right thing to say.

Soon we were on the road and somebody said something funny, so we dived into that conversation and stopped thinking for a while.

WEEK 90
1 October 2002
18st 1lb (115kg, 253lb)
7st lost (44.5kg, 98lb) – 6st 4lb to go (40kg, 88lb)

It seems stupid even mentioning this right now, but I'm still losing weight. After eight weeks of plain yoghurt and unlimited cucumber, I'm down to 18 stone 1 pound. It just keeps coming off in hefty chunks and I'm almost back to my Weight Watchers lowest.

SureSlim is suiting me well right now. The repetition and lack of choice is a relief. It leaves my mind free for work, friends, exercise, and most of all my family. My body feels strangely calm; I'm not fighting against it any more. I'm sticking to the plan when I can and trying not to panic when I can't. The café near the hospital doesn't sell SureSlim salads, but I'd rather eat an illicit sandwich and be with my family.

Meanwhile, my clothes are fitting again. Some are

getting too big. They measured me at my weigh-in last week and I'd lost two inches off my bust and waist and two and a half inches off my hips. My flesh is on the move. I'm not sure where it goes exactly, but there seems to be less of it hanging around.

It's only a month until my birthday. Despite last year's projected figures, I'm not going to attain my projected figure by my twenty-fifth birthday – the body is still lumpy and bumpy and miles from goal. My spreadsheet couldn't predict life getting in the way of weight loss.

WEEK 90.5
6 October 2002

They've moved Poppy back home. Well, home to the hospital in Cowra.

Rhiannon and I drove up to see him today; Mum was already there. We sat with him and Nanny and we could all feel that we don't have long.

There was a moment when Rhiannon and I couldn't help smiling in spite of ourselves. Nanny has diabetes and often tells us about her brave battle with the blood sugar. Today she was going on about the Glycaemic Index and recalling all the Times She'd Been Naughty. She spoke of a mouthful of cheesecake with the same forbidden glee most people reserve for skinny dipping or shoplifting. It was reassuring to discover that comfort eating is in my genes. She recalled the dearly departed family members of 2002 (it's been a very rough year) and what she ate on each occasion.

'When my brother Mick died, I ate half a family bar of chocolate. And it was damn delicious. Then when Colin died, I had a packet of crisps. Salt and vinegar, I think . . . ooh, I do love crisps. And when Rick died the other day, what did I have? Hmm. Let me think. Oh yes, I had a KitKat. That's right.'

She held Poppy's hand, stroking it tenderly and talking over the top of his fractured breathing.

'If anything else traumatic happens, I might have to eat a whole cake.'

WEEK 91
8 October 2002
17st 13lb (114kg, 251lb)
7st 2lb lost (45.5kg, 100lb) – 6st 2lb to go (39kg, 86lb)

Why did I go to my weigh-in today? Mum called me at work with the news but it didn't sink in. I hung up the phone and told Sue I was going out to lunch.

I kept slipping out of my sandals as I walked past the casino. I'd stupidly slathered my feet with moisturizer this morning in an attempt to make them feel soft and spring-like.

They're always playing some cheesy song over the PA to persuade gamblers to enter and leave their kids in the car. Today it was 'Don't Worry, Be Happy'. The background singers sounded so mournful and I just couldn't believe he was gone.

I weighed in then went back to the office, still in a trance. I was half-heartedly typing up a press release when it hit me like a wave. I started bawling right there at my desk. Sue was kind and told me I should go home.

'No, it's cool! I'll be fine in a minute.'

Rhiannon called not long after. 'How are you doing?'

'Not that great. How about you?'

'A bit crap. Want me to pick you up?'

'Yes.'

Rhiannon and I have always had some sort of cosmic food thing happening. As soon as I got in the car we looked at each other and said, 'Passion fruit cheesecake.'

I've never felt so grateful for my sister and our unspoken understanding of all things. We needed cheesecake. It was huge, like the face of an old school clock, glowing orange with the promise of passion fruit crunch.

We sat in front of the telly and ceremoniously cracked open the box.

'I'm sure Poppy would have wanted us to have this,' said Rhiannon with a sly smile.

'Yes!' I cut two fat slices. 'To Poppy!'

It tasted smooth and cool, almost easing the hollow ache in my stomach. We sat there quietly watching *Neighbours* with the volume turned down. I tried to block out the last time I saw him with his face so grey and twisted with pain. I thought of him back on the farm, sitting at the kitchen bench, digging out stray bits of lunch with a toothpick, cracking jokes, smelling like the shearing shed; being the guy I idolized all my life.

It's only been a few hours but I just want to tell you, I miss you miss you miss you so much.

WEEK 91.5
11 October 2002

When I was a little kid, straight out of the bath on a winter's night, Mum would make me wear a turtleneck under my pyjamas for added warmth. For some reason I used to freak out about this. I couldn't stand the suffocating feeling of that tight neck dragging over my head, squeezing down over my forehead and nose, plastering freshly shampooed hair to my cheeks. I'd wave my arms and stomp around with a muffled squeal. 'It feels yucky! Yucky!'

That's how I feel today. Grief is clinging to me like cheap polyester. I just want to scream: Get it off me!

It doesn't seem to fit quite right. I'm saying lines I've never had to say before, words that feel strange and tight on my lips.

I'll have to skip the meeting next Tuesday because it's my grandfather's funeral. (Finally, a legitimate excuse!)

The more I say it the easier it gets, so long as I don't stop and actually listen to the words.

Is there anything more exhausting than grief? My body feels like an old teabag, paper thin and full of tiny holes, all scrunched up and drained after being dunked in and out of a cup of hot shittiness.

My friends have been amazing. Peita wrote me an email about losing her own grandma and she just described how it feels so perfectly that I went and cried in the loos at work. Then yesterday afternoon my friends Belinda, Matt and Rachael showed up on the doorstep with flowers and ice-cream. They didn't say a word, they just held out their gifts like the Three Wise Friends. I was overwhelmed with gratitude. I wanted to grab them and never let go and tell them how much their presence meant, but I felt too tired and stupid to express it. I will have to write some superlative thank-you notes.

On the other hand you get the Standard Issue phrases from people. *You'll be OK. Time will help.* That just makes me boil. I don't want to hear that it gets easier; that I should be happy Poppy's not suffering any more, that he's gone to a better place. I'm not sure I believe in a better place. I just miss him like hell and want someone to say something that will take away the rock in my stomach. Somebody must know the magic phrase. Why won't anyone speak up?

I've been acting like a bratty child all week. I don't feel I have any control over what I say or do, I'm just floundering. I want to curl up in a ball and not think about anything.

I'm being selfish and pathetic just when there are people around me who need me to be strong. Rhiannon and I have to stand up there in front of a churchful of people on Tuesday. I'd rather write a thousand stinky press releases than one eulogy.

It's such a wake-up call. I've been cruising along for almost twenty-five years, thinking that the Grown-ups know what they're doing; that they are in charge. But I've been so busy being fat, depressed and directionless that I didn't notice all the wrinkles and hardships collecting on their faces. It's only just occurred to me that I'm supposed to be a Grown-up too. They asked Rhiannon and me to do the eulogy because they're too wrecked from losing a son, a brother, a nephew, all in the space of two months.

Sometimes you need to set aside your own shit and be there for someone else. I want to do them proud. I want to pay a worthy tribute to my grandfather.

I didn't expect all these crazy emotions. Why can't I be more dignified? Why am I behaving like such a loon?

WEEK 92
14 October 2002

All my memories are tangled up with food. When I sat down to write Poppy's eulogy, the first thing I thought of was how every year we'd buy him a jar of chocolate-covered almonds for Christmas. He'd always rattle the parcel and smirk, 'Hmm, I wonder what this could be?'

I seem to measure my milestones with meals. Some people remember what they were doing or what they wore but I can always tell you what I ate. Ask me in ten years about tonight – how my mother, my aunt and uncle, Nanny, Rhiannon and I all gathered around the table – and I will recall every mouthful of Chinese takeaway. I will remember the sound of the plastic containers ripping open and the purposeful clatter of forks. I will remember the steam rising from the rice and how a bellyful of MSG dulled my senses.

How do you cope without stuffing your face? Without food to keep you busy, there are only words and feelings. I need a hobby like knitting, so I've got something else to do with my hands.

151

25 Things Thought at the Funeral of Malcolm James

1. *Look at all these people, you popular fella.*
2. I better start being nicer to people. I want crowds, too.
3. Stop looking at the coffin.
4. But the coffin looks so small. He was taller than that!
5. We are crammed so tight into this pew. What if my skirt schloops off when I stand up to do the eulogy?
6. Why the bloody hell did I wear a skirt?
7. Actually, I think I look pretty good in this skirt. I wonder if anyone else is thinking that?
8. Of course they're not, you idiot! This is a funeral, not a fashion parade.
9. Oh, we're on!
10. You're doing great, Rhiannon. Keep going, tiger.
11. My turn. I don't recognize my voice. It's calm and clear and upbeat.
12. They're listening to every word. We made them laugh and cry. I feel like Billy Graham!
13. If I squeeze Rhi's hand a little harder, we will get through this together.
14. I wish they could raise the speed limit of funeral processions.
15. I wish they could lower the speed of the coffin into the ground.
16. *And now you're really gone.*
17. *I loved how whenever Rhi and I used to argue as*

kids, you would say in sage tones, 'As the dead sheep said to the crow, stop picking on me!'

18. Ooh goody! Looks like those little old ladies have done the catering for the wake.

19. Little old ladies make the best cakes ever. SureSlim can bite me today!

20. If one more person tells us we did a beautiful job of the eulogy, I will explode with pride and there will be little fluttery bits of pride all over the sponge cakes and egg sandwiches.

21. The underwire of my bra is attacking me.

22. I hope Rhiannon is thinking what I'm thinking. Pizza from Zeffirelli tonight. Sometimes only carbs and mozzarella will do.

23. One can never get enough hugs.

24. Life is so much bigger and better than worrying about the size of your thighs.

25. *I just want there to be some sort of heaven. Full of chocolate-covered almonds with a Johnny Cash soundtrack, all for you.*

Week 93
22 October 2002
17st 9.5lb (112.5kg, 247.5lb)
7st 5.5lb lost (47kg, 103.5lb) – 5st 12.5lb to go (37.5kg, 82.5lb)

Ever since the funeral I've been feeling oddly energetic. It's as if the last of the fog has lifted and life is coming back into focus.

It's been comforting to ease back into an everyday routine. Today I had my first weigh-in for two weeks and I'd lost three and a half pounds. I had my measurements taken too – two and a half inches off both chest and hips and *four* inches off my waist! I knew something funny was going on because I've had to pull my trousers up all the time. I thought they'd stretched in the wash!

I'm amazed by the dramatic results. I put it down to clean eating and trekking up Mount Ainslie every Sunday afternoon.

The first twenty minutes are still purest hell. My thighs scream, my chest rasps and I bitch to Rhiannon, 'There is no fucking way I am going to fucking climb this fucking hill any fucking further!' She just laughs and hands me a bottle of water.

Once we get to the top, I limp around triumphantly like Rocky until my jelly legs force me to sit down. On the descent I have enough energy to appreciate the quietness, the rustle of the trees and the crunch of gum leaves and kangaroo shit beneath my shoes. By the time we get back to the car I've forgotten all about the uphill bit and say, 'Hey that wasn't so bad. Same time next week?'

During BodyPump today I realized my attitude to exercise is changing. Last year I was so obsessive – it was not about fitness but about weight loss and punishment. I saw my sweat and red face and screaming muscles as signs that I could wield control over my wayward body. But now I crave exercise because it soothes the soul. It's hard work squatting 40 pounds for six minutes but it's peaceful too. I like the camaraderie of being in a group class yet slipping away into my own thoughts at the same time. My trembling legs and flushed cheeks are now signs that I'm getting stronger.

Lately I feel calm; full of hope and possibility. I want to move forward and make the most of everything. I need to make some plans.

WEEK 95
4 November 2002
17st 6lb (111.8kg, 246lb)
7st 9lb lost (47.7kg, 105lb) – 5st 9lb to go (36.8kg, 81lb)

So my twenty-fifth birthday came and went. There were no goal weights, wild parties, champagne or size 14 dresses, but I had a good time anyway.

I stayed the same at weigh-in today. I'd vowed to be SureSlim super strict at my birthday dinner; but my resolve cracked after three sips of red wine.

I sat at the head of the table gazing at my friends like it was an episode of *This Is Your Life*. There was Jenny, so hilarious, loyal and down-to-earth. And Peita, who unwittingly helped me through my university days with her wicked humour and sharp mind. Then Emily, who brightened my public service days and cheered me on when I started Weight Watchers. And of course Rhiannon, my long-suffering sister and best friend. Where would I be without her?

I stared at them through my wine glass and felt a surge of gratefulness. I wanted to crash-tackle them to the floor with ferocious hugs. They've stuck with me through thick and ... less thick. So many times I thought I didn't deserve their friendship; sometimes I still do. But I know I've got to stop wasting time and energy being paranoid, and start being a better friend instead. No more hiding, no more doubts, no more sitting back feeling sorry for myself while my friends have fun.

'Screw it, ladies, it's my birthday.' I drained my glass and slammed it on the table. 'Let's get some dessert!'

'Yeah, baby!' cheered Rhiannon. 'More vino, too.'

I picked the apple and blueberry crumble, the least rich of the desserts, but still the richest thing I'd eaten for months. I can still taste it right now. Because I haven't brushed my teeth since Friday. Well actually, just because the memory of cinnamon and sugar still lingers. But most delicious of all was the rush from eating something sweet in public – openly, surrounded by friends; without shame or apology. I'm not hiding in cupboards any more.

WEEK 97
18 November 2002
17st 2lb (109.1kg, 240lb)
7st 13lb lost (50.4kg, 111lb) – 5st 5lb to go (34.1kg, 75lb)

'Oh girls, you are going to have a great time!' Anna smiled. 'You have no idea what you're in for!'

Rhiannon looked at me and grinned. I bit my lip and looked at the floor.

'Go on!' she hissed. 'Hand over the cheque!'

We were in Flight Centre today, buying plane tickets. One-way plane tickets.

I've lost nearly eight pounds over the past four weeks but I think I've also lost my mind. Remember last year when Jenny got back from her UK jaunt and Rhiannon said we should do the same? I laughed her off, and part of me still wants to laugh her off. But today we bought one-way plane tickets to Edinburgh, Scotland. We're leaving four months from now on 26 March, armed with a two-year working holiday visa.

There's a long tradition of young Australians doing a stint in the UK and travelling around Europe. It's so commonplace it might as well be compulsory. I never thought I'd be one of the masses. I'm too fat for adventure! That's not the sort of thing I do!

But it's time to be bold. As Aunty Marg said, you never know what's around the corner. Make some plans, she told us. I don't want to ignore the little voice inside me that's screaming, Get out there! Push your boundaries! Do something scary!

Ever since Poppy passed away and I emerged from this last blast of depression, I've become increasingly aware of a new Shauna that wants to do something with her life. It's the Shauna that was there all along, but I'd hidden her under a layer of blubber and convinced myself she didn't exist.

We've decided to base our adventures in Edinburgh. London sounded too big and scary for me, plus Scotland has all those hot men wearing kilts.

Why now? Why pack up and leave now when life in Canberra is pretty much perfect? I'm blessed with great friends, I'm finally losing weight, I've finally scored a great job, I'm finally getting my act together.

The fact that it's going so well makes it the perfect time to go. I want to push forward before I have a chance to falter. And as Rhiannon declared, 'It's high time we had some proper fun.' We're young and we should be having adventures, darn it. And why should I wait until I'm skinny to do that? I've spent too long waiting for life to happen to me.

Anna handed us our receipt and actually spun in her chair with delight. 'This is almost as good as going again myself! You do realize this is going to change your life.'

'Bring it on,' I said, and I really think I meant it.

WEEK 99
2 December 2002
16st 13lb (107.7kg, 237lb)
8st 2lb lost (51.8kg, 114lb) – 5st 2lb to go (32.7kg, 72lb)

Here I am after another weigh-in. Three pounds down and I've squeezed under 17 stone! I'm trying to be less obsessive but my inner geek still loves a good milestone on the scale.

In other news, I leaned forward to brush my teeth last night and I saw my *collarbone*! Oh my goodness. A visible collarbone! You can't see it if I just stand up normally, but this is progress! I'll continue to develop it in secret for a few more months and then I'll flaunt it to the world.

It's all happening, folks. My trousers are starting to fall

down so I went to the hideously named My Size yesterday. The saleslady was bigger than me! I'll probably go to hell for thinking that, but it was incredible not to be the largest person in a room for a change.

What's going on with clothes this season? Every garment has that bohemian peasant hooker thing going on. I spied a shirt and thought, 'Ooh lovely!' only to pluck it from the rack and discover ruffles spewing down the front like an old man's beard. Ruffles rarely look good on waifs, let alone buxom mamas like myself. Who the hell are these designers kidding? All I want is simple, classic clothes I can wear near a naked flame.

No luck in My Size, so I ventured back into one of the 'normal' chains to see if their XL would fit me yet. The shirts were still a bit too snug. I stormed home and whined to Rhiannon that I'm never going to be normal and I'll die alone because no one will ever want to see me naked and furthermore I don't *want* anyone to see me naked because my body is so utterly horrible.

'That is the saddest thing I've ever heard,' she said.

But I wiped my tears and went back to the shops today, because I really do need those trousers. We went to Katies where they stock the '16–26' label for fat chicks. In January 2001 the size 26 was too small but now I'm a size 18! I know it's a Fat Shop and the sizes run big, but doesn't it sound nice? Eight. TEEN! I'm a twenty-something no more!

Most of the clothes were of the peasant hooker variety, but I found a few nice tops for work. At first I bitched that they were too fitted, but as Rhiannon pointed out, 'That's why they're called *clothes*, not potato sacks!'

'Wow, Shauna!' said the SureSlim ladies today. 'You're really shrinking!'

It's nice to be getting compliments again, but these days I'm pretty damn pleased with myself too.

WEEK 101
19 December 2002
16st 9lb (105.9kg, 233lb)
8st 6lb lost (53.6kg, 118lb) – 4st 12lb to go (30.9kg, 68lb)

Well, people, can you believe I've just returned from the company Christmas party? It's the first time I've actually stayed for the duration instead of running away at half-time!

I drank a whole bottle of red tonight, which is approximately 10,000 Weight Watchers Points! and strictly forbidden on SureSlim. I also walked into a tree on the way home, but at least I walked, right? It's all exercise.

I haven't written much about my job lately because I love it so much. If I say it too loud a piano will surely drop on my head. But tonight I'm drunk so I confess, I love being the communications officer chick and writing things and being creative and working with lovely people who make me forget about my fat and feel like I actually have a brain.

SO WHY AM I LEAVING THE COUNTRY THEN?

I forgot to mention I've lost another four pounds, which means I've got less than five stone to go! Doesn't that sound far less horrendous, now?

It's been 101 weeks of marvellous fat-fighting adventures, my friends. This year was chock full of ups and downs and I'm glad there's a new one coming soon. And there might even be a white Christmas at the end of it.

YEAR THREE
2003

WEEK 105
15 January 2003
16st 2.5lb (103kg, 226.5lb)
8st 12.5lb lost (56.5kg, 124.5lb) – 4st 5.5lb to go (28kg,
61.5lb)

And so begins another year of lard busting. Can you believe it's been two years since that fateful moment when I was shocked by the sight of my giant pants on the clothesline?

I'm happy to report the smalls situation is much less dire now. I've ditched the Bonds Cottontails, but I kept one souvenir pair. I like to put them on sometimes and marvel at how I can pull the waistband up over my boobs. How did one arse manage to take up so much space?

These days all my knickers are black. Not because they're dark like my tortured soul, but because they make me feel almost sexy. They have alluring hints of lace at the hips. Sure they're a size 20 but they're more dainty and daring than I'd ever thought possible!

Speaking of daring, there's just over two months until Rhiannon and I leave for the Land of Kilts. Already I'm

165

pondering what to pack for a colder climate. All last year's winter clothes are too big. I wonder what the Fat Shops are like over there? Do big lasses get decent clothes in the UK or will I be donning a thermal mumu?

WEEK 106
20 January 2003
16st 2.5lb again (103kg, 226.5lb)
8st 12.5lb lost (56.5kg, 124.5lb) – 4st 5.5lb to go (28kg, 61.5lb)

Something strange is happening lately. The days in which I like myself and feel somewhat attractive are starting to outnumber the Die You Fat Ugly Cow days.

How did this happen? Perhaps the vanishing pounds and the prospect of skipping the country are making me feel cocky and reckless. All I know it's high time I stopped telling myself that I'm the obese incarnation of the devil.

The Mothership once said that I exuded 'Go away, don't get too close' vibes that scared off all the boys. I thanked her for the amateur psychoanalysis but insisted the problem was actually my voluminous arse. But now I'm wondering if she wasn't entirely batty. I went to a party on Saturday – which was an achievement in itself – and tentatively tested out a different vibe.

I had an internal pep talk as I put on my lipstick. *Forget the sprawling stomach and the dimpled thighs tonight. Don't think about the 62 pounds you've still got to lose. Focus on your cute nose and not-bad boobs. Let's get out there with the humans!*

A little confidence and red wine went a long way. I actually *talked* to people. I smiled and listened and did not hide behind a plant pot. Instead of the Sad Fat Chick at a Party, I was just another chick at a party. It was so wonderfully ordinary I could have wept.

I think you could even classify some of my conversations as flirtatious. I started to chat up a cute bloke over the punchbowl and he gave me his phone number! I had a brief playground flashback, and looked over my shoulder to make sure his friends weren't sniggering behind a tree, but he seemed genuinely interested. I couldn't hide my grin as he volunteered his number and suggested we meet again. That's item number 2 on my 'Things to Do When I'm Skinny' list done and dusted while I'm still a plus size!

I tucked the little scrap of paper in the back of my diary. I don't want to actually do anything with it. I just want to keep it there and savour the idea that I could be someone who gets phone numbers from men.

WEEK 108
3 February 2003

I went to the dentist the other day for a simple check-up and to enquire about a nagging pain way up the back of my mouth. X-rays and painful poking revealed that all four of my wisdom teeth are 'severely impacted'. This means they're growing at crazy angles and my mouth is not big enough to accommodate them.

So the only way is *out*. Three weeks from now, I'll

be clobbered over the head with a brick then the evil butchers will extract my freaky fangs with pliers. Well, apparently it's gentler than that, but try telling that to the tumble-drier nerves already gathering in my stomach.

I predict a Fat Girl Freak Out. Anyone with a white coat and an authoritative manner chills me to the bone. They had to hold my hand and bribe me with jellybeans when I got a tetanus shot, and I was 20 years old. And the last time I had a blood test, they couldn't find a vein! I'm sure it was because of my size. They prodded me for twenty minutes but the little blue buggers refused to swim to the surface. Perhaps my body was pumping with pure lard, not blood? They sent me home and told me to come back the next day, and have a very hot shower beforehand. In the end they finally drained me, and ever since I've gone out of my way to avoid medical procedures.

But now there's no escape! Here is my ever-growing list of fears:

1. Ending up on *A Current Affair* in a tragic 'I Woke Up During My Surgery and Couldn't Cry for Help' story.
2. Saying stupid things when I come out of the anaesthetic.
3. Terrifying small children with my swollen chipmunk face.

The first one is my greatest concern. What if I'm so fat that there aren't enough drugs in the world to knock me out? What if I wake up and hear them laughing, 'Who's this fat chick under the knife?' This worries me more than the actual pain and gore.

WEEK 109.5
14 February 2003

I've been wheeling and dealing. All I need is a cheap tweed coat with leather patches at my elbows and I'd be the salesman of the month. If someone says hello I'll pounce: 'Hey, do you need a microwave?' or 'You look tired, want to buy a chair to park your arse on?'

There's less than six weeks until Rhiannon and I abscond so we're selling most of our worldly goods. We'd planned to have a garage sale tomorrow, but we've fobbed off so much stock to friends and colleagues that there's not enough left to have one. We've had bidding wars and fights over furniture, plus one emotional Mothership attempting to hijack the whole event.

'You're not selling that toaster, are you?'

'Yes,' said Rhiannon firmly. 'We are selling that toaster.'

'Can I have it?'

'You already have a toaster!'

'But my toaster might die!' She hugged it to her chest protectively. 'There could be a toast situation. I need backup!'

It's all so surreal. It would appear things are winding up; doors are closing. Our gym membership has expired, we've given notice on our flat, there are removal boxes everywhere and they've found a replacement for me at work. I'm watching this flurry of activity with my usual absent-mindedness and can't comprehend that I'm actually leaving.

I don't want to stop and think about it, because then the panic kicks in. I start running around in small circles and wailing – *What if I can't find a job what if no one understands my accent what if my friends forget me what if we can't find somewhere to live what if I get fatter what shoes should I pack?*

WEEK 110
18 February 2003
15st 12lb (103kg, 222lb)
9st 3lb lost (56.5kg, 129lb) – 4st 1lb to go (28kg, 57lb)

Today I broke up with SureSlim. I'm insanely busy with our Scotland preparations and next week I'll be eating mush after my teeth get wrenched out, so the SureSlim ladies agreed it was best to wind things up now.

It was an amicable parting. Unlike Weight Watchers, I had no emotional attachment to the place. It was more like being sent to rehab – expensive, brutal and mercilessly strict; but exactly what I needed to get back on the straight and narrow.

I haven't precisely followed the programme since Christmas, which meant I've not even lost five pounds in the past five weeks. But it's impossible to get into my usual lard-busting routine with everything going on right now – preparing to move house, finishing things off at work, touring up and down Australia saying goodbye to our nearest and dearest. And I can't weigh out my birdseed and chicken breasts because I've sold the kitchen scales. So I'm just trying to be as healthy as I can in between *bon voyage* drinks with friends and afternoon teas with my aunties.

So what did I learn from SureSlim? I've learned that diets *do* work – if you can stick to them. But who can do that without going insane? I think my $700 was well spent just to blast off my mammoth regain, but I knew I couldn't keep it up for ever. I can only abstain from chocolate for so long.

SureSlim has also taught me that my body feels better with less processed food so I now I try to eat food that's full of nutrition, rather than fretting about the calories. So my next challenge is to find a middle ground between the chocolate fiend and the nutrition nerd. I'll just muddle along as best as I can in the midst of madness until we leave Australia. After 110 weeks it's rather daunting to be leading a scale-less existence.

Week 111
26 February 2003

First I conversed with the anaesthetist.

'I hear you're going overseas.'

'Yeah, but don't think I haven't noticed that huge needle.'

'Are you taking a year out before university?'

'No!'

'Just finished your degree then?'

'No! I've been out for years!'

171

'Oh! Well I hope you've got some sort of qualification, if you're intending to unleash yourself on the world?'

'I've got a degree, mate.' My vision grew cloudy. 'Hey, did you really think I just finished high school? It's the chubby face that makes me look young, isn't it?'

The next thing I remember was hearing my voice talking and it wouldn't stop. It was saying a lot of stupid things. My brain was soggy and numb as it pleaded with my mouth, *would you please shut up*?

But the mouth wouldn't comply. It was its own entity, completely detached from the body. I'd been put under intravenous sedation, as opposed to general anaesthetic. So apparently you can't feel a thing but you can get quite talkative when you come around.

I faded back in just as the surgeon was winding up. I felt something tugging at my tooth, but there was no pain. I babbled away in a wounded monotone, trying to make him feel bad for attacking me, 'HEY. Hey. Ow Ow. OW!'

Then I chatted to a nurse.

'You guys are lovely,' I slurred. 'You are doing a lovely job. Really you are. You have all been so nice.'

'Thank you, dear.'

'I was so worried you wouldn't be able to knock me out. I thought I'd be un-knockout-able and feel everything!'

'Well we managed just fine.'

'Yeah, but I'm a big girl. It can't have been easy. You know, half the reason I'm trying to shrink is to avoid doctors?'

'SHUT UP!' (That was my brain speaking)

'Is that so, love?'

'I've lost nine stone, would you believe.'

172

'That's very impressive!'

I launched into what I thought was an articulate and detailed outline of my diet and exercise regime and secrets of well-being, weight loss and eternal happiness, but I'm sure was actually a saliva-drenched numb-tongued blur. As they wheeled me out of theatre my brain cringed because my mouth was still moving and there seemed no way to stop it.

Half an hour later, I was able to sit upright in a chair. I flashed a dopey smile as Rhiannon arrived to take me home, my mouth stuffed with cotton swabs.

'This one's a talker,' said the nurse. She handed Rhiannon my bloodied wisdom teeth in a jar. 'She told us all her secrets.'

'Ha ha!' I said. 'Oh. Shit.'

It's now 5 a.m., two days later. I can't sleep because my head is massively swollen like a mutant potato. I was hoping for a cute little chipmunk face, but instead I'm a slab with eyes, like those statues on Easter Island. My lips are numb too, so when I spoon gruel into my mouth it slithers down my chin as if I'm a helpless baby. Somebody should just strap me into a highchair and make the aeroplane noises.

I am hideous. Look away. Look awaaaayyyy! No hang on, fetch me some more drugs, *then* look away.

WEEK 113
10 March 2003

We're now officially homeless. I felt sulky and betrayed as

I watched the last relics of our cosy Canberran lives walk out the door with their new owners. My bed, the television, and the crappy coffee table we painstakingly stripped back and restored. And how one forms an emotional attachment to a microwave beats me.

Finally on Friday afternoon, Rhiannon and I dropped off the keys to the estate agent. We've now moved in with the Mothership.

My eating has gone out the window. Now that I'm back on solids, I'm desperate to eat at my favourite Canberra restaurants one more time. Luckily Rhiannon feels the same way, so we organized a dozen different farewell dinners with different groups of friends. We've had Thai, Vietnamese, Chinese and Italian. I had my final potato wedges from Tilly's, my last Gus Café chocolate shake, my last sausage roll from Cornucopia, my last pumpkin pesto pizza from Babar. The food is always delicious, the company sublime and every meal ends in tears.

With friends like these and food like that, why am I walking away?

WEEK 114
17 March 2003

I tell you, if one more person tells me how they gained *so* much weight while travelling overseas, I will punch them in the face. If I am to believe what I'm told, the streets of Edinburgh are paved with lard and it rains pure beer.

All this saying goodbye has left me rather emotional

and pathetic. Sue looked at the calendar today and said, 'You're leaving in a week!'

'I don't wanna go!' I croaked, and promptly burst into tears.

This was the second incident of workplace bawling in six months. At least last time Poppy had just passed away so I had a decent excuse. But today poor Sue looked quite alarmed as I hiccuped away.

Tens of thousands of Aussies go off to the UK every year; it's a cultural institution! So why am I so afraid? It's only two years. And we're so lucky to be doing this, as everyone keeps reminding me. We're on the cusp of a great adventure.

But I feel like a fraud. None of this sounds like a very Shauna thing to do.

WEEK 114.5
22 March 2003

Tonight I drove back to Mum's house in Goulburn in the middle of a thunderstorm. Lightning scribbled across the sky, illuminating random bursts of sheep and gum trees.

It finally hit me as I rattled alongside the vast emptiness of Lake George. I'm leaving this beautiful country in four short days. I'm going to Scotland. I'm going to Europe. I'm going to see places I've only known from books. It's terrifying – but holy shit, it's exciting too!

And then suddenly my thoughts turned to chocolate. It's almost Easter. Should I buy one last Red Tulip Bunny? They're not going to have Red Tulip chocolate in

Scotland. What if I never get to bite off those creamy ears again? Oh I'll have to get one. Maybe just a baby one.

The first thing we did when we arrived in Frankfurt was phone Mum to let her know we hadn't been shot down over Iraq. I tell you, George Bush had a lot of nerve starting a war two days before we left the country. And that SARS outbreak was most untimely too. As if the Mothership wasn't worried enough about her children leaving the country!

Rhiannon and I were the only ones not crying as we left Canberra airport. Our friends were tearful and Mum was sobbing, but even as I hugged everyone for the seventy-fifth time I couldn't quite comprehend that I wouldn't be seeing them all again in a day or two.

As the plane took off, Rhiannon squeezed my hand and grinned. Her eyes were wild and glistening, as though she'd just spent twenty years digging out of prison with a teaspoon and had finally tasted freedom.

So now I realize just how far Australia is from the rest of the world. I managed to distract myself with Tetris from Sydney to Singapore, but I thought the fifteen-hour flight from Singapore to Frankfurt would never end. At least I had time to marvel at how easily I fitted in the seat. I'd put the Fat Girl Logistics Department on high alert but I had plenty of room to spare.

We made it to Scotland!

Edinburgh is stunning. It's particularly beautiful at 6 a.m. We had the privilege of seeing it early, thanks to the snotty fuckwit in our hostel room. He was very polite and sweet in daylight, but when night fell he morphed into an evil flu-ridden snoring machine. It sounded like he was boiling a huge vat of snot in his nostrils, and another vat of putrid phlegm in his throat. His girlfriend was wide awake in the bunk below, but did she once tell him to shut up? No! As his travelling companion it was her duty to be on Snore Watch.

We gave up on sleep and went for a walk up the Royal Mile, plotting their demise. But they were soon forgotten as we went past the crumbling closes and tacky tourist shops all the way up to Edinburgh Castle. You couldn't find a greater contrast from the clean lines of Canberra.

I swear the sunrise is a different colour over here. In Australia it's a riot of red and orange, here it's gentle pinks and blue. We stood out the front of the castle and gawked down at the city, trying to drink it all in.

I wonder how long it will take before I can hear a British police car siren without automatically humming the theme tune from *The Bill*?

Our first meal in Scotland was McDonald's. We arrived late on Friday night and were too knackered to look beyond the familiar arches.

'The Big Mac seems much smaller in Scotland,' said Rhiannon.

'Do you think that means everyone will be less fat?'

Since then we've been feasting from supermarkets. They're big on ready-made sandwiches. They come in boxes or cellophane, many oozing with mayonnaise. How very curious. I'm used to the sandwich shops in Australia where they have all the ingredients in little dishes and you tell the sandwich wench exactly how you want it. Yes, I predict this will be about as profound as my cultural observations get.

Today we each purchased a mobile phone in readiness for our job and shelter search. I added Rhiannon's number to my phone book. She added mine to hers. And that was it.

I felt slightly nauseous. Will we ever have other numbers in our phones? What if we don't make friends? What if it's just the two of us for the next two years? What if we can't find a job? What if we can't find somewhere to live? What if I have to slink back to Oz and live with the Mothership? Why did we come here?

But my fears were temporarily soothed by the sight of a dozen kilted men walking down Princes Street. I though this was standard procedure but it turned out they were rugby supporters on their way to a match. Still, all those pale hairy legs felt like a welcome mat.

I've become even more besotted with this country. In between job interviews, Rhiannon and I did three different bus tours this week. The tour guides point out the sights in a monotone, struggling to disguise their boredom, but I'm too enthralled to care. We've seen castles and mountains and Highland cows with hair more violently ginger than mine. We've seen Glencoe and the Wallace Monument and the bonny banks of Loch Lomond. We did not see a monster in Loch Ness. There's something so wild and raw about the landscape I could just hump the heather-clad hills in ecstasy. And I can't believe how much of Scotland you can see in a day! In Australia you can drive for a week without seeing a change of scenery.

Every tour ends with the bus pootling back over the Firth of Forth and by the third tour Rhiannon and I would chant in unison with the guide, 'On your left is the Forth Rail Bridge, which was the greatest feat of Victorian engineering.'

It's so bloody great to be here.

WEEK 118
14 April 2003

The romantic part of me thought living in a shared house in the UK would be a bit like an episode of *This Life*. I would do a lot of shagging, drink lots of wine and perhaps snort some illicit substances. Or at the very least I'd scamper around in my sexy bathrobe and scoff cake at midnight by the light of the refrigerator, Nigella Lawson style.

But it isn't quite turning out that way. For a start my bathrobe is pink and hideously fluffy. It was a size 24 but it was on sale. I look ridiculous in it, especially when it's combined with my purple slippers with the sequinned love hearts, also on sale. We are on a tight budget now, so I am a vision of frumpiness. I look like the lost Jedi Knight, Porky-Wan Bathrobi.

There are seven women living in our house. Luckily there are two bathrooms, but there is just the one tiny fridge. My flatmates seem to live on tinned soup, diet yoghurt and ready-to-eat lasagne from Sainsbury's with barely a vegetable in sight. Instead the fridge is crammed with condiments. I've never seen such an impressive assembly of relishes and mayonnaise. Then there's the Jams Throughout the Ages, topped with bursts of mould. We managed to carve out a third of a shelf for our own food, but I think the Glaswegian Chick's radioactive Cheddar has plans to invade.

Amazingly, we found a place to live on our second day in Edinburgh. We saw an advert in the *Evening News* and the cheery landlord invited us around immediately. It's a lovely Victorian flat in Bruntsfield, close to the centre of town. There's a constant pungent stench of yeast in the air, thanks to the nearby Fountain Brewery. It makes me think of Vegemite and home.

The landlord leased us each a room right on the spot, no reference checks required! We moved in on

Wednesday. My room looks rather sad, just a bed and a suitcase and a mobile phone, but it's my own wee space here in Scotland.

Already we're trying to establish new customs. Rhiannon and I are like small children or dogs: we're best behaved when we have a routine. We made a weekly meal list just like we'd do in Australia and headed off to Tesco.

The plan was abandoned as soon as we hit the aisles. The supermarket proved more thrilling than all those castles put together! We spent two hours cooing over the foreign brands and products and packaging and sights and smells. And all the funny names! Courgettes instead of zucchinis; peppers instead of capsicum.

The fruit and veggies are a bit odd. Many of them are wrapped in plastic and come from faraway countries. Peruvian Kiwi fruit, Italian tomatoes, South African butternut pumpkin! (Or butternut *squash*, to use the local lingo.) It makes everything seem exotic, if environmentally troublesome.

Our next mission was to find a gym. There's a huge one ten minutes' walk from our house; I'll call it Fancy Gym. The saleswoman gave us the grand tour, and we were dazzled by the vast bank of cardio machines, the sauna, the pool, the bar, the plush leather chairs, the ambient lighting and the spectacular class timetable. But then she revealed the monthly fee – £55! That's like 130 Australian dollars. It's more than double what we paid back there. She said she'd waive the joining fee but we still can't afford it. Especially since we don't have jobs yet.

It was so depressing that we stopped for British Mars

Bars on the way home. They seem to taste different from the Aussie ones. How will I survive without a gym? I feel my fat coming back already.

WEEK 119
23 April 2003

Rhiannon and I are working as administrators for a company we've codenamed Geriatric Rescue. They install alarms in the homes of elderly people and give them a pendant to wear, so if they have a fall or need help they press a button on their pendant and it sends a call to Rescue Headquarters. What a great idea. They've just taken on about 10,000 new clients so we have the thrilling task of adding them all to the database.

I can't believe I'm Secretary Girl again. If I'd known I'd have packed my staple remover. But I'm not complaining; I'm just relieved to have a job after four weeks of fruitless searching. I'd naïvely hoped I'd waltz into a marketing-internet-writer-geek job like I had in Australia, but I hadn't done my research. Edinburgh is a financial town so that's where the jobs are. It makes me wish I'd got a proper career like teaching, nursing or accountancy. They're always in demand, unlike arts degree layabouts.

So we're stuck with temporary work. We dumbed down our résumés and signed up with half a dozen recruitment agencies. I felt the cobwebs settle over my qualifications as each agent asked, 'Can you do Word and Excel?' After taking what seemed like a dozen different typing tests they informed us the minimum hourly rate was £5.50. We'll be earning far less than we did in Australia in a country that is twice as expensive. Well, they did say travel was character-building.

At least Rhi is working with me. We're going batty together. We spend our days in a tiny attic office, typing in medical details. It gets rather depressing, seeing all this information about people in their twilight years. Some of them are really in a bad way. I wonder if they're happy, if they're alone in their house watching *Emmerdale* or if they've got enough legs to pop out to the bingo. I type in their contact details and wonder who'll be *my* contacts when I'm old and grey. I must start sucking up to people in advance.

It scares me, all these things that can go wrong with your mind and body. We've seen stomach ulcers and paralysis and hernias and cancers and dementia. It makes me want to run away from the office and climb some hills, write a book or shag some kilted men while I'm still relatively sprightly.

All musing aside, the urge to be unprofessional quite often prevails. It is dull, repetitive work, so we amuse ourselves by setting challenges to find the oldest client (101), the most common names (Mary and Alex) and the one with the weirdest ailments.

'Right,' I said today. 'The first one to find a goitre wins a fiver.'

Week 120
28 April 2003

I've made contact! I've found a friend. Two, actually!

Tonight I met up with Rory in a cosy pub on the Royal Mile. Rory is a fellow Australian that I've 'known' online for many years. Since we have the dubious honour of both being Canberran expats in Edinburgh, we had to meet up.

His wife Jane came along too and they were both friendly and hilarious. It was heartening to meet people who've successfully existed in Scotland for nearly two years. We bitched about the weather and the food and reminisced about things we missed from Australia. Best of all they told me all about their European travels, which had me squirming in my seat with excitement and remembering why we literally turned our lives upside down.

It wasn't until I got home that I realized I'd done two very un-Shauna things tonight. Firstly, I went to a pub and not once did I fret about breaking chairs or knocking over drinks with my enormous hips. Secondly, I talked to strangers! Sure, I'd known Rory from the internet but he could have been a serial killer or stamp collector, so it was somewhat bold of me. I'd say the evening was a dazzling step forward for this reformed hermit. And now I've got two new numbers in my mobile phone.

Week 121
5 May 2003

I've discovered that the bacon over here tastes amazing. I

don't know what the Scottish pigs are rolling in but they're doing a great job. I keep telling myself that eating bacon sandwiches for breakfast is helping me become immersed in local culture, but the tightening of my pants – sorry, *trousers*, as they say here – indicates that it's time to crack on with the lard busting.

WEEK 122
12 May 2003

Cabin fever set in last week. Well, attic fever, to be more precise. Chronic boredom has pushed us to the brink of madness. Every time the secretary leaves the room we degenerate into behaviour not seen since kindergarten. There's hair pulling, tickling, stomping on toes, Chinese burns and nasty insults. And the graffiti-ing of limbs with highlighter pens. As soon as we hear the secretary on the stair, we drop our weapons and nonchalantly resume our typing.

We're just plain sick of the sight of each other. We trudge home from work together and someone will say over dinner, 'How was your day?'

'Oh, I did some typing and some filing.'

'I *know*. I was there!'

Moving overseas is nothing like I expected. It's such a well-worn path, Aussies doing their two-year stint in Britain; so I thought I'd slip into my new life as easily as a Scottish pizza slips into a deep fryer. Instead I'm feeling paralysed and overwhelmed. Rhiannon and I enjoyed such a comfy, middle-class lifestyle in Canberra and now

185

we're struggling to get by each week, let alone save money for travelling, which is our whole bloody *raison d'être*.

I'm glad Rhiannon's here, but I miss my other friends. I miss the Mothership and affordable mangoes and avocados. I miss our old routine, I miss my former salary. I miss not living in a house full of strangers.

WEEK 123
19 May 2003
16st 7lb (105kg, 231lb)
8st 8lb lost (54.5kg, 120lb) – 4st 10lb to go (30kg, 66lb)

Britain would be a great place for a spot of depression. You could really work up a good gloom here, with all the grey skies, grey buildings and grumpy grey faces on *EastEnders*. Depression never seemed quite appropriate in the midst of glaring sunshine and drought, but over here it's more atmospheric.

But I'm not going to let that happen again. For the third consecutive week, I spent Saturday night holed up in my room watching the National Lottery Draw and ploughing through a large bar of Dairy Milk. It was only when I reached for another square and found nothing but an empty packet that I realized where I was heading.

What's going on here? I huffed. *You're a disgrace. Are you planning to spend the next two years like this? Being a miserable bastard and gaining all your weight back?*

And what about the *last* two years, and all that effort I put into losing it? I couldn't let that go down the gurgler. Did I really want to fall in a heap at the first sign of hardship? Especially when it's *voluntary* hardship! I chose to move to Scotland, to challenge myself and do things I'd never done before. That was hardly going to happen while sitting on my bed.

My recent behaviour and emotions were all too familiar – the gnawing dread, the fatigue, the crushing self-doubt, the anxious binges. I've been circling the drain, in danger of being sucked back down at any moment.

But this time I've recognized the signs before it's gone too far. That's one of the advantages of keeping such an angst-ridden diary; you can poke through the archives and see patterns of behaviour.

So we can see, Doctor, that the patient has a strong tendency to hide from the world when things get scary. And to shovel food down her gob in an attempt to numb her angst.

Diagnosis: Freak Out!

Moving to the other side of the world is a daunting thing and I think I've simply been overwhelmed. So instead of waiting for it to get worse I sprang into action. I went upstairs to Rhiannon's room and declared dramatically, 'I'm not happy!'

Where would I be without my sister? This move has been equally crazy for her yet she still puts up with my whining.

We made an executive decision to join the gym. Sure it's expensive, but I've been spending the equivalent on junk food anyway. I know I could exercise for free by walking the hilly streets of Edinburgh, but I've missed having a gym; Rhiannon has too. I miss classes and shouty instructors. I miss having somewhere to go that isn't work

187

or my bedroom. I miss having an oasis of sweat where I can escape from the world. Most of all I've missed the sanity and smug satisfaction I get from a good workout!

I went to my gym induction tonight and discovered I'm back up to 16 and a half stone – a nine-pound gain since February. Damn those bacon sarnies! But I'm ready to resume the battle and get those endorphins buzzing again.

WEEK 125
2 June 2003

How the hell do people lose weight in Britain? It seems easier and cheaper to eat badly. The supermarkets are chock full of ready meals, fresh or frozen. And if the microwave is too much effort, you can always rock up to one of many chip shops for some lard-covered delicacies.

Fruit and vegetables, on the other hand, are rather pricey. Back in Australia it was cheaper to buy raw ingredients than a packaged meal. I know I must stop converting prices back to Australian dollars, but fresh produce seems so expensive. And I still feel guilty for eating all those imported veggies, wondering how much air was polluted and how many workers were exploited for those baby corncobs.

But we've discovered that busting blubber on a Scottish budget just requires a little more imagination and planning. In fact the effort is perversely pleasurable. Rhiannon and I used to cringe when the Mothership raided the bargain bins and bought generic food, but now we've embraced our frugal genes. We scour the greengrocers for the cheapest carrots then trek a mile in the opposite direction to fetch bulk rice and lentils from the health food shop. It makes us feel rather righteous too, lugging groceries in our backpacks while other people load up their Land Rovers. We slave over a vat of veggie chilli while our flatmates zap their over-packaged ready meals. We're saving money, we're eating healthily, we're getting bonus exercise and we're being nicer to the environment. I could spew from all this smugness!

At work today I drew many curious stares as I crunched on my packed lunch of mixed lettuce, cherry tomatoes, avocado, peppers and chickpeas.

COLLEAGUE: What's that you're eating?

ME: It's a salad.

COLLEAGUE: Ooh. That looks complicated.

WEEK 126
9 June 2003

Tonight I had my first pint of beer. Well, it was a half-pint. And I only drank a quarter of it. But still, I tried. It's important to at least attempt to embrace the culture of your new home.

This was a Proper Scottish Pub too – ancient black beams, low ceilings and red pressed-tin walls. There were grumpy men propped up at the bar half hidden in the cigarette haze. It was like being trapped in an episode of *Coronation Street*, or the Scottish equivalent. None of it was good for my lungs or liver, but I loved being right in the thick of it.

We had come for the pub quiz. Jane and Rory had formed a team with their friend David and invited Rhiannon and me to join them. I pounced on the chance, as pub trivia is the only place my passion for useless information is actually useful.

I felt happy sitting there with my pint and my new friends. I'm on a high lately and it's not just the exercise endorphins. For once, my fat hasn't been the first thing on my mind. Suddenly I'm embracing the uncertainty and unfamiliarity of my surroundings. It's so liberating to live in a city of strangers and freely roam the cobbled streets, safe in the knowledge that nobody's going to pop out from behind a statue and ask after my mother or demand to know if I've found a boyfriend.

Moving to the other side of the world has given me a brand-new perspective. The past finally feels like the past. It doesn't matter how fat I used to be, where I went to school or what my first pet cat was called. All that matters is who I am, right now. No one has to know anything I don't want them to. I could completely reinvent myself, like a less dangerous version of a witness relocation programme!

There was one late addition to our team, just as the first question was read. He came huffing through the door, flush-cheeked, bald-headed and hauling a bag of books. He apologized for being late and no one looked surprised.

His name was Gareth. He was a Ph.D. student at the university where Jane works. He was a gorgeous, quiet Scottish accent, in contrast to the shrill, competitive tone I seem to adopt for pub quizzes. He was unpretentious, warm and witty. He listened to people when they talked to him. And he shot way up in my estimation when he knew the answer to an obscure question. I like a guy who knows stuff about nothing.

When Rhiannon mentioned we were off to Paris at the weekend, Gareth piped up and said he went there a few years ago. I asked what he'd done and he replied that he went to Euro Disney and rode all the rollercoasters. This was back in the pre-budget airline era so he had to take a three-day bus trip from Edinburgh.

'Next time I'll do the proper tourist stuff,' he smiled.

For some reason I found that incredibly charming. I don't know if it was my eighth of a pint of Stella Artois, but there was something about him. He was so laid-back and easy to talk to, not trying to impress anyone. I had the briefest glimmer of a grandchild sitting on my knee as I told the story, 'We met at a pub quiz in Edinburgh. He had *all* the answers!'

I really need to lay off the beer.

In other news, our team won, which really capped off a good night.

WEEK 127
16 June 2003

As we jumped off the train at Gare du Nord in Paris an aesthetically pleasing young man appeared and asked if we were lost. We immediately assumed he was going to kill us, because this would prove correct the Mothership's theories about Young Ladies Out in the Big Bad World. But no, he was simply a hunky lad with a strong sense of community. He spent fifteen minutes explaining the intricacies of the Paris métro system then ran away while I was still figuring out how to say *en Français*, 'Take her, she's got more cash!'

Before long we were on a sightseeing bus, our cameras clicking in unison. Disgustingly famous and fabulous sights lurked around every corner. When the Arc de Triomphe loomed into view we couldn't help crowing, 'Holy fucking shit! We're in Paris!' It felt unreal, as if we'd run away from boarding-school and would get busted by Matron at any moment.

We hopped on and off the bus, trying to do as much as possible while spending the least amount of money. The pace didn't slow until late afternoon when, after wandering around Notre Dame, I barrelled back on to the bus and whacked my head on the roof as I ran up the stairs.

On Saturday morning we went out to Versailles super early in order to beat the crowds. Not a bad little château, I tells ya. Then we wandered around the town and argued over who would buy lunch:

'*You* ask for it.'

'Noo. *You* ask for it!'

'No. *You* ask for it! You're the one who did the classes!'

'I wish I knew how to say "Rhiannon's being a bitch" in French!'

Rhiannon is always making me ask for things. It must be part of my Fat Girl rehabilitation. I used to hide behind her and make her be my spokeswoman, but ever since we moved overseas she's had me making phone calls, ordering meals, asking for directions and buying bus tickets. It still makes me nervous to draw attention to myself like that, but I'm gradually overcoming my wimpy ways. At least in English, anyway.

Somehow we ended up with three croissants and a tiny quiche, but it was all very tasty. That was about as French as our cuisine got the whole weekend. Not only had we run out of money, we had run out of nerve. I'm ashamed to say we ate from the supermarket or Quick (the local equivalent of McDonald's) because we were too chicken to try out more French. We ate far too many *baguettes avec jambon et fromage* because that's all I could ask for. We also ate yoghurt in our hotel room by sticking our noses in the pots and slurping it out because we didn't have any spoons. But it was our first proper European jaunt, so I'm sure we'll be better tourists next time!

WEEK 128
28 June 2003
15st 13.5lb (101.6kg, 223.5lb)
9st 1.5lb lost (57.9kg, 127.5lb) – 4st 2.5lb to go
(26.6kg, 58.5lb)

The scale at the gym is an old clunker like the one at Weight Watchers all those years ago. It's plonked right next to the abs station where the nubile bunnies perform their perfect crunches and it intimidates me greatly. So instead of being a slave to the scale I've tried to adopt a general policy of three gym sessions a week, lots of incidental walking and eating a Frugal Tourist Diet. It seems to be working because I can once again breathe in my jeans.

But my inner statistician cried out for cold hard data, so I weighed myself tonight – 15 stone 13.5 pounds. Half a stone gone in five weeks! I'm a loser in the northern hemisphere!

WEEK 131
13 July 2003

There's this running joke in our family. Whenever we're too lazy or tired to do something, we whine, 'I can't. I'm too fat!'

It all started with the Mothership, who asked my sister to change a light bulb for her one day.

'Do it your bloody self!' snapped Rhiannon.

'I can't, I'm too fat!' came the reply.

The phrase quickly passed into our lexicon. It's perfect for those lazy arguments over who should do the dishes or who should nip round to the shop for some milk.

But seriously, I have an exhaustive list of things I didn't do because I was too fat, or believed that I was. I've waddled away from job opportunities, roles in school plays, writing gigs, concert tickets, boyfriends, holidays and party invitations. When I was sixteen I was selected to spend a year in Japan as an exchange student. Mum and my teachers were flabbergasted when I refused to go, but the thought of being a red-haired whale amongst all the delicate Japanese people was too terrifying.

Sometimes I was quite literally too fat – like for canoes or amusement park rides. But most of the time it was all in my head. I've spent so many years cutting myself off

194

from new experiences because I felt like a worthless butterball.

But now I'm desperate to make up for lost time, so today I confronted one of my longest-running Too Fat fears – the rock festival.

I've always been passionate about music but thought festivals were best left to the skinny people. If you couldn't fit into a tour T-shirt and drainpipe jeans then you had no right to be there. I convinced myself that I preferred a dark room and headphones to a live show. A mosh pit was no place for a fat chick; the hipsters would bounce off me like a trampoline! A few years ago some friends had tickets for the Big Day Out festival in Sydney, but I concocted an elaborate work emergency to worm out of it. My size 26 body didn't belong in a crowd of thousands on a summer's day!

So it was terrifying and exhilarating to find myself at T in the Park on an uncharacteristically scorching Scottish day. Rhiannon and I wandered around the various tents and ended up at the main stage, eating ice-creams while the Proclaimers and thousands of Scots belted out 'Five Hundred Miles'.

After that was a blur of bands – some I knew, some I'd only read about in expensive imported copies of Q magazine back in Australia. The crowds were obviously familiar with them as they sang every word with drunken joy. It was fantastic. And violent and insane. I felt so very old; surely they all needed permission notes from their mums? With acne on their chins and beer on their breath, they jumped and jumped and jumped, so I jumped and jumped and jumped too.

And then finally it was time for REM. Michael Stipe skipped on to the stage, dripping charisma from every pore. The shoving and kicking resumed in earnest. My shoelaces got shredded, a bottle of Fanta exploded over my hair, a topless woman toppled off her boyfriend's shoulders and landed on Rhiannon's head.

The long arm of the TV camera swept over us periodically and we'd jump and flail with even more vigour. On the big screen it just looked like a sea of happy faces with no hint of the stomping and vomiting and groping and fainting going on beneath.

It was wonderful. I feel far too crumbly to ever do it again, but today was really for the spotty teenager with the *Smash Hits* posters taped to her walls. I'm glad she got her day in the sun.

It's now 3 a.m. and I'm counting all the bruises on my legs. Each one is proof that my Fat Girl thinking was wrong. Today I danced and sweated and sang and not for a single moment did I think I was Too Fat to rock. Suddenly the world feels open and ripe with opportunity and all I have to do is decide what's next.

'I'm too fat' no longer.

WEEK 132
21 July 2003
15st 6.5lb (98.4kg, 216.5lb)
9st 8.5lb lost (61.1kg, 134.5lb) – 3st 9.5lb to go
(23.4kg, 51.5lb)

I wish I could live at Fancy Gym. I wouldn't be any

trouble; I'd just curl up on a treadmill and let the techno music lull me to sleep.

I'm in love with the fancy lighting. Our Aussie gym had fluorescent strips that illuminated every lump and bump in the mirrors, but Fancy Gym has calm flattering light throughout. Even the loos have a soothing glow. Bright lights have always made me feel exposed, so at Fancy Gym I can happily skulk about in ambient shadows.

I'm mad for the classes too. They have my old favourites, BodyPump and BodyCombat, plus a galaxy of other options – spinning, yoga, kung fu, Pilates, circuits and ballet. I have copies of the timetable on my wall and in my handbag so I can pull them out at any time and drool over all the possibilities.

My new routine involves racing home from whatever crappy temp job I have this week, scoffing down my dinner then hurrying to the gym. I do a couple of classes or just plonk along on the treadmill, watching programmes about grumpy British people buying houses in the sun.

I weighed myself again on Sunday – 15 stone 6.5 pounds. It's metric milestone day! I'm now 98.4 kilograms which means after nine years I'm back in double digits. It just sounds skinnier without a 'hundred' in the number. All hail the metric system!

My weight loss is quite slow compared to the dramatic superhero efforts of 2001, but I don't miss obsessing over crazy deadlines. I'm enjoying my new life in Scotland, and that happens to involve the occasional drink or chocolate bar. It may take me longer to get to my goal, but I'd rather have a slice of cake with friends than sit home alone with a diet yoghurt and an Excel spreadsheet.

197

WEEK 134
6 August 2003
15st 4.5lb (97.5kg, 214.5lb)
9st 10.5lb lost (62kg, 136.5lb) – 3st 7.5lb to go (22.5kg, 49.5lb)

Life is rattling along at a hectic pace. The Edinburgh Festival has started so the population has swollen with tourists and wacky performers. Just walking down the street is an exciting adventure.

Even more exciting are my new jeans! My Aussie ones were slipping so low I was flashing my undies. Both old and new pairs are a size 20, but the UK ones are much smaller.

Last night we met up with Jane and Rory to see Dave Gorman's show. We went for a drink afterwards and I found myself standing under a tree talking to that Gareth guy again. That seems to happen a lot lately. I don't know if it was the confidence that comes with jeans that don't show off your knickers, but I was buzzing after our chat. How do you know if someone is interested in you? It's been so long that I don't remember how it works. Is the inability to make eye contact an indication of attraction? He makes me feel shy yet talkative at the same time. I gravitate towards him, much as I used to gravitate to a buffet. It's an irresistible urge. We got so lost in conversation that he almost missed the last bus home. As he sprinted off into the night it occurred to me, *Hey, I was talking to a man! And I wasn't even thinking about my belly rolls!*

There was a disturbing incident at Fancy Gym this morning. I'd taken the bold move of hitting the showers after my BodyPump class, which meant facing my fear of changing rooms. After all these years I still race home after my workouts, as the crowds of naked toddlers and mothers yelling, 'JUST PUT YOUR PANTS ON!' make me feel panicky.

Today I was surrounded by chicks who were stripping off with great aplomb. They slapped moisturizer on to tanned thighs and happily fluffed their pubes with a towel. After ten minutes I finally summoned the nerve to remove my shoes and socks but then I froze.

It was then I realized that, despite my newfound positive body image and happiness, I was still a trembling prude.

'Don't worry about it,' Rhiannon reassured me as I toyed with the hem of my T-shirt. 'No one is looking!'

'Yeah, yeah.' I huddled in the corner with my head low and shoulders rounded in my traditional Fat Girl Hiding stance. Alas, there is no practical way of removing bra and undies while covering yourself with a towel at the same time (how do you secure the towel? with your teeth?) so I just had to strip and be done with it.

Once I'd had my shower I felt a lot better. I padded back to the locker in a towel and realized that Rhiannon was right. Nobody was paying the slightest bit of attention.

But then as I started to dress, who should saunter in and

sit down on the bench opposite me but our BodyPump instructor! She fetched a water bottle from her locker then just sat there, for what seemed like an eternity, sipping her water, all of ONE METRE directly behind my naked arse.

I looked at my sister. We held an alarmed eyebrow conversation. *What is she doing?* I don't know. *Is she going to go soon?* Doesn't look like it. *I don't want to get changed now!* Me neither, and I ain't no prude. *She is RIGHT THERE near my butt!* I know; it's too weird!

It was extremely unsettling to be naked near one's fitness instructor. It's not a position you expect to be in. Instead of mixing with the mortals after class, I always imagined the instructors went to a private temple out the back to have their beautiful muscles kneaded by chiselled boys in loincloths.

In the end I held the towel around me by holding it on my chest with my chin, then executed a dainty wriggle/slide motion to pull my undies on without the towel dropping. I knew I was being ridiculous, but once you start these things you just have to see them through.

Afterwards Rhiannon and I went out for brunch, where I devoured a big plateful of scrambled eggs and bacon without a trace of self-consciousness. I just operate so much better with clothes on.

Rhiannon and I went to Jane and Rory's for afternoon tea today. It makes me feel disloyal to Nanny to say this, but Jane is a master cook. She churns out quality cakes and scones that are almost impossible to resist. That's one annoying irony of losing weight and becoming a social animal: the more you leave the house, the more you fall in the path of tasty treats.

Gareth arrived late and the only seat left was beside me. It was then I noticed his lovely forearms – strong and lightly tanned from the balmy summer we've been having. I've always liked a nice forearm. And a great set of eyebrows too. His have a good strong arch. What is it about this guy?

He became even more appealing when Rory held a Vegemite Tasting. Rory's parents had sent over a jar of New Zealand Vegemite and wanted to see if we could tell the difference between the Kiwi and Aussie stuff. I'm proud to say Rhiannon and I immediately detected our native spread.

Then Gareth volunteered to join in. Foreigners usually run screaming from the room when you offer them the black stuff but not only was he up for it, he enjoyed it and asked for another slice! I know it was just a sandwich but to me it was a manly feat of strength and character. I just love his quiet curiosity about the world. Maybe that appeals to me because that's how I'm starting to live my life.

201

Iceland! On the bus into Reykjavik, there was a crazy man beside me with a grizzly beard and a camouflage jacket. He muttered about how he 'got done' at Customs for having two bottles of duty-free whisky too many. Rhiannon rolled her eyes and made her 'Well, *dickhead*!' face.

Meanwhile, a blond girl was rummaging through her swanky handbag and looking confused, as if she had no idea how she'd ended up in Iceland and the answer was hidden beneath her Evian and breath mints.

'Do you have any idea where I could stay tonight?' she asked the bus in general.

'You've got nowhere to stay?' asked Crazy Man, leaning over the aisle. 'I can help. How much are you willing to spend?'

'Oh, money isn't a problem,' she replied as she slopped on some lip gloss. 'I'm here on my own, I've got no plans.'

I heard the voice of the Mothership on my shoulder: 'Tell her to shut up! She's giving him *way* too much information! And you know he has a collection of large knives in that duffle-bag. She's sushi tonight, I tell you.'

But one look out the window and I forgot to care. All the guidebooks waxed lyrical about Iceland's 'lunar landscape', but the clichés were true. The contrasts and emptiness were overwhelming. The silvery highway slashed through the middle of an endless stretch of lava rocks, all weird and clumped and covered in brilliant green moss.

Crazy Man bragged that he'd been to Iceland five times before and offered to show Blondie around town. I just wanted him to shut up and go home so we could have this strange, beautiful place to ourselves.

Rhiannon and I spent the rest of the day wandering around Reykjavik. Having squandered our money on the flights and day trips to spectacular geysers and waterfalls, it was a case of lots of looking but not much touching. We turned into those annoying Oh My God tourists, cooing over brightly coloured houses and weird boutiques and road signs with names we couldn't pronounce.

I saw a duck out the front of the Hallgrímskirkja church. You can't help go crazy over a duck in a foreign land, especially when it's a land so completely removed from your own. I used to roll my eyes at Japanese tourists in Cowra, squealing as they snapped twenty photos of a fat old sheep. But now here I was crouched beside the duck, yelling to my sister, 'You have to come see this Icelandic duck!'

I don't know what I expected; perhaps when it opened its beak it would issue weird glacial soundscapes. But no, it just gave me a withering look and said quack in the usual manner. Then Rhiannon informed me it was actually a goose.

Next stop was Bónus, the local supermarket, where we bought our rations for the trip – a loaf of bread, four apples and a jar of peanut butter. Along with the two-minute noodles and chocolate bars we'd bought from home, I'm proud to say our entire food expenditure was a mere 400 krónur. I honestly think supermarkets are the best part of foreign travel. We cruised the aisles, poking each other when we found something exotic. 'Look at these Icelandic *beans*!'

203

I took four extra Bónus shopping bags as souvenirs. I wonder if Icelandic tourists in Scotland save their bags from Tesco? Maybe they would if they had a little pink pig on their logo, like Bónus.

Iceland continued to astound us over the next three days. It was worth every penny to see the massive waterfalls, gurgling hot springs and the steam rising from the barren hillsides.

But the happiest moment was on the first day, sitting by the harbour with the fog obscuring the view of almost everything. The temperature plunged as we ate like savages, dipping chunks of bread into the peanut butter jar and not thinking of the calorie content. I sang the praises of Icelandic peanut butter until Rhiannon pointed out it was American peanut butter. Of course. Iceland is hardly the ideal climate for peanut growing, nor does it have the economic clout to lord it over a country that does.

Still, it was a delicious meal. We sat there in the drizzle with our hair doubling in volume, and I couldn't quite believe that I'd travelled from a couch in Australia to a park bench near the top of the globe.

WEEK 140
16 September 2003
15st 2lb (96.4kg, 212lb)
9st 13lb lost (63.1kg, 139lb) – 3st 5lb to go (21.4kg, 47lb)

The travel bug has taken hold. Rhiannon has put a giant

map of Europe on her bedroom wall and every night we congregate beneath it for dinner, plotting our next move. Since we got back from Iceland all we can think about is where to go next. Who put so many countries in Europe? How are we going to have time to see them all in the next eighteen months? I want to see Russia, Scandinavia and the Baltic States. I want to soak up the sun in Spain and eat a giant, calorific sausage in Germany.

But we realized that none of this will be possible on our current paltry incomes, so we've taken on second jobs in the call centre at Geriatric Rescue. This means giving up the occasional weekend but it's the only way we'll afford to see all these crazy places in the limited time we have over here.

I've started yet another new weekday job too. I'm a personal assistant at a government agency that I shall call the House of Sport. After six jobs in six months, I've finally scored a long-term contract!

After all my job woes last year, it seems hilarious now that I'm excited about a new secretarial gig. But moving to Scotland has stripped me of all employment snobbery. I used to be terrified of job interviews; but I've had at least two dozen this year. I no longer have the luxury of fretting over whether I am bursting out of my trousers or if the interviewer is counting my chins; I just have to put myself out there because I've got to pay the rent in Scottish pounds! Do I want to travel or do I want to slink back home?

I'm beginning to think moving to Scotland was the best decision I've ever made. If I'd stayed in Australia I doubt I would have found the inclination to push myself and confront my fears. I may have taken a few steps down the career ladder, but it's been worth it just to stop living in my head and start engaging with other humans! I've been a receptionist, a personal assistant, a call centre slave, a filing lackey and a data entry automaton and with each new gig I feel more outgoing and practical, instead of insular and clumsy. I've even overcome my fear of making tea and coffee – I dreaded wobbling into meeting rooms with the tea tray, positive that everyone was sneering at my incompetence, but now I realize nobody gives a shit. I've stopped worrying what people are thinking and have learned to laugh at myself and my myriad mistakes.

So this is my roundabout way of convincing myself I'm glad to be broke and working two crappy jobs. It has been character building. I'm so full of character now I should be in a Dickens novel.

WEEK 141
24 September 2003

Unexpected advantage of being fat: I have excellent balance.

I went to a Body Balance class tonight and discovered an uncanny ability to hold the tree pose for a lengthy period. Gravity is on my side!

Do you remember the first time I tried BodyBalance? I got stuck on my back like a cockroach. Now almost four years later on the other side of the world I'm as uncoordinated as ever. But I muddled my way through all the moves, albeit with less grace and flexibility than my classmates. And not once did I curse my reflection; instead I chuckled to myself when I arsed things up. I'm amazed at how my body keeps adapting and evolving as this lard-busting journey drags on. I floated out of the room afterwards, utterly mellow and relaxed. It was a beautiful high like after an orgasm or a particularly good dessert. I'm a dying cockroach no more.

WEEK 142
2 October 2003

Tonight we met up with Jane, Rory and Gareth at David's house. It's turning into a regular little expat gathering – four Aussies, an Englishman and Gareth. He lives 15 miles away in Dunfermline, and apparently Fife is like a whole other planet, so that sort of qualifies. Each week we order an Indian takeaway and watch a DVD.

When Australians living in Scotland congregate, at some point the conversation will inevitably swing to 'Is The Food Shit Over Here Or What?' Which is unfair, as I've found scores of British delights like oatcakes, afford-able raspberries and Green & Black's chocolate. But when you meet your fellow countrymen you're obliged to get misty-eyed about vegetables that don't come in Mexican plastic jackets and checkout chicks that don't ask 'What the hell is this?' when you buy some passion fruit. That cost £1.50 each.

Last week we were all pining for Mint Slices. They are a true Australian classic – a delicious chocolate biscuit with a layer of peppermint cream, elegantly coated in smooth dark chocolate. They marry the adultness of an after dinner mint with the dunkability of a biscuit.

'Oh yeah,' Gareth piped up. 'That sounds just like a Viscount!'

We shot him doubtful looks, certain that the country that gave the world the deep-fried pizza would be incapable of producing anything near the standard of a Mint Slice biscuit. But he bravely faced the panel of Australian critics and brought a packet tonight.

I was excited, as I am by anything that combines chocolate and mint. You get the goodness of chocolate then as a bonus your mouth is left minty-fresh as if you've just brushed your teeth. It's like the calories never happened!

The Viscounts came individually wrapped in green foil. We turned them over in our hands, slowly unwrapping, regarding them suspiciously. After examining from all angles we all took tentative bites.

'Pretty good,' I said diplomatically.

'No,' said Rhiannon. 'It's all wrong.'

'It's not quite the same,' said Rory. 'The biscuit isn't chocolate, for starters.'

'And the coating should be *dark* chocolate. This is a low-grade *milk*.'

'The mint isn't evenly distributed across the surface of the biscuit.'

'It's basically nothing like a Mint Slice at all.'

'Oh!' said Gareth.

'Well I think they're all right!' I said brightly, and promptly shovelled down three more. One, because I am a big greedy-guts and two, because I'm increasingly

Cheeky & cheerful
at three years old,
1981

Rhi

Me

I was a skinny
five-year-old,
but had already begun
to feel otherwise.
1983

With Nanny,
Poppy & Rhi,
1996

17 STONE

Me & my chins on
Graduation Day, 1996

22 STONE

At Rhi's Graduation
on the eve of
Operation Lard Bust,
December 2000

25 STONE

16 STONE

Nine Stone lighter on
the day I left 02, 2003

15 STONE

Swinging in
Estonia,
2004

Windswept
at John o'
Groats,
2004

15 STONE

14 STONE

Wedding

PART I
GRACELAND WEDDING CHAPEL

March 2005

13 ST 8LB

WEDDING PART II
Scotland,
July 2005

WEDDING PART
III
Australia, October
2005

13 ST 7LB

Dr G, me & The
MotHership!

22 STONE

21st Birthday, November 1998

A TALE OF TWO CAKES

My body shape
may have changed
considerably,
but my undying
love for chocolate
cake has never
wavered!

13 ST 7LB

Wedding Part III, October 2005

Half the girl I used to be
in my old size-26 jeans,
October 2005

Finally done with the lard busting & just happy being me.

May 2007

12ST 7LB

convinced that I want to get into Gareth's pants. Surely a hearty appetite has got to impress him?

WEEK 143
6 October 2003
15st 1lb (96kg, 211lb)
10st lost (63.5kg, 140lb) – 3st 4lb to go (21kg, 46lb)

I'm paranoid about Scary Bastard, one of the gym instructors. He's a wonderful instructor; all bulging biceps and flirtatious manner. He works us hard and is a stickler for technique, which is what you want in a teacher.

But I seem to be invisible to him. I've seen him make eye contact with everyone else, from the nubile lasses down the front to the old grannies and the token males. But he never ever looks my way. He never corrects my form. He never tells me to kick harder or to squat deeper as he prowls around the class.

So I seethe beneath my barbell, my brow beading with perspiration and paranoia. What the hell is wrong with *me*, buddy? Why won't you acknowledge my presence? Is it my freakish lack of coordination? Is it because I am usually (still, after all this effort) the fattest person in the room? Why? WHY?

I must learn to channel this petty rage into my workout. Thighs of Steel shall be mine.

I'm probably just projecting, anyway. I feel like a big fat Blobby McBlob lately, despite the fact I've now lost 20 pounds since we moved to Edinburgh. My body is the smallest it's been for almost a decade, but it's disguised by my sad and baggy clothes. I came to Scotland with just one suitcase and didn't think very hard about what I tossed inside. I've got twenty pairs of undies and quite a few books, but for six months I've been wearing the same lonely pair of jeans, three pairs of trousers and five tops for both work and play. Now they're all faded and ratty, not to mention too big. My gym pants have reached the point of indecency, so now my pyjama bottoms are doubling up as workout gear. The new jeans I bought in August are getting roomy, and even my watch is too big! I never knew wrists could shrink so much.

Since Rhiannon and I have ploughed all our money into travel and rent I kind of forgot about clothes for a while. But now that I've got some semblance of a social life I'm conscious of my dishevelled appearance. Meanwhile, the Mothership keeps asking me when am I going to find a Nice Scottish Boy? It's hard to feel attractive when you're constantly hauling your trousers up.

WEEK 143.5
11 October 2003

Gareth and I have been corresponding! It all started with one of those unwieldy group emails about the next Curry Night. David had asked ages ago if he could borrow Gareth's copy of *Breakfast at Tiffany's*:

David, my memory is pants! Would you like me to bring Roman Holiday as well? I love that film as it combines lots of my favourite things – Italy, Vespas and Audrey Hepburn.

My heart leapt to my throat. *Roman Holiday* is my favourite film! Could this be – a heterosexual Audrey fan? I immediately hit Reply and in my excitement I abandoned my grammar and punctuation.

no bloody way . . . you are my hero! i can't believe you like roman holiday! audrey! rome! gelato! Gregory Peck's eyebrows!

Twenty minutes later he replied:

Excellent, another Audrey admirer! Roman Holiday is one of my cheery-up movies. My favourite parts are when she first escapes from the castle in the back of the moped/van thingamajig and she's looking out at the city streets, when she batters the dude over the head with the guitar and when they're at the place where you stick your hand in the hole and Gregory Peck pretends his hand has been bitten off (can't remember what it's called).

It's called the Mouth of Truth, as I so helpfully responded. He thanked me graciously and continued:

It's such a sad ending with Gregory Peck's long, lonely walk out of the palace. And no matter how many times you see it you want Audrey to come running after him . . .but she never does!

Next time I'll have to look out for Gregory Peck's eyebrows.

And it just went from there, back and forth for three days. We talked about music and movies and books and travel and I found out so much about him. He's 30 years old and has one brother. He just passed his motorcycle test and he plays bass guitar in a band and he's going to Amsterdam next weekend. He has a tattoo on each biceps and his Ph.D. thesis has something to do with electrical engineering. And he seems to be the most thoughtful, genuine and witty guy I've ever met. He's so positive and enthusiastic about life and just seems to match the headspace I'm in these days.

I wonder if he likes me. How are you supposed to tell? Maybe he only writes back so quickly because he's procrastinating with his thesis. And do I like him? I think I do, because I'm poring over every word of my replies, correcting my spelling and striving for a balance of wit and cool intelligence. No more lower-case babble, this could be courtship!

WEEK 144
13 October 2003
14st 13lb (95kg, 209lb)
10st 2lb lost (64.5kg, 142lb) – 3st 2lb to go (20kg, 44lb)

The Mothership called yesterday to get her weekly Status Report.
'So how goes the Being Healthy?'
'It goes pretty good.'
'And how much do you weigh these days?'
'Just a peep under 15 stone!'
'Wowiee! So what does the body look like?'

'Well, my waist is getting smaller but the hips and thighs don't seem to change.'

'Oh, so you're an hourglass.'

'Sorta.'

'You must look like Oprah.'

'Oprah?'

'You know! Curvy hips, defined waist, impressive bosom . . . like Oprah!'

'I do not look like Oprah!'

'What's wrong with looking like Oprah? She does a lot of good for this world!'

Despite the recent bout of curries, I'm still shrinking. The scale isn't doing much, yet the inches are inching away. Life has settled into a rather mundane routine now that we're working six- or seven-day weeks with our two jobs. The travel fund is fattening up nicely but I'm so exhausted that I've been taking naps after work and not waking in time for my gym classes.

I must refocus! Sometimes I forget that I'm still 44 pounds from a healthy weight. I'm so absorbed in my new life in Scotland that I don't notice those belly rolls or how my thighs still smack together as I amble along to the bus stop. And my arms! I'm so impressed by my growing biceps that I block out the turkey gobble beneath. I'm sure if I flapped my arms long enough I could fly back to Australia for free.

The fact is, I never thought I'd get this far. I never thought my brain and body were capable of such dramatic change. So squeezing into a size 18 feels like a miracle. It almost feels like enough.

But I've still got a long way to go. I may *feel* positively slinky but when I stand beside 90 per cent of the population I'm still quite a hefty lass. Next time I take a progress photo I'll have to pose beside a skinny person to give a more accurate perspective. Or I'll put a milk carton or television or other inanimate object in the frame. Then you could say, 'Oh yeah, now I see! Her arse is still huge when you look at it in relation to a telephone box.

WEEK 144.5
16 October 2003

Last week Jane and Rory got back from two weeks in Australia and they brought us back a packet of Mint Slices!

It's not that Mint Slices were particularly precious to me back home, but now I'm on the other side of the world it was like receiving a shipment of illicit substances. Rhiannon and I gleefully divided the goods then devoured them throughout the week, because surely the calories don't count when it's contraband.

But I saved the last one. For Gareth. What madness is coming over me when I would willingly sacrifice a chocolate biscuit?

At Curry Night tonight, I went into the kitchen for a glass of water and he followed me.

'Hiya Shauna!'

'Hello!' I squeaked.

'How are you?'

'Good!'

Oh, the unbearable agony of eye contact. I fiddled with cups and cutlery and foil takeaway dishes.

'I have a wee something for you,' he said, handing me a small paper bag.

'Ooh, cheers!'

It was postcards from Amsterdam.

'I forgot to take your address with me, I'm a bit disorganized.'

'No worries,' I smiled. One postcard was a canal boat scene, the second dazzling tulips at the Bloemenmarkt. The third was a shop window in the Red Light District, featuring a display of vibrators and dildos in all the colours and girths of the rainbow. He looked nervous as I stared at it.

I burst out laughing. 'Bloody brilliant. That's going on the wall in my bedroom.'

He grinned, relieved. 'Glad you like it.'

'Ooh, I have something for you too, I just remembered.'

I dug the Mint Slice out of my handbag. I'd carefully wrapped it in cling-film.

'Jane and Rory brought this back from Australia. I saved it for you.'

'It's not . . . is it really?'

'Yes. It really is.'

'A genuine Mint Slice! I don't believe it.' He cradled it in both hands and petted it like a baby bird. 'I'll save this for my first cuppa tomorrow.'

'You have to let me know what you think. If you fall to your knees at the superior taste of Australia.'

There were more awkward smiles and my cheeks blushed a Tandoori red. Then someone yelled out that the movie was starting so we were excused.

215

Rhiannon and I went out for dinner tonight, to the Thai restaurant where we'll all be going for my birthday on Saturday week.

'Consider this meal a warm-up,' she said. 'We're just casing the joint, making sure it's suitable for everyone else.'

'But of course!' I grinned. Hey, I'd been to BodyPump earlier; I felt virtuous enough to indulge.

We got all dressed up, as much as our tatty garments allowed, then headed to the restaurant. Back in Australia we'd eat out at least twice a week, such spendthrift care-free middle-class socialites we were! We never imagined that we'd wind up working two jobs and feeling deliciously guilty about one Thai meal.

I'd forgotten how much I enjoyed our sisterly nights out. Ever since Iceland it seems we've done nothing but work. But now as we attacked our pad thai and fishcakes, we forgot about the monotony of call centres and photo-copying and talked more openly than we had in months.

'So,' Rhiannon said suddenly. 'Have you met anyone interesting in sunny Scotland?'

'What do you mean?' I stared at the little bowl of chilli dipping sauce, wondering if it would be rude to pick it up and lick the last few drops.

'You know. Like *men*.'

'Me? I don't meet men. I'm Too Fat for men.'

We both laughed.

'No, seriously,' Rhiannon pressed. 'What about Gareth?'

'Gareth!' I coughed. 'What about him?'

'Oh come on. It's obvious to everyone. You're all over each other like a rash.'

'Really? Do you think so?'

She rolled her eyes and I couldn't help grinning.

'So you like him?'

'I dunno,' I mumbled. 'I think so. Maybe?'

'Honestly,' she said, 'you're both hopeless. You'd be perfect together.'

'What should I do? I don't remember how this works.'

'Well . . .' Rhiannon leaned forward conspiratorially. 'Your birthday's the thing. He's coming, right? That'd be the perfect time for a move.'

'A move? I've never made a move before!'

'You'll be fine.'

I picked up the bowl of coconut rice and emptied the last of it on to my plate. If I was going to be courageous I'd better do some carbo-loading.

WEEK 146
27 October 2003

BIG AUSSIE LASS MAKES BOLD MOVE ON SCOTSMAN

EDINBURGH, AP – Amateur Antipodean seductress Miss Dietgirl was embroiled in attempts to woo Dunfermline resident Gareth Reid this week.

'I decided a direct move was not my style so I used a cowardly, lazy girl's way to let him know I'm kind of interested,' she said.

217

Dietgirl sent Mr Reid a copy of the Audrey Hepburn/Cary Grant classic *Charade* from Amazon. 'They only had it on VHS, but I'd told him about the film in an email. We both love Audrey movies and he hadn't seen this one. I thought it was a good way of showing him I'd been paying attention.'

Dietgirl spent the past seven days in a heightened state of agony, wondering if her move was too bold or not bold enough. But today Mr Reid notified her by email that the goods had been received. Dietgirl read his message out to the assembled press:

'*At first I was confused as although I'm a notorious impulse buyer (damn that One Click Purchase thingy) I couldn't remember buying any-thing. I was dead chuffed when I opened the box and realized what it was. I sat on the couch with a big happy smile on my face for about an hour!*

'*Oh the power of human kindness. You're a real star, Shauna (and a bit of a honey if you don't mind me saying so!). Thanks very much. You made an old man very happy!*'

Dietgirl says she was delighted with the outcome of her crafty plan. 'He called me a star! And a honey,' she said. 'Honey's good, isn't it? It's got to mean something, right?'

Dietgirl's only concern was whether Reid actually owned a VCR in this day and age. 'But I must say I like this idea of conducting a romance entirely via email and Amazon parcels,' she concluded. 'I can choose my words carefully and no one need ever know about my stretch marks.'

Still Week 146
31 October 2003

The Mothership sent me birthday money so I splashed out on some new workout gear from TK Maxx. Designer gym trousers for only £10! Size XL. I've never been so proud to fit into an overpriced, over-hyped garment made by child slaves. I thought I'd be banished to Target Plus Size workout gear for the rest of my life. Now I can finally see that my body has changed. I've got a waist! Tonight at Body Pump I couldn't stop admiring my significantly smaller arse and thighs in the mirrors. Now I'm desperate to be near the mirrors instead of wishing I could smash them. I quite like what I see these days.

Week 146 *(will it ever bloody end?)*
1 November 2003

Twenty-six today and my first birthday in the dark, damp northern hemisphere. My first ever birthday that required a coat!

Gareth was late as usual, but Rhiannon had strategically seated Jane and Rory so the chair next to mine was vacant. He gave me a Godspeed You Black Emperor album and a Far Side card with my favourite ever Far Side cartoon on it. There's a tumble dryer with the word CAT FUD written on the open door and an arrow pointing inside. There's a cat peering inside it while a dog watches from around the corner murmuring, 'Oh please, oh please!'

Of all the dozens of Far Side greeting cards in the

world, Gareth somehow picked my favourite. Is that some sort of sign? We seem to have so much in common, both trivial and profound.

But nothing happened all night. We were both too bashful to mention the whole *Charade* thing. The five of us went out for drinks after dinner and Rhiannon pointedly raised her eyebrows at Jane and Rory so Gareth and I had to sit beside each other again. But I was too nervous and crap to make any eye contact.

Now it's 2 a.m. and I'm brooding back at home. Gareth is staying over at Jane and Rory's, just five minutes down the road. So near and yet so far.

What did I expect to happen? Was he going to lunge at me in front of our friends? I don't know. I'm rubbish at this stuff. I'm going to be alone for ever.

WEEK 147
3 November 2003

The tide has turned, people!

After sulking all night that He Doesn't Even Know I'm Alive, Gareth called in the morning! Jane and Rory must have given him my number. My heart thumped as his mellow accent wafted down the line.

'Do you fancy coming out to Dunfermline today?' he asked. 'I can show you around the town.'

'Oh!'

'It's only a wee place. It'll take about ten minutes.'

'I'd love to.'

An hour later, the train rattled over the Forth Rail

Bridge and I searched for something profound to say.

'Ahh, the Forth Rail Bridge. The greatest feat of Victorian engineering!'

Gareth smiled. 'Hell, yeah. It makes me proud!'

Could I be the biggest twit in the world? As the train pulled into North Queensferry I considered hopping out and hurling myself on to the tracks.

'So . . . Dunfermline's a fair distance from Edinburgh,' I said. Shit!

'Aye! And my flat is twenty minutes' walk from the station too.'

'Aha. So is that why you're always running late?'

He laughed. 'Guilty as charged.'

'Excellent.'

I was all out of words.

Mercifully we arrived in Dunfermline. He showed me around the Abbey and walked me back to his flat via the local park where I saw my very first real live Scottish squirrels!

Gareth's flat was incredibly tidy with enormous piles of books and CDs. Always a good sign.

'Can I get you a cup of tea?' he asked.

'Oh no thanks,' I blurted out automatically. 'I don't drink tea!'

I remembered a time about five years ago when a guy asked me did I want to come in for coffee when I dropped him off at his house. It was just like that *Seinfeld* episode where George turns down a late-night cuppa and it sparks a lengthy 'Does coffee mean sex' debate. I didn't think of that at the time, even though it was 1 a.m.; for why would someone want hanky-panky with a lump like me? So I said cheerily, 'Oh no thanks, mate! I don't like coffee!' and drove away into the moonlight.

Gareth's question was perfectly innocent: tea really did mean tea. We couldn't even look at each other, let alone make sweet love down by the fire. But he was astounded that I was a tea virgin at twenty-six years old. Eager to establish myself as a wild adventurer, I agreed to try it. As he fiddled with mugs and spoons, I examined the box of teabags and took another stab at conversation.

'So . . . it says here this tea is Scottish Blend. How does that work?'

'Oh it's genuine Scottish tea,' he replied, 'from the Scottish tea plantations.'

'Tea plantations? In Scotland?'

'Aye! It's special cold climate tea. They grow it down in the Borders!'

I grinned. 'Oh I see.' He could have told me that the Scottish tea plantation was right next to the haggis fields and across the road from the oatcake orchard and I still would have said, 'Really, how fascinating!'

I'll never forget that first sip. It was scalding hot; I hadn't thought to let it rest for a while. It burned a path down my throat until POW! It exploded like a punch in the chest. With minimal calories!

'What do you think?'

'Not too shabby!'

I proceeded to drink five more cups during the evening. We chatted non-stop, side by side on his couch, tantalizingly close yet not touching. I've never felt such ease and warmth talking to a guy. I was deliriously happy just to be near him, or perhaps that was the effects of tea on a body that had been a stranger to caffeine for the previous two and a half decades. Well, aside from all that chocolate.

We talked and talked, then somehow it was midnight. I'd missed the last train back to Edinburgh.

'Um, you could crash here if you like?' said Gareth.

'Really?'

'I'll sleep in the spare room,' he said hurriedly. 'No worries.'

He made another round of tea, this time with Vegemite toast. 'I'm completely hooked on this stuff now,' he said.

I poked through his record collection, looking for a clanger that would spoil my opinion that he was possibly the most perfect bloke in the world. But there was nothing incriminating!

Finally at two o'clock this morning I crawled into his bed. I was still so wired that I kept yapping, even though he was in the spare room.

'Why don't you just come in here?' I said after a while, all bold like an oversized Mae West.

So he slipped into the bed beside me and we lay on our backs, too timid to look at each other even in the dark. Eventually he reached over and took my hand and traced the back of it with his thumb, neither of us skipping a beat of the conversation. My heart pounded wildly, but again that could have been the caffeine. I had to keep getting up to pee and agonized over whether he could hear me through the flimsy walls.

By 6 a.m. he was starting to drift off but I was still staring at the ceiling and squeaking, 'I can't sleep! I can't sleep! Hee hee!'

At 8 a.m. I called in sick to work because I couldn't bear

for the conversation to end. Then we finally slept for three hours.

When we woke there was more tea and Vegemite toast but it was back to the extreme shyness. We watched DVDs and chatted all afternoon then finally at six o'clock we walked back to the train station in awkward silence.

Standing on the platform in the chilly night air, my breath shot out in anxious, near-hysterical puffs. It had been five long months since our fateful meeting at the pub quiz: now the time was ripe to finally make that move!

With the train rattling towards us there was potential for a dramatic and memorable moment, like *Brief Encounter* or something. But an ill-timed lunge, an awkward hug and my kiss landing somewhere up his left nostril was hardly something to tell the grandkiddies. Neither was me blurting, 'You rock!' before fleeing on to the train. All executed without any eye contact whatsoever.

Now it's eleven o'clock and here I am cringing in my bedroom. *You rock*. You ROCK? Why did I say that? What kind of crap seductress am I?

WEEK 147.5
7 November 2003

For the past three days Gareth and I seem to have returned to chaste emails. I'm starting to panic. Was that wonderful weekend entirely my imagination?

I went shopping to console myself and bought a new pair of jeans – size 18! And a normal size 18 from a normal shop. Finally! There's no elastic in the waistband either. If I weren't so anxious I'd be feeling pretty darn foxy right now.

WEEK 148
10 November 2003

'Shaunie Prawn. It's the Mothership!'
  'Hello!'
  'How's life treating you?'
  'I'm fine. Well . . .' I couldn't contain my glee. 'I'm about to head out, actually!'
  'Oh *really?*' I could hear the wheels turning. 'Going anywhere special?'
  'Just the pub around the corner.'
  'Oh yes. With anyone special?'
  'Well . . .'
  'Spill! Spill!'
  'He could be. Oh, Mum. I really think he might be.'
  'Shauna, you sly dog!' she howled. 'Who is he? Why wasn't I informed earlier?'
  'He's Scottish. He's smart . . . oh bugger, he's just rung the doorbell. I'll put Rhiannon on. Wish me luck!'
  'Good luck. You'll be hearing from me soon!'

I was just beginning to give up when Gareth called and asked me out for a drink. A few hours later I was fumbling with Walker's crisps and a gin and tonic. The MTV Awards were on the telly, live from Leith. Christina Aguilera ponced around the stage in a tiny kilt. I was so nervous that I couldn't think of any zany anecdotes to charm him with, so I resorted to probing intellectual debate: 'Speaking of Michael Hutchence – would you rather people thought you'd committed suicide or wanked yourself to death?'

He made me laugh. He made me feel like I didn't have to be anyone else but me. Before I knew, it was last orders and he'd missed the last train back to Dunfermline. We walked back to my house in the drizzle, stopping outside a lighting shop. My heart clattered against my ribcage as we made inane conversation about lampshades. I was considering attempting another Move when I felt his hand curl warmly around mine.

Simple and effective. Why hadn't I thought of that?

And then finally we kissed, and everything fell into place.

WEEK 150
24 November 2003
14st 13lb – still, after five weeks! (95kg, 209lb)
10st 2lb lost (64.5kg, 142lb) – 3st 2lb to go (20kg, 44lb)

Has anyone ever lost a stack of weight and felt like it was a dirty secret? No one in Scotland needs to know about my former size unless I tell them. But if I don't tell them, they'll never understand why I'm so paranoid about my body. They won't know about the decades of misery that came before because they don't have the historical context!

Yesterday I was having lunch with some House of Sport

colleagues and we were talking about exercise. One chick said she wanted to try BodyPump classes, and I said I'd been doing it for two years and loved it.

As soon as the words were out my old friend paranoia was back in town. *Quick! Tell them about all that weight you've lost! Otherwise they'll think, 'She's been doing weights for two years and still looks like THAT?'*

Even though I'm happy in my size 18 body these days, I feel I should explain to everyone that I'm still trying to get smaller. Why can't I just be out and proud about the way I look right now, instead of explaining away my supposed freakiness?

And if I tell someone about my loss I always understate the number. I usually say five or six stone, when it's actually ten stone now! If people knew precisely how obese I used to be, would they look at me differently? Would they think I was some gluttonous weirdo?

I just know that non-fat people find such figures hard to fathom. A few months ago at Jane and Rory's tea party we were looking at some old photos and there was a very large guy in one picture. Rory said he weighed about 22 stone.

'How can anyone weigh 22 stone?' asked David. 'How is that physically possible?'

'Wow . . . that's nearly two of me,' said Gareth.

They weren't being mean or judgmental; they were genuinely awed that the human body could scale such lardy heights.

It can happen! I wanted to say. *I used to be 25 stone!* But I couldn't bring myself to speak up. What would they think of me then?

It's funny to have such a huge (forgive the pun) part of your life a total secret. I can't bring myself to tell Gareth about it. Our love feels so lovely and shiny and new, but inside I'm *brickin' it*, as they say over here. I may be a lot smaller, but I'm more neurotic than ever about my body. I look fine with my clothes on, but underneath it's a disaster. My stomach is flabby and my gelatinous arms depress me.

I'm terrified of this romance going further. He may just well be the most incredible guy I've ever met, and possibly be very understanding about my issues. But if it ever comes to us getting naked, there will be soft lighting. And I will explain why my body is such a wreck and reassure him that efforts are being made to rectify the situation. Then I will probably feel the need to outline my gym schedule, nutrition plan and highest squat weight, just so he knows I am aware of the problem!

WEEK 152
14 December 2003

I'm sending Gareth deranged mixed signals re: Getting My Gear Off™. We've been taking things slow and he seems to be letting me set the pace, as though he senses a neurotic, insecure freak lurking beneath the clothes.

Last night I crashed at his place after we'd been out to see some bands. My top was reeking of second-hand smoke but I'd forgotten to bring my pyjamas. We were lying there in the dark when he said, 'Man, that pub smell is really clinging to me tonight!'

'Oh! That would be my stinky shirt,' I said. 'I left my PJs in Edinburgh.'

'Let me get you one of my T-shirts!'

'NO! I mean, no thanks!'

'It's no trouble,' he said. 'You shouldn't have to sleep in your nice clothes.'

'I'll just take off the T-shirt.'

'Well that I don't mind,' he laughed. 'But it's freezing.'

'It's OK, honest.'

I could just make out his puzzled frown in the dark. 'I demand to know why you're refusing to wear my crappy clothes!'

I gave a weak laugh and told him not to worry, then whipped my top off and slunk under the covers.

Yes, I'm so ridiculous that I'd rather go topless and freeze than risk the humiliation of not fitting into his T-shirt.

WEEK 153
21 December 2003

Tonight it snowed. It wafted down slowly, not looking like much at first. After an hour I took a break from the Geriatric Rescue phones and stared out the window in amazement. The world wore a marzipan coat. It looked surreal, almost fake.

My Canadian colleague told me that I should try living in Calgary if I wanted a proper winter, but it was impressive enough for me. It was my First Snow! Even as she shoved a snowball down my shirt I couldn't stop grinning.

229

Until tonight it was as though I believed I'd still been living in Australia, just in some remote pocket where people talked funny and ate a lot of lard. After my shift I got the bus back into town, along the same road we'd come in from the airport nine months ago. Only now, gawking at snow-covered cars, did it truly sink in that I'm in Scotland.

It took me half an hour to get home from Haymarket, shuffling through the sludge. My shoes were drenched and my thighs were frozen. I smiled at people going by as they stabbed at greasy chips in polystyrene boxes.

By then it had stopped snowing and the sky was soggy and pale. I stopped on the canal bridge and watched the shivering swans, wondering what other Firsts are in store for me next year.

YEAR FOUR
2004

Week 156
5 January 2004

After two solid months I think it's safe to say I've acquired a boyfriend. Jane even has a nickname for us . . . SHAG. *SH*auna *A*nd *G*areth, geddit?

I can't believe I'm part of an acronym! I hadn't been looking for love. Surely that sort of thing wouldn't happen until I was a size 14, or a 16 at the earliest? I was perfectly content flying solo. But as I keep discovering, life has a habit of wandering off in crazy directions you never planned for.

So now there's this wonderful guy who seems to want to be around me just as much as I do him. Gareth makes me laugh, he makes me tea and the smell of his skin makes me purr. Sometimes when we're apart my Fat Girl fears creep in, wondering how he could possibly be interested in a blob like me. Surely he'll change his mind soon? But whenever he shows up on my doorstep or I cross the Forth Bridge, my doubts melt away. When we're together it all makes sense, it's as natural and easy as breathing.

I never had any great longing to be in a relationship but

233

now that it's happened it's like someone turned up the colour and the contrast on the telly. I was already enjoying the picture, but now things look even more vivid and alive.

Week 157
15 January 2004

Today marks the third anniversary of my lard-busting adventures. To celebrate I stripped off in my room and had a good look in the mirror. I admired my collarbone and glared at my belly flab. Will I ever get there? I'm stuck halfway between loving and loathing my body. I'm proud of how far I've come but I'm aching for the day when I can say I'm DONE. If you'd told me in 2001 that after three years I'd still be miles from my goal, I would have hurled the scales out the window and given up before I'd even tried. Shouldn't I have things figured out by now?

Someone who does seem to have it sussed is Gareth. I've always liked to observe the habits of skinny people, and he's been a fascinating case:

- He never has seconds. He dishes out his portion then puts the leftovers straight into a container.
- He's surgically attached to his water bottle and guzzles regularly throughout the day.
- Since he's surviving on the dregs of his Ph.D. grant he only buys what food he needs and makes simple meals packed with fresh vegetables. He uses up everything in

the fridge before it turns into mouldy pulp.
- Most astoundingly, he made apple crumble and ice-cream six weeks ago, and the same tub of ice-cream is still in the freezer! He hasn't touched it, because I've been checking the levels as part of my research. He hasn't scoffed the rest of it straight from the tub in front of the telly, like any normal person would do. Or maybe that's just me.

At first I thought, *what a freak! He's not eating enough!* But then I realized I'd been comparing him to me, who dreams of bacon and sees snacking as a leisure activity. He's not a saint – he loves crisps or a biscuit with his cuppa – but he has modest portions and eats slowly. He doesn't feel the need to demolish everything in sight.

I demanded to know how a Scottish guy could be so sensible about food. That's not natural! It turns out Gareth has lost a lot of weight himself – three stone, in fact! He went through a slothful period of beer and curry a few years ago, and when his belly spilled over his trousers he decided to take action.

I grilled him for answers. *What's your secret? How did you do it?* But it was infuriatingly simple. He cut out the crap and bought a bicycle. At first he could barely huff along a flat road, but after a year of steady effort he was powering up mountains and the beer gut was gone. He's kept it off for ages now and says he just tries to be healthy the majority of the time, so he doesn't have to worry about a few indulgences.

He makes it sound so easy; like he just jumped on a bike and pedalled away from his paunch! If he wasn't so modest about it I'd probably punch him. I know I'm just jealous of his ability to keep things simple. He saw his weight as a practical problem, not an emotional catastrophe. Maybe if I had his sensible, engineering brain I wouldn't be dragging my weight into a fourth year!

Oh well. It's nice to have found weight loss inspiration right under my nose. He knows I'm trying to lose weight and has been very supportive and understanding. But I still can't bring myself to tell him just how big I used to be.

WEEK 158
20 January 2004

I've never had a vegetarian boyfriend before and my digestive system is struggling to adjust. Gareth came over last night and I cooked up a delicious spicy dahl. As soon as we'd finished I felt the lentils preparing to wreak havoc. I'd yet to fart in front of him; and vice versa. It seemed far too early in the relationship for such familiarity.

'Quick, hand us your plate and I'll take it down to the kitchen,' I said.

'Oh no, let me do that!' He jumped off the bed. 'You did all the cooking, after all!'

'No! You're the guest. Stay where you are!'

After a brief tug-of-war I triumphed and scurried down the stairs. Thankfully the kitchen was empty, as I couldn't help releasing a most unsexy trumpeting sound.

I giggled as I returned to my room. And there was Gareth, his denim-clad butt poised over the window ledge with a guilty look on his face.

'You're back!' he said.

'Were you just farting out the window?'

'Maybe!'

'You're such a gentleman to direct them outside!'

'It's your cooking!' He blushed furiously as I slumped on the floor with laughter. 'It's delicious but lethal!'

'Don't worry, I just let one rip in the kitchen.'

Somehow that's taken us to a whole new level of intimacy. I almost did the same with my BodyPump classmates tonight. Heed my warning, people: don't squat too deeply if you've just had lentils for dinner.

WEEK 162
16 February 2004

Dear Neglected Diary,

You know that old saying, 'mind over matter'? I've really stopped minding my matter lately. The mind keeps trying to persuade me that my expanding matter doesn't matter. I can feel my jeans getting tighter but my mind shrugs it off: 'They must have shrunk in the wash!' But they haven't been washed for weeks.

I'm such a slob. A tired, tubby, chocolate-scoffing, scale-avoiding slob. Do you want to hear all my excuses?

First there's work. This is our mighty Year of Travel: so far we've planned a Scottish jaunt with the Mothership in April, a three-week tour of Russia and Scandinavia in June, plus a fortnight's backpacking around the Baltic States in September. I can't believe I'm going to Russia! I've been obsessed with the place since we studied the

237

revolutions in high school. Sometimes we'll be eating dinner or waiting for a bus and Rhiannon and I will look at each other and scream, 'RUSSIAAAA!' But in order to pay for it all we're doing extra weekend shifts at Geriatric Rescue. We've just finished an epic sixteen working days in a row, during which time our precious weekly routine fell apart and we resorted to takeaways or toast for dinner.

Secondly, there's the lovely Gareth. We're ships in the night at the moment, with my work schedule and his frantic dash to the thesis finish line. He's stressed and I'm tired so when we manage to meet we open a bottle of wine, bitch about our days then fall asleep in front of the ten o'clock news.

Finally there's complacency. Sometimes I forget that I need to shift a few more stone, especially with Gareth telling me I'm foxy all the time. Who cares that my knickers are still a size 18 when there's a lovely bloke trying to get into them?

But the fat won't let me forget it's still around. When I woke this morning I was suddenly hyper-aware of my flesh. It felt alive, like it had doubled in size overnight and was hogging the whole bed.

Gareth opened one eye and mumbled, 'Are you OK?' but I turned away from him, trying to crunch my body up into the smallest possible space.

Eventually he persuaded me to come down for breakfast. There were only two pieces of bread left and I insisted he eat them.

'Why?'

I pointed to my stomach and shrugged. 'Well, come on!'

He shook his head, bewildered. 'Why should you say something like that?'

I burst into tears. I didn't know why I'd said it. I hadn't even *thought* such negative things for months, let alone actually said them aloud. I guess I feel like things are getting out of control, and you know I'm not good with that. I've been living in a bizarre state of bliss, stress and fatigue and I've allowed bad habits to creep back – taking the lift instead of the stairs, neglecting mundane tasks like laundry, skipping my gym classes, stopping for junk food on the way home from work.

I've got to get back on track and find a way to cope with all the variables in my life. I don't like being an anxious grump, running round my room hiding chocolate wrappers every time Gareth comes over.

WEEK 163
23 February 2004
15st 1lb (96kg, 211lb)
10st lost (63.5kg, 140lb) – 3st 4lb to go (21kg, 46lb)

I finally made it back to the gym tonight. It was supposed to be yesterday but I wanted to have a Last Supper (two Topic bars and a bag of sweet chilli crisps) before I resumed the fight.

Miraculously, I've only gained two pounds since November. But that's probably because I've lost all my precious muscles. I had to lighten all my weights at Body-Pump and I was soaked with sweat after just the warm-up!

As I squatted and lunged I tried to remember how good it feels to take care of my body. I'd had muesli for breakfast and a salad sandwich for lunch and now I was back at the gym. *You've fallen off the wagon so many times before,* I told myself. *You know how to get back on track!*

But that would be much easier if I could stop thinking about muffins. Banana muffins, blueberry muffins. Or chocolate chip. Or chocolate chocolate chip. Surely muesli and aching muscles were more satisfying than muffins? But I could almost taste them. I could feel the stray chocolate chips clinging to the roof of my mouth. All I needed was a cool glass of milk to hose the crumbs off my teeth.

How did I get back to this place where I'm constantly thinking about food? What happened to the part of my brain that makes me stop and think before I eat? But I've made it through today, so I'll just try and do it again tomorrow.

WEEK 164
3 March 2004
14st 13lb (95kg, 209lb)
10st 2lb lost (64.5kg, 142lb) – 3st 2lb to go (20kg, 44lb)

I've lost those two pounds again; it feels rather accidental. But I'm setting myself small challenges so it feels like I'm heading somewhere positive. This week's task was simply Drink Two Litres of Water per Day. Not that I think I can flush out the flab, but it's good exercise running to the loo eleven times a day.

I think I'm getting a bit obsessed, though. I read that you can tell your body is properly hydrated if your urine is a 'pale straw colour with no discernible smell'. So I've been doing this mad dance of pee, wipe, jump up, spin round and peer into the bowl to examine my handiwork. I even considered finding a piece of actual straw to get a more accurate colour comparison. I have not, however, gone so far as to get down on my knees and sniff at the bowl.

WEEK 165
9 March 2004

'So how's the Body looking these days?' asked the Mothership.

'Oh, it's looking all right!'

'So do you feel good about yourself?'

'Indeed I do.'

'So do you feel . . . sexy?'

'What?'

'I said, do . . . you . . . feel . . . sexy?'

'I'm not going to talk about that with you!'

'Aww c'mon, why not?' she insisted. 'I was sexy once, you know!'

As much as I enjoy our rambling long-distance phone calls, I draw the line at discussing my sex life with the Mothership.

So do I feel sexy?

I've certainly always been a hot-blooded creature. Extra pounds have been no barrier to an active sex life, although much of it took place in my imagination. It just felt safer there, under the covers in the darkness with my trusty friend Mr Shakey. I could block out the belly rolls and dimpled thighs and let my thoughts run wild. Instead of criticism or rejection I only heard the steady buzz of two AA batteries.

241

But falling in love has made sex scary. The problem isn't desire – just his laugh or the arch of his eyebrow makes me hot – but the way I feel about my body. Although I can look in the mirror these days and appreciate my curves, I'd hardly say I was ready for public exhibition. This wasn't supposed to happen yet! I was going to lose all my pounds, shed my body issues and only then would I become a sultry sexpot and consider falling in love.

Most times I can just close my eyes and surrender to all that lust and longing, but other times it feels like there's huge neon arrows floating in the air, pointing out my flaws. HEY GARETH, CHECK OUT THE ARM FLAB! or DANGER! THESE THIGHS COULD KILL!

I've always hated moving my body. I remember nearly crying at a piano recital when I was ten years old; I was so paranoid that my arms were jiggling as my fingers roamed the keyboard. I've only just learned to walk past a bunch of strangers without worrying they're laughing at my wobbly bottom. So moving my body *while naked* is a whole new level of terror. So many positions, so many unflattering ways to arrange my flab! Every time he closes his eyes I pray it's because he's overcome by passion, not because he's avoiding the sight of my bouncing boobs.

I think my bedroom anxiety runs parallel to my general relationship anxiety. I've always liked to keep people at a distance, so being in love makes me feel vulnerable. Sometimes I look at Gareth and see our future unfolding, all the way until we're crotchety pensioners shouting at the television, but I can't decide if that thrills or scares me. I feel exposed when I'm naked, all pale and streaked with stretch marks, trying to trust the tenderness of his touch. I

242

worry that it's all too good to be true, that it's more happiness than I deserve.

But most of the time my heart and body are not afraid. This wasn't what I expected to happen but why not let go? Some day soon he'll be able to run his hand over my body without me hurriedly sucking in my stomach.

WEEK 166
15 March

Gareth has just left for a two-week Canadian holiday. He's trying to juggle his thesis with starting a full-time job so the poor lad has earned his break.

The first thing I did after waving him off at the airport was bawl for two solid hours. It's not that I'm a jealous loser who doesn't want her fella having fun without her; I just hate saying goodbye. It felt like reality biting me in the arse. I'm Australian, he's Scottish, and my visa expires in twelve months' time.

I've stopped short of drawing up an actual Excel spreadsheet, but I've tallied up all the time we'll be apart this year, with my travel plans and his holidays and business trips. So far it's six weeks for me and five for him, which adds up to *sweet bugger all* time left together!

I shouldn't even speculate about the future after just four months together. But it still gnaws at my gut, knowing sooner or later I'll have to face up to it.

I'm such a lovesick twit. And still paranoid. I'm convinced he's going to wake up one sunny Vancouver morning and realize he really could do better.

You know what's funny about losing a stack of weight? Nothing really changes. All that happens is that you lose the thing upon which you used to hang all your neuroses. Fat has shape and substance; you can poke it with a stick. It's a scapegoat and a handy excuse. Once you start to lose it, you realize you're stuck with the same moronic core.

WEEK 167
24 March 2004
14st 10.5lb (93.9kg, 206.5lb)
10st 4.5lb lost (65.6kg, 144.5lb) – 2st 13.5lb to go
(18.9kg, 41.5lb)

OVERBLOWN WEIGHT-LOSS ANALOGY OF THE WEEK: The fat-busting process is like having a delicate dish simmering on the stove. If you don't constantly watch the pot, it will boil over or stick to the bottom. You've been whisking so hard and so long that your wrist is sorer than that of a fifteen-year-old boy with a stack of *Playboy*. You're frowning at the recipe, *Shouldn't something be happening by now?* But you have to stay there at that stove, baby! Stay there until the dish is done!

Today, at least, the kitchen feels somewhat under control. I've lost weight again. I've stopped moping about Gareth and I'm savouring my solo time. I even had a day off work yesterday and did all these little Edinburgh things I've wanted to do for months. I wandered through Dean Village and over to the Modern Art Gallery. I lingered over scones and tea in the café, then I sat outside on the grass writing postcards until, in fine Scottish tradition, it started to rain.

244

I saw one of my Geriatric Rescue colleagues at the café, and it made me smile to think I've lived here long enough to 'bump into' people.

'You're looking well, Shauna!' she said. 'Have you lost more weight?'

I was secretly pleased that she could see a difference, but quickly mumbled, 'Maybe a little bit. But I'm not done yet!'

Just to flog that kitchen analogy some more – this lard-busting business makes me feel like an over-zealous cook, slaving over Christmas lunch. People keep coming into the kitchen to lift saucepan lids and peek in the fridge, demanding to know when it will be ready. The cook starts screaming, '*GET OUT OF MY KITCHEN!*' Nobody's allowed to look until it's perfectly done!

It happened last Saturday at the hairdresser's. My stylist looked me up and down as she helped me into the cape. 'Are you shrinking?' she asked. 'Your trousers are huge on you!'

'I don't know,' I blushed. 'Perhaps. Maybe. Either way, I'm still working on it!'

Don't look! Work in progress! Not finished yet!

WEEK 171
14 April 2004
14st 8.5lb (93kg, 204.5lb)
10st 6.5lb lost (66.5kg, 146.5lb) – 2st 11.5lb to go (18kg, 39.5lb)

There was a moment today when I had a glimpse of what

245

it's like to just have a body, as opposed to the Body; that capitalized Thing that I spend so much time and energy worrying about.

I spent Easter Monday with Gareth and his lovely family. Not only did our love survive his Canadian jaunt; we've progressed to Meet the Parents level! I wish it were physically possible to kick my own arse for all that unnecessary angst.

After our pub lunch we went to a park to roll hard-boiled eggs down a hill. I was watching his little cousins playing on the swings when Gareth slipped his arms round my waist. 'I see you're busting for a go on those,' he said.

'Me?' I snorted. 'I don't think that seat is designed to contain an arse like mine.'

'Of course it is. Let's go!'

To my surprise, I fitted with room to spare.

The two of us swung back and forth and made lame jokes about always wanting to be swingers. We yelled at his parents like five-year-olds, 'Look at me! Look at meeeeeee!'

It was thrilling to feel so light and carefree and . . . normal.

WEEK 172
30 April 2004

Until she was toddling towards us at the airport, I never quite believed the Mothership would make it to Edinburgh. But there she was with her huge grin and ridiculous sunglasses perched on her head.

'Hello darlings! I only just realized, I've had these on my head all the way from Canberra!'

Suddenly she dropped her handbag and did a dramatic double-take. 'Wow!' she crowed. 'Lookin' good, girl!'

'Don't exaggerate, Ma.'

'Seriously! You're so skinny!'

Rhiannon and I had expected tears aplenty after a year apart, but she launched right into her usual blathering.

'Would you look at this shirt? I'm a bloody disgrace!' She pointed to various crusty blobs. 'That's lunch at Sydney. And here's my ravioli on the way to Singapore. And here's a bit of breakfast before we got to Heathrow. Did you know I've had *two* breakfasts today? They gave me another one on the way to Edinburgh. I got two bits of bacon, scrambled eggs, half a tomato and a bread roll. A stale bread roll.'

The strongest bond between my mother and me will always be our ability to collect meals on our clothing.

The three of us sat on the top deck of the airport bus and headed into the city. She frowned at the grey houses and concrete gardens and asked casually, 'So . . . do you *enjoy* living here?'

She came bearing gifts of affordable Australian clothing. Twenty-dollar trousers, cheap T-shirts and multi-packs of socks and undies. Jackpot!

But all of the clothes were too big. I don't know whether to celebrate finally outgrowing the Aussie Fat Shops or be crushed that I won't be expanding my skeletal wardrobe.

Mum eyed me critically as I made my way through the pile. 'Look at you!' she crowed. 'You've got a *waist* now!'

'I'm getting there. Sort of.'

247

* * *

Scotland is small. If you tore it off from England and dumped it in outback Australia, it would take the Federal Police, Interpol and a herd of Alsatians ten years to track it down again. But this tiny country is beautiful, and we only had one week to force-feed the Mothership as much of it as possible.

It's ridiculous after just a year how protective you feel about a place. Mum would make an innocent comment like, 'It's raining!' or '*How* much for a cup of tea?' and we would splutter defensively, like she was a playground bully picking on our baby brother. Even though we'd whinged about the same things last year.

We just wanted her to love Scotland like we do. So the grand tour kicked off at South Queensferry beneath the Forth Bridges.

'The red one is the rail bridge,' I explained. 'Built in 1890. Look at it. Look at it!'

'I'm looking!'

'Take a picture!' said Rhiannon. 'It was the greatest feat of Victorian engineering!'

We trundled through the gentle greenness of Perthshire. Look at the cows! Look at the castle! Are you looking? And again as we wound our way through the Highlands. Look at that loch! Get a load of that glen!

Finally we arrived on the Isle of Skye.

'Those mountains are the Cuillins, Ma,' I announced, with such ridiculous pride you'd think I'd given birth to them myself. 'Don't you think they're beautiful? Eh? Eh?'

And so it went, all the way to Mull and Iona.

* * *

'Mothership,' I said as we drove along Mull's nerve-racking single-track roads, 'you're doing that staring thing again.'

'I'm allowed to look at you! I haven't seen you in over a year!'

I got the feeling she was slightly overwhelmed by our whirlwind tour. Not so much the packed itinerary but the poise with which we shuttled her around the countryside. We were assertive and organized, which was no surprise with Rhiannon; but I'd always been a passive creature. Now I was confident and opinionated, and when Mum kept applying the phantom brakes and muttering about my driving skills, I pulled the car over and said, 'If you don't shut up I'll make you sit in the back seat!'

All week long she kept looking at me with bewilderment, perhaps even envy. I know she is struggling with her own weight problem, and that struggle was something we've always had in common. It feels as if the balance has subtly shifted in our relationship. I just hope she's proud of me; I want her to see that I'm not so helpless and hopeless any more.

On her last night in Scotland she finally met Gareth. It was hard to tell who was the most nervous. After half a glass of wine I calmed down and enjoyed the treat of seeing my three favourite people in the same place at once.

I could tell Gareth was charmed by the Mothership's playground anecdotes, but it was hard to tell if the feeling was mutual. The strained smile and frequent nodding indicated she was struggling to comprehend his Scottish accent.

'So! What did you think?' I demanded, once Gareth had left to catch the train.

She smiled. 'He's wonderful! So down-to-earth. And he certainly thinks the world of you.'

'How could you tell? You didn't understand a word he said!'

'Love transcends language, Shauna,' she said sagely.

'I see.'

'You're quite serious about each other, aren't you?'

'I think so.'

'Have you talked about the Future?'

'The future?'

'Yes, the Future. With a capital letter!' she said. 'What will you do when your visa runs out next year? Should I start saving for another air fare in case of a certain special event?'

'A *wedding*?' I laughed. 'We've only been together for five months!'

'I'm serious! Mothers have a nose for these things. I heard it in your voice the first day you mentioned him, and now I've seen it for myself.'

'Well Nostradamus, I'll keep you posted.'

Mum was sobbing when we left her at the departure gates. She looked so forlorn with her red eyes and perennial sunglasses on her head. I felt guilty for not summoning up the tears but the sheer force of her personality means I never feel all the miles between us. Each time her chirpy voice blasts down the phone line, crapping on about her students or the latest motivational book, we grow closer than ever before. Besides, I'll be home again soon. I guess.

WEEK 174
10 May 2004
14st 5.5lb (91.6kg, 201.5lb)
10st 9.5lb lost (67.9kg, 149.5lb) – 2st 8.5lb to go
(16.6kg, 36.5lb)

Happy days! I just found out that I'm contributing to a book called *Tales from the Scale* that my fellow weight loss blogger Erin Shea is editing. I'll be paid for something other than making coffee! I wasn't going to tell anyone but since I'm going to be in a Real Live Book, I couldn't resist blurting the news to Gareth.

'Shauna in print!' he grinned. 'That's great news. So what's the book about?'

'Umm . . .' How could I explain without betraying my secret? 'It's just about chicks,' I said vaguely, 'and their weight loss experiences.'

'Cool! How did you get involved with that?'

'Well, I know Erin . . . from the internet. It was a message board or something. Where chicks gather to talk about their fat.'

Yeah, that'll do.

This morning Gareth was still snoozing in my bed when I left. That's one of the perks of working for a small consultancy: he sets his own hours and works from home, while I must trudge to the office. When he went to leave a few hours later, one of my flatmates had locked the mortice on the front door, which he didn't have a key for.

He phoned me at work. 'I'm trapped inside your house! I'm the only one here!'

'Oh crap!' I said. 'I'll come home right now.'

251

'No, don't worry. If you don't mind me borrowing your laptop I can crack on with some work. I'll be fine!'

He'd be fine, but what about me, sitting at work all nauseous while he roamed about my room unsupervised? And *the folder*! Oh Lord, the Folder. I'd printed out my entire Dietgirl diary ready to plunder for my book submission. The same Dietgirl diary I still haven't told him about. It was sitting right there on my desk in a shiny silver folder that would be impossible to ignore. Shit shit shit!

I pictured him reading away, curled up on my bed with a cup of tea and a digestive biscuit, discovering that his neurotic girlfriend actually has another fifteen levels of neurotic with her compulsion to tell the world about her belly rolls and binges.

At 3 p.m. I could stand it no longer. I feigned a headache and made my escape. I did my very best approximation of a sprint all the way home from the bus stop. I was gasping when I burst through the door to find Gareth engrossed in an engineering textbook. The Folder had not moved.

'Hiya.' He kissed me on the cheek. 'You're home early!'

'Oh yeah. Quiet day!'

I felt foolish but more so relieved. I know he knows I used to be bigger, but I still can't bring myself to tell him the whole story. Deep down I know it wouldn't matter to him, so why does it matter to me?

Later on I tested the waters and showed him a photo taken the day we left Australia. 'Check this out,' I said. 'You can tell I've lost a bit of weight this past year.'

'Whoa!' His eyes were wide. 'Wow, you can really see a difference.'

'I've got worse pictures than that,' I said quietly, feeling a surge of panic. 'But don't worry, I'll never look like that again!'

He shook his head and wrapped his arms around me. 'Why are you so hard on yourself?'

I would like to reach a point where I could be proud instead of ashamed. When I read through the Folder the other day I was amazed by how far I've come – not only my body, but my health and my attitude. Yet there's still a part of me that thinks I'm just a big useless lump that doesn't deserve affection and attention. What the hell is wrong with me?

WEEK 176
24 May 2004
14st 6.5lb (92kg, 202.5lb)
10st 8.5lb lost (67.5kg, 148.5lb) – 2st 9.5lb to go (17kg, 37.5lb)

I gained a pound over the past two weeks. No doubt I've made it worse by working two late shifts this weekend and consuming my weight in chocolate HobNobs. The biscuit tin is always full at Geriatric Rescue and I can't help nibbling anxiously between calls, wondering if the next one will be critically injured or dead.

Anxious is my default state these days. What's not to worry about? Will we earn enough money for Russia, will I ever get skinny, what will I do when my visa expires, will I understand the client's accent, will Gareth notice my hairy legs, will I remember to get out of bed, what day is it, which job am I meant to go to today?

'Do you realize,' Rhiannon said after a particularly harrowing call, 'that if we'd stayed in Australia with our old jobs, we could have saved enough money for all these trips in half the time?'

'Oh man,' I mumbled, spraying crumbs over my keyboard. 'Don't say that.'

'We could have just taken a few months off and done all the travel in one hit, without destroying our careers!'

'And without the ugly dark circles under our eyes!'

She sighed. 'Why did we put ourselves in this idiotic position?'

'Well, it's not just about the holidays,' I said. 'It's the life-affirming experience of living and working in another culture.'

'Ahh, of course!'

'If we'd stayed in Oz we'd never have known the joy of haggis.'

'And the joy of seeing a rainbow of pubes in the shower that don't belong to you!'

Our laughter was delirious, near-hysterical with fatigue. We've only had two days off in the past month. Working one mind-numbing job is a challenge, but *two* mind-numbing jobs have us teetering on the brink of madness. And our precious meal-planning routine has gone out the window, my gym attendance is patchy and I've barely seen Gareth in weeks. He's bonkers with stress over his job and thesis plus his band has been arsing around in the recording studio at the weekends. I treasure the tender scraps of time we have together, although often I'm too tired to do anything but coax him into going to the shops to fetch chocolate.

But I am determined to remain positive and Think of Russia. There's only two weeks before we leave on our epic tour, and each night we ceremoniously cross off another day on the Official Countdown Calendar. When I fall asleep doing chest presses at the gym or spend another Saturday night answering distress calls, I just remember that soon I'll be fulfilling a lifelong dream. We may have taken the most ridiculous, roundabout route to Russia but I know it's going to be worthwhile.

WEEK 179
15 June 2004

I'll never forget my first glimpse of Red Square. We approached in the Contiki tour bus; orange and obnoxious amongst the local black Mercedes and crumbly Ladas. We rounded the Kremlin then finally the multi-coloured domes of St Basil's Cathedral came into view.

While the rest of the group were still fumbling for their cameras, Rhiannon and I were off the bus and running. Have you got some little thing that you always wanted to do? Some place you always longed to see? The Pyramids, the Great Wall, the Cumberland Pencil Museum? Your obsession may sound batty to most, but it's your silly dream and it means everything to you.

I opened my mouth to say something profound to mark the momentous occasion, but could only manage a squeak. I was overwhelmed by all the things that had happened there: the military parades, the demonstrations, the Paul McCartney concerts. My breath caught in my chest and my legs felt weak. It wasn't because my heart was about to explode after that short jog. It was simply the pure elation of being in Red Fucking SQUARE!

I take it for granted these days that I can walk as far as I want for as long as I want. I take it for granted that I can find clothes that fit me, talk to strangers, lift heavy objects and catch trains in strange foreign cities. I normally avoid congratulating myself because I don't want to substitute a fat body for a fat ego, but today I had a little moment. I couldn't believe it was *me* on Red Square, the same scared person who said three years ago she was Too Fat to travel.

Hours later my body is still tingling with excitement. I keep thinking about all the things I'd had to change to get to this point, and now I just want to eat up the world and all its scrumptious possibilities. If I could get myself off the couch and over to Russia, what else can I do?

Bloody *anything*, really.

WEEK 181
28 June 2004

I survived twenty-one days on a Contiki tour! At first I thought three weeks of enforced socializing was going to kill me, as I've never been good with backpacker types. I hate all those tedious, competitive conversations about Where Have You Travelled and How Cheaply Did You Do It. And though I'm far more confident than I used to be, I'd still panic whenever someone sparked a conversation or bought me a drink or asked me to sit at their dinner table. At first I couldn't stop the Fat Chick's automatic assumption that they were only talking to me out of politeness.

But soon I noticed everyone else was just as nervous, and that cheap Russian vodka was a wonderful way to kill off shyness. Suddenly I felt bold and eager to meet people and hear their stories. One night in St Petersburg we got chatting to a bunch of locals about fast cars and koalas. As the vodka burned in my belly I thought how seven countries in twenty-one days seemed obscene because we could only skim the surface of all these people and places. I wished I could stay longer and plunge right in, because I've been skimming the surface for too long.

I missed Gareth, so deeply and pathetically it made my bones ache. I drunk-dialled him on my mobile on the ferry from Stockholm to Helsinki, determined to finally tell him I loved him. But I rambled for so long about the Musik Museet in Stockholm, where Rhiannon and I played the eighties-style electronic drum kit and pretended we were in Mike and the Mechanics, that I ran out of calling credit. This meant we were incommunicado for the next two and a half weeks. I stood beneath a plastic palm tree and howled, 'No! Noooo!'

Two hours later Rhiannon found me wandering the decks and took me to the bar. I had yet another wine and morphed into one of those dreary people who babble on and on about their boyfriends when drunk.

'I love him,' I slurred to Tamie and Liz, two lovely Australian girls. 'He's funny and sexy and bald and I knew right away we'd end up together.'

'Aww Shauna, that's so sweet!'

257

'I know! I'm sorry!'

I'm too much of a control freak to ever get so drunk that I don't know what I'm doing, but I can push it to the point where I can't shut up. The alcohol makes my limbs feel liquid and dreamy and I feel a desperate need to vocalize all the emotions I'm normally too scared to acknowledge.

'I want to be with him,' I mumbled, draping my arm over Tamie's shoulder. 'Always.'

'Really?'

'And I know he wants to be with me. I can just feel it, Tam. *Feel it*. He wants us to stay together, too.'

'You mean after your visa runs out?'

'Yes.'

'Ooh! Shauna's in love!'

'Yes!' I hiccuped. 'Shauna's in love!'

There was still a tiny, deranged sector of my brain convinced that three weeks was plenty of time for Gareth to realize he didn't want to be with an insecure, lard-armed Aussie. But when I got home today and heard that warm Scottish accent on the phone, life was instantly sweeter than all the chocolate I'd scoffed in Finland.

'Can I come over later?' he asked.

'Well, only if you want to,' I said coyly. 'If you're not busy. I mean, I can see you on the weekend if that suits you better?'

'I haven't seen you for three weeks!'

'Oh yeah!'

You'd think after eight months of blissful togetherness I could accept that someone could want to be around me on a voluntary basis, but I am still bewildered by it all.

When he arrived on my doorstep tonight I blurted, 'I love you!' before I could lose my nerve. I handed him a can of Russian Irn-Bru and deposited a furry Russian hat on his lovely head.

He smiled, and to my immense relief said, 'I love you too.'

WEEK 181.5
1 July 2005

I'm still coming down off my Russia high. Everyday life is so bloody dull. There's no breakfast waiting for you when you wake up, no itinerary, no exciting new city to explore and no 30p vodka shots.

I was back at the House of Sport today, typing letters and removing staples and daydreaming about our travels. I have to admit, despite all the spectacular churches and museums and historical sights I saw on our tour, my holiday highlights revolve around food. From the pickled herring in Stockholm to the peirogi in Poland to the obscenely fat sausages in Berlin, I was determined to sample it all. Even McDonald's seemed exotic when it was on Red Square!

The sweets were my downfall. I was inspired by Jane's impressive collection of international candy wrappers and decided to start my own. It was a great excuse to scour the supermarkets in every city. Who knew the Finns were so good with chocolate? I fell for the mint chip Fazer bar, the delectable hazelnut goodness of Geisha bars and the squishy malty whatever-it-is of the Tupla. And what

259

warm-blooded creature could resist a chocolate bar actually named 'I Love Chocolate'? Because we all do!

There should have been some respite for my waistline in Russia and Belarus, where the chocolate tasted of dirt, gravel and perhaps the remains of former dictators. Luckily I'd smuggled a dozen Finnish treats over the border. Our included meals were universally awful, and I'm sure that's not a reflection on Russian food so much as on our budget accommodation. One breakfast in St Petersburg consisted of a cold frankfurter sausage and a spoonful of green peas, so I preferred to live off Geisha bars, vodka, and a bag of almonds I'd bought from Tesco.

Needless to say, I'm too scared to go back to the gym and get on the scale. Tonight I examined my candy bar wrapper collection instead. It's alarmingly impressive. Why didn't I buy smaller bars? What was I stockpiling for? In case the tour bus broke down or the Russian food queue came back in vogue? The Iron Curtain came down years ago, but try telling that to my stomach.

WEEK 185
26 July 2004
14st 10lb (93.6kg, 206lb)
10st 5lb lost (65.9kg, 145lb) – 2st 13lb to go (18.6kg, 41lb)

Just half an hour ago at the supermarket I spotted a pint of Ben & Jerry's Chocolate Chip Cookie Dough ice-cream.

'Yeah baby!' I crowed, picking up the tub and heading for the checkout. 'You were meant to be in my belly!'

Now I'm sitting here peering down into a half-empty tub. What possessed me? I've absolutely demolished it. You know you've eaten too much ice-cream when the edges have melted away and you're just left with this ice-cream *ball* that spins around and around as you chase it with a spoon.

I feel quite ill.

I've gained four pounds and have shown no sign of getting back on track since Russia. It was only Wednesday night that Gareth and I were reflecting on eight months of bliss, and how we seemed to have turned into inactive slugs since hooking up. He's still knee deep in thesis and has turned to Hula Hoops instead of mountain biking. And I'm back to my hectic work schedule, in readiness for our Baltic jaunt, and still scrambling to get into a routine. My weight goes down, my weight goes up; my jeans squeeze and release my thighs like a concertina.

We decided to make more of an effort, starting with cooking a healthy dinner. Without guzzling two bottles of wine. That's how I ended up at Somerfield with my virtuous basket of stir-fry veggies, noodles and fruit. But I couldn't help detouring down the frozen aisle thinking, *Rhiannon's at work, I'm home alone. I could scoff some ice-cream and no one will ever know! And Gareth will think I'm a legend for whipping up this nutritious meal!*

Oh how crafty was I for concocting such a cunning plan! Not bloody clever at all, since now I feel like a whale and will no doubt be trying to suppress my gurgling stomach all night.

I wish I could get over this 'Quick! Eat! While No One's Looking!' mentality. The world is not going to run out of ice-cream. It's always going to be there, so I'm not going to be deprived of some wild pleasure if I leave it alone for a while. Do you ever feel you're so eager to be skinny and tap into the sexy clothes and supple flesh, but part of you is afraid of missing out on something if you don't stay fat?

WEEK 189
24 August 2004
14st 10lb (93.6kg, 206lb)
10st 5lb lost (65.9kg, 145lb) – 2st 13lb to go (18.6kg, 41lb)

After another four-week hiatus I weighed in last night – 14 stone 10 pounds.

What? STILL? What the hell is going on? I actually stomped on the scale in fury.

But then I remembered out of those four weeks, I've only really been eating properly for one of them. Somehow I thought seven days of perfection would make up for months and months of half-hearted effort. Shouldn't I be instantly rewarded for finally saying no to chocolate? I thought the scale needle would land triumphantly on my goal weight and my trousers would fall down, right there in the middle of the gym.

Maybe next week, then.

Gareth has gone gallivanting again. This tag team relay across Europe is getting tiresome. To celebrate the Submitting of the Thesis he's gone to France with his friend Steve to scoot around on motorbikes for a fortnight. He'll only be back for one day before Rhiannon and I head off for two weeks in the Baltic States.

Just two hours before catching the ferry, Gareth was showcasing his inability to multi-task. The stress of finishing his thesis *and* preparing for his trip was all too much. He was frantically trying to attach the luggage box to his bike, but turns out he'd ordered the wrong kind. He had to pack all his belongings in a plastic shopping bag and tether it to the bike with rope. Oh dear.

Unlike last time, I had no tears when he departed, because I was too busy cackling at the sight of that Asda Bag for Life. But I do wonder what will become of the intercontinental star-cross'd lovers? There's only seven months until my visa expires. I'm still bemused and baffled that I even have a boyfriend, let alone thinking about the authoritarian cloud of the Home Office looming over us.

WEEK 190
30 August 2004

One of my colleagues has lost a hefty slab of weight this year. Grant used to have a sprawling beer belly and quite the collection of chins, but now they've melted away.

I'd observed how he'd stopped buying hot chips and greasy curries from the staff canteen. Instead he'd just have soup and oatcakes, chased by a few pieces of fruit. Even more shockingly, he stopped partaking in the Cakes.

We have a lot of cakes at the House of Sport. It's like the public service morning teas back home, but here you only need the flimsiest excuse – a birthday, the anniversary of your start date in the company, a particularly sunny day – and someone will head to the shops then email the invitation, 'Cakes at 3 p.m.!'

'Cake' is the umbrella term for anything sweet and gooey – we've had donuts, cookies, muffins, éclairs, Bakewell tarts and brownies. Sometimes I'm strong but sometimes I'll get stuck in, if I'm tired or rebellious or just want to feel like one of the boys. Especially when there's Marks and Spencer's Caramel Shortcake, which gives Nanny's recipe a run for the money. But they always go down far too quickly and leave me full of remorse.

Now that Grant's all svelte he allows himself a cake now and then. Why do blokes make it seem so simple? During today's session he undid his belt and paraded around, showing the lads how baggy his trousers had become. I felt a stab of jealousy as I chomped on my shortcake. I wanted *my* trousers to be falling off! Well, maybe not in front of my colleagues.

I miss the golden days of being a weight loss superhero. I don't get the double-takes and shocked gasps now my loss is practically non-existent. Not that my UK friends would ever notice a startling difference since they never saw me at my heftiest.

At least my Aussie pals are good for my pathetic ego. I got an email from Jenny today – I'd sent her some photos from Russia and she claimed she wouldn't recognize me in the street now. That sounded a bit optimistic, but I gobbled up the compliment anyway.

I'm such an attention whore lately! I suppose after all those years of hiding behind jokes and baggy clothes, I'm tired of being invisible. I wouldn't mind getting the occasional once-over. I like to imagine Gareth and I having a night out on the town when a handsome stranger saunters by.

'That bloke is checking you out!' Gareth would say.

'Damn right, buddy!' I'd reply.

There's a multiple-choice ending:

a) Gareth punches the guy in the face and says, 'Step off pal, SHE'S MINE!' But since Gareth is a pacifist who catches spiders in jars instead of mashing them with shoes (maybe that's just an Australian thing?) the more likely conclusion is:

b) I suggest Gareth takes me home immediately for hot lovin' before the handsome devil steals me away.

I have dozens of similar fantasies, but my point is, I want to feel foxier. And I want to be a fat-fighting superhero again! I must remember that next time the Cakes come out.

WEEK 191
6 September 2004
14st 8.5lb (93kg, 204.5lb)
10st 6.5lb lost (66.5kg, 146.5lb) – 2st 11.5lb to go (18kg, 39.5lb)

Gareth called me on Sunday night from a payphone near a vineyard somewhere in Beaujolais.

'I just ate *coq au vin* for dinner,' he confessed. 'I'm the world's most rubbish vegetarian!'

I melted at the sound of his voice. 'So are you having fun?'

'Shit, yeah! We rode around the Monaco Grand Prix track the other day. I thought I was going so fast but I got overtaken by a chick on a moped!'

'Hee-hee. Is the wine good?'

'Oh aye. You should see this place, Shauna, it's beautiful. I'll have to bring you back some time.'

'How about next summer?' I said boldly. I might as well get the ball rolling *vis-à-vis* the Future.

'Next summer?' I swear I could hear his smile. 'So do you want to stay in Scotland?'

'Of course I do!' My heart was hammering. 'Do you want me to stay?'

'Of course I do.' He paused. 'But I thought maybe you'd be missing the food back in Australia too much or something.'

'Very funny.'

'Anyway,' he chuckled, 'I was calling to see if you want to go out for dinner on Friday. How about Italian?'

A date! Due to budget constraints we don't do that kind of thing too often. I spent the week in a frenzy of room cleaning, brow plucking and nail painting. I even de-forested my legs.

Gareth looked so tanned and handsome when he arrived tonight that I went all quiet and bashful. But then he confessed he'd forgotten to make a reservation. The Edinburgh Festivals were in full swing so when we finally phoned they were booked out!

I'm ashamed to admit that I sulked. I wanted romance! I wanted cheese and garlic! I wanted him to be more bloody organized! I hadn't seen him for two weeks and then I was away tomorrow for two more and my visa expires in less than seven months, so we should be having romance while it's still legal.

'So what do you want to do instead?' he asked.

'I dunno,' I said airily. 'What do *you* want to do?'

'I dunno.'

'Well neither do I!'

This went on for half an hour.

He produced two cookies from his backpack. 'I bought you these from France; they're a bit squished up from being in the Bag for Life.' He put them behind his back. 'Pick a hand. Brown wrapper is for the dodgy pizza joint, white wrapper for the Indian up the road.'

He looked so ridiculous I couldn't help laughing. I picked his left hand. Indian.

We walked up the hill to Himalaya. Well, he walked and I stomped.

'You don't want Indian, do you?' he said.

'I don't care!'

He smiled.

OK, I was being a brat. I was just so relieved he'd made it back on that motorcycle in one piece, and that meant more to me than a posh dinner.

We had a terrible seat in the restaurant, right next to the coffee machine. Our conversation was punctuated by the constant *ssccchhh* of frothing milk. But my sag aloo was great, the room was cosy and I loved how happy Gareth looked as he told me about his trip. It felt strange to feel so happy for someone else, to realize how much his happiness meant to me.

I know none of this has anything to do with losing weight. It's just about realizing what's really important. Losing weight is quite important to me, but naan bread and a lovely Scotsman rate pretty highly too.

WEEK 193
20 September 2004

We're back from the Baltics! Rhiannon and I spent two weeks wandering through beautiful Latvia, Lithuania and Estonia. We soaked up unforgettable sights like the Hill of Crosses and Tallinn's crumbling Old Town, but I must say it was equally magnificent to discover that all three Baltic countries stocked Finnish chocolate. Mmm, Geisha bars.

Since our return we've been embroiled in various schemes to stay in Britain. That's the problem with travelling; the more you do it the more you want to do it again! I only used to feel this way about chocolate cake, and similarly my eyes have become bigger than my stomach.

But as of next Sunday there's only six months left on our visas before I can no longer live and work in the UK. And we haven't even been to Italy! Or Portugal or Turkey or Morocco or Luxembourg.

Rhiannon and I spent four hours poring over the Home Office website. There's no option to extend our Working Holiday visa, our jobs are too menial to qualify for the Highly Skilled Migrant visa and we have no British grandparents to get a British Ancestry visa.

'Bloody hell!' screamed Rhiannon. 'Why must our ancestors be convict scum?'

I even tried worming my way into a work permit by applying for permanent jobs at both my workplaces, but both attempts were disastrous. It seems work permits are reserved for the likes of brain surgeons and engineers. To get a work permit the employer has to prove that there were no suitable British candidates. Unfortunately there are British secretaries and phone answerers in abundance. I was naïve to believe I was so spectacular that either employer would wade into an expensive pool of red tape just to keep little old me.

Rhiannon is contemplating applying for jobs in London in her old field of Extremely Posh Hotels, as they are more receptive to work permits. But since my career had barely started when I left Oz, I've got to be more realistic. My options boil down to:

1. Go back to Australia
2. Quickie wedding.

Both of these options make me weep.

Number One obviously sucks because I don't want to go home! I'm not done by a long shot. I've still got to eat olives in Spain and *frites* in Belgium. And above all I don't want to leave Gareth.

Which brings us to number two. We've only just said the L word, how can we be ready for the M word? I know they're alphabet neighbours but matrimony is a crazy leap when we haven't even clocked up a year together. I think back to our bumbling courtship, and it's quite hilarious to think two lazy, daydreaming bums like us would progress to the next level so soon. Gareth is an easygoing type who likes to let things unfold at their own pace, and I just don't like anything involving change!

I know we both want to stay together but I also know we both like things the way they are right now. My visa situation means we could be forced to speed things up because of circumstances beyond our control. The idea of a rushed proposal and a quickie wedding seems so tacky. I just want to talk about music and holidays and what to have for dinner, not about how we'll divide household chores or whether to put plastic people on top of a wedding cake.

But I guess the most important thing is to have faith that we'll find the best way to handle this. There's still six months to decide. And I need to look after myself and get back to the gym after my Baltic break. I can't think clearly when my jeans are so tight.

WEEK 193.5
26 September 2004

I have to tell you the sad and sorry tale of the Nutella. You may recall the brown stuff was one of my favourite binge foods, but I've been clean for eight long years.

Unfortunately there was a moment of weakness in Germany. You must understand we'd been eating those vile Russian sausages for a week! Our mouths were full of ulcers and our gums hurt. So when we arrived at the Berlin

Youth Hostel and found that not only were their bread rolls *not* stale, but they provided those darling foil packs of Nutella to spread upon them, I was powerless to resist.

A few weeks later at Chez Gareth I spied a familiar jar in the back of his pantry.

'Is that Nutella?'

'Yep. Do you want some?'

'Oh no. I have a problem with Nutella.'

'How can anyone have a problem with Nutella?'

'Trust me,' I muttered darkly. 'It can happen.'

A whole month passed and I was at Chez Gareth again, chatting on the couch with a cup of tea.

'Sooo,' he began, 'I went to make a Nutella piece today.'

Piece, I've discovered, is a Scots word for sandwich.

'Yeah?' I searched for an innocent tone.

'Yeah. I took the Nutella jar from the shelf and it looked like a normal jar of Nutella; about three-quarters full. But then I opened the lid!'

'Oh?'

'Much to my surprise the jar was nearly empty! Except for a *very thin layer* of Nutella right around the edges and bottom. Like someone had very carefully excavated the contents, spoon by spoon. They took great pains to make it appear full from the outside, when in fact the lot had been scranned!'

'How ridiculous!'

'I know!' he laughed. 'Can you believe that?'

'Maybe you have mice. Some very precise mice!'

'That's one theory!'

'Yeah! Well!' I bristled, 'you shouldn't eat that stuff anyway. It contains partially hydrogenated oil, don't

271

you know; and that's very bad for you. Very very bad.'

I assuaged my guilt by buying him a fresh jar. But another month has gone by and he hasn't even opened it!

We were watching a movie last night when I finally exploded.

'How come you haven't opened that Nutella yet?'

'What? Oh, I totally forgot it was there.'

'How could you forget Nutella?'

'Well I dunno. I just did.'

'But haven't you been *thinking* about it? Hasn't it been *taunting* you?'

'Has it been taunting *you*?'

'I'm just amazed that it's still there. Don't you just crave it?'

'Well, I tend to crave things like chips or cheese. I'm more a savoury guy; you're the sweet tooth in this relationship.'

'Oh I have a sweet tooth *and* a savoury tooth,' I said. 'I've got *many* teeth.'

I don't know what came over me, tiptoeing into the kitchen while he was in the bath or on the phone and helping myself to a spoonful, week after week, over and over again until it was gone.

I can feel the Old and New Shaunas at war again. The Old Shauna feels the sting of shame and disgust, and annoyance for getting caught. Back in my sneaky prime I'd have replaced the jar before he had a chance to notice!

But the New Shauna looked into that neatly emptied jar and joined in the laughter. Gareth was completely sweet about it, by no means accusing or angry like my parents used to be. Yet I still wonder why I didn't just eat it in front of him? What am I afraid of?

WEEK 194
27 September 2004

I had a crisis coffee with Jane and Rory tonight. I'm desperate to talk to Gareth about my doubts re: the Future, but he's busy preparing for his viva, the torturous ritual in which a panel of academics will grill him about his Ph.D. thesis for hours. So I thought I'd bend my poor friends' ears instead.

'All I know is that I don't want this to end,' I said. 'We're SHAG. We're an acronym! You can't break up an acronym!'

'Why would you have to break up?' asked Jane.

'Because! I'm going to get deported!'

'There's no need for that. Why don't you just get married?' asked Rory.

'Married?' I snorted into my tea. 'That's a bit much.'

'Why?'

'Because! That's what *grown-ups* do. You've witnessed our immaturity.'

'But you love each other.'

'We haven't been together long enough to get married.'

'You've been together longer than Britney Spears and her bloke were before they did.'

'But we're too young!'

Rory smiled patiently. 'Gareth is 31 and how old are you again?'

'Yeah, all right.'

'You know what? If you love each other and want to be together, you should just go for it.'

Why does everyone else think the situation is so clear-cut? It's all too surreal. It was only a year ago I was wondering if Gareth would ever ask me out on a date, and now everyone's sending us down the aisle?

WEEK 195
4 October 2004

'Hello?'

'It's only me,' said the Mothership. 'Just wanted to say hi.'

That didn't sound right. She always takes great pleasure in announcing, 'It's the Mothership!' Her voice was flat and dull, and she kept asking questions instead of telling me school stories or a scene-by-scene recap of the last episode of *Taggart*.

'What's the weather been like?'

'Crazy!' I replied. 'Freezing one day, unseasonably warm the next.'

'Oh well, I'm sure you can handle all temperatures now that you're skinny.'

'Sorry?'

'And how's Gareth? Done his exam yet?'

'Another few weeks. He's so busy that we haven't really talked about the Future yet. I'm crapping my pants.'

'You've got no reason to be nervous when you have that fabulous body!'

274

'Mum!' I spluttered. 'What the hell does that have to do with anything? Why are you so obsessed with weight today?'

'I'm not obsessed!'

'But you keep bringing it up!'

'Because, because!' Her voice wavered. 'I just . . . admire you for what you've done.'

'What I've done?'

'Losing your weight.'

'Oh.'

'I don't know how you do it.'

'Well I'm not really doing it very well lately, I've barely lost a thing all year!'

'You're doing it!' she insisted. 'You're skinny!'

I didn't know what to say.

'How did you do it?' I could hear the despair in her voice. 'How did you stop making food the answer to your problems? Where did you find the courage? I've got to do something but I just don't know where to start.'

'Oh Mum.'

'I'm just watching my life pass me by and I don't know how to stop it.'

Why can't you just dive through the phone line and hug somebody? She was saying the exact same words I'd said nearly four years ago. I've been lounging in this 'not quite fat, not quite skinny' stage for so long now that I've almost forgotten what it's like to be seriously overweight, how difficult it is to take that first step. Or maybe I just don't want to remember.

I felt helpless as she started to cry. I always thought Mum was so strong and in control. I'd watch her in action at Weight Watchers, bubbly and warm with the ladies clinging to her every word as if she was the Weight Loss Messiah. But then I saw her marriage erode that confidence, and now ten years after it ended she still sounds so lost.

'Anyway,' she sniffed, forcing a laugh. 'Have you got any words of wisdom for me?'

'Seriously?'

'Yes.'

'Umm. Don't do anything radical,' I began. 'Don't try and change everything at once, even though everything might feel like shit right now.'

'That's exactly how it feels.'

'Just pick one thing. Think of one healthy thing and do it tomorrow.'

'Go for a walk?'

'Yeah! Just try twenty minutes. I used to go early in the morning so no one could look at me.'

'That's a good idea.'

'Seriously, Ma. Don't beat yourself up. Don't worry about what you're eating and don't even think about what you weigh. Just try doing one positive thing this week. That will give you courage to add something else next week. I know it sounds simplistic but it's much less daunting, and starting small really can lead to something big.'

'OK.'

'OK.' My heart was pounding. It felt ridiculous to be giving diet advice to my mother. Did I sound too glib? Did I sound like those patronizing weight loss magazines? But when I think about my lard-busting methods, it really does boil down to baby steps. Why do I always lose sight of that?

Suddenly she was sobbing again. 'I'm so sorry I put you in this position.'

'What position?'

'All the things I said to you when you were a kid. All the diets I put you on.'

'Ma, you don't have to apologize. We had this out a few years ago, remember?'

She just cried harder.

'We weren't living in a happy environment. It wasn't easy for anyone. There was a lot of crazy shit going on.'

'I'm so proud of you both for turning out so well, considering everything I put you through. I should have left the farm years before I did.'

'I kept on eating for five years after I left home. I had to take responsibility for my own actions.'

'But you and your sister had to move to the other side of the world to get away from all those memories.'

'Oh,' I sighed. 'It wasn't like that.'

'You don't have to lie!'

'Well . . .'

'Do you remember what you were like when you were really young?' she said suddenly.

'Umm . . . aside from ginger?'

'You were the most outgoing little four-year-old. Confident and bright, always chatting to people. Don't you remember?'

'No.'

'When your father and I split up you changed overnight. It was like someone turned the light out behind your eyes.

I think you blamed yourself, somehow. You just withdrew into yourself, you were so fragile and insecure.'

'I don't remember that.'

'You were never the same after that. We were so worried about you that I took a whole term off school just to be with you all the time.'

'Oh.' My throat felt tight. 'That kind of explains a lot.'

'That's why I was always sending you to drama classes and swimming lessons, trying to help you find your confidence again. But now I know that I was too overbearing and pushy.'

'Don't worry, Ma, I was too busy thinking I was fat and ugly to notice.'

'Shauna! I'm trying to apologize!'

'I know.' I couldn't help it, I was crying too. 'I'm glad you told me all this, but I'm OK now. I've moved on and I'm doing fine.'

Mum honked into a tissue.

'I'm happy how things have turned out,' I said. 'So please don't worry any more. I think you need to start worrying about yourself.'

There was a long pause. 'I'll go for a walk tomorrow morning.'

'Good.'

I still don't know what to make of that conversation yet. But I am aching to go back in time to that four-year-old me and say, 'Chin up, ginger. Twenty-three years from now you'll think you're great!'

On Tuesday night Gareth's band played a wee gig at the Liquid Rooms. It was the first time I'd ever seen him in musical action. He's always been so bashful about playing the bass in front of me, so I'd started to suspect he just goes to the studio to chat with his pals and eat pizza.

But he was all business as he walked on stage with his slouchy shuffle, wearing his trademark faded jeans, T-shirt and beanie. He picked up his bass then squinted through the spotlights in a searching fashion. Finally we made eye contact. He flashed a grin and held up the Fist of Rock.

And in that tiny moment I felt like I'd been punched in the stomach. With that smile of recognition and that cheeky rock fist, everything fell into place. Finally I just knew, *knew knew knew*: that I had to have this guy in my life no matter what.

Whatever it takes for us to be together, I'll do it. And I'll be happy to do it.

He looked so at home on the stage, a faraway look on his face as he plonked away with skill and swagger. That's what I loved about him right from the start: his serenity, how he looks so comfortable in his own skin. He always looks as if he's thinking about something deep, although it's usually motorbikes or equations. But I love how there's no big dramas with Gareth. No jealousy, no arrogance, no smothering self-doubt. He just is who he is, in a completely unassuming way.

And that's how he's always made me feel. Calm, at ease.

I remember the night we met at the pub, with me

279

resplendent in my size 20 jeans and faded T-shirt. I was already happy and content and finally learning to like myself just the way I was. I didn't think I was looking for love but now I see it was the perfect moment. I was ready. It's not that he changed me; he enhanced what was already happening. Meeting him was like taking the final step towards being the confident, joyful person I always hoped was hiding inside the fat suit. For years my life was ruled by doubt, but our relationship is something I've always known was right. Even if it's taken me a while to believe that it really could be that simple.

All my fears about our future suddenly seemed trivial. They were just annoying technicalities that we could work through somehow. I saw the future with perfect clarity, what I wanted and where I wanted to be. And in the midst of wailing guitars and thundering drums I'd never felt so peaceful.

Let's hope the feeling's mutual.

WEEK 197.5
23 October 2004

I got brave today and brought up the Future with Gareth. The timing was rubbish – he's snowed under at work and his viva is just a week away. But we were having a pub lunch in Cockburn Street and he looked rather relaxed after his pint.

'The Mothership called again yesterday,' I began.
'Oh?'
'You wouldn't believe it. She said she's found a piper in

280

Goulburn and she's got him on stand-by in case of any sudden . . . important events.'

'A piper!' He went slightly pale.

'Aye! I couldn't tell if she was serious or not.'

(She was perfectly bloody serious. She also asked if Gareth's family had an official tartan.)

'Well,' Gareth said, 'my mother keeps saying stuff like that too. She wants to know if she needs to start shopping for a new hat.'

'Oh dear.'

We smiled awkwardly.

'It's crazy, isn't it?' I said nervously. 'This situation?'

'Yeah,' Gareth admitted. 'But don't get the wrong idea, it's not that I wouldn't want to. It just feels as if our hand might be forced.'

'Yes! That's what I've been thinking.'

'I've always liked letting things happen naturally, in their own good time, you know?'

'Rather than the Home Office making us . . . accelerate?'

'Yeah.'

'I totally agree.'

Later on, back at my place, I introduced him to the Home Office website and explained the intricacies of the UK immigration system.

'So as you can see I don't qualify for work permits, Ancestry or the Highly Skilled Migrant programme.'

He nodded.

'But I *could* qualify for a Prospective Marriage visa, which is a fancy name for a Fiancée visa, but that wouldn't make any sense.'

'Why's that?'

'Well it's just not value for money. It's five hundred quid and only valid for six months, plus you're not allowed to work. I'd just have to sit on my arse until we got hitched, then we'd have to pay even more dosh to get the Marriage visa. So I'd be broke and unemployed just for the sake of six months.'

'Right,' said Gareth. His eyes were glazed over from a combination of confusion, fatigue and Guinness.

'Anyway,' I said quickly, already feeling nauseous having said the M word so many times. 'No need to worry about that now. Just keeping you informed!'

'Well I appreciate it,' he said and kissed my cheek. 'Don't worry. Everything will work out fine.'

WEEK 198
25 October 2004

I'm getting back to basics. There's no point sitting around getting tubby and worrying about the Future. Onward and downward!

With no further excursions planned at present, Rhiannon and I have scaled back our work at Geriatric Rescue. We're trying to rebuild our trusty routine of cooking, shopping and gymming.

I've really missed our weekly treks to Tesco. We have turned grocery shopping into sport. We synchronize our watches, catch buses from our respective workplaces so we arrive at the same time. We pause at the magazine rack then glide up and down the aisles with a shopping list that's ordered in harmony with the supermarket layout.

Then we waste half an hour browsing the chocolate so we always have to sprint across the car park to make the bus on time.

Once the pantry was full and the meals were planned I decided to start tracking my food again. I'd lost touch with just how much I'd been putting away. I signed up with an online food diary service, like a high-tech version of the dreaded Points tracker. It's got a huge database of UK foods so I just type in what I eat and it spits out the nutritional information. It tells me where my calories are from (fat, protein, carbohydrates) and logs my weight, measurements and exercise.

Once I did the sums I could see where I've been going wrong. One tiny ounce of mild Cheddar cheese is 115 calories, yet so many times over the past few months I've sliced a fat wedge off the block then wondered why my jeans were strangling me. So this week my goals were to fill in the diary, avoid the vending machine at work and get back to wholesome foods in sensible portions.

I have to say it's mildly arousing having so much data at my fingertips. There's *graphs*, too! I haven't indulged my inner statistician for so long – maybe that's what's been missing from my lard-busting efforts? Of course I'll have to make sure I don't get too obsessed.

I've now racked up seven healthy days in a row. I didn't skip a workout or fall into a pile of buttered toast. I haven't had a week this good since . . . I can't remember when. I was scared that I didn't know how to do this any more. I thought I'd never want it bad enough to get back into the groove. But I do want to see Operation Lard Bust right through to the end, so here's to another healthy week.

Gareth passed his viva! We can now officially call him Doctor G!

I took him out for dinner to celebrate. He sat on my bed while I ran around trying to find something to wear. All my knickers were in the dryer so I had to dig out an ancient pair in a size 22. When I pulled them on, the waistband came underneath my boobs.

'Now that's sexy!' he said.

'Why thank you, Doctor! I bet I could pull them over my nipples.'

And I could.

When we finally stopped laughing I said solemnly, 'These used to fit, you know.'

'Well I figured as much,' he said. 'Unless you've got a large lady lover who's gone commando today!'

I almost told him that when I first bought those knickers they'd seemed incredibly tiny to me. What would he make of my old size 26s? I bet if he put those on he could pull the waistband over his head.

The other day I asked him how much he weighed, and the scrawny bastard is only eleven and a half stone. I'm more than three stone heavier! How have I managed not to crush him to death?

He wouldn't believe that I was heavier than him, even after he tried to pick me up and spin me around. I'm sure that move is romantic if you're a waif in a Flake commercial, but I just shrieked, 'Put me down unless you have a good chiropractor!'

I can't help being hysterically secretive about my journal and my starting weight, even though he's never made any judgement about my size, or batted an eyelid at any mentions of my lardy past. I feel guilty for holding back on something so important to me, especially now we're vaguely contemplating making a serious commitment. But I guess it takes time to feel ready to share certain pieces of yourself.

WEEK 203
29 November 2004
14st 7lb (92.3kg, 203lb)
10st 8lb lost (67.2kg, 148lb) – 2st 10lb to go (17.3kg, 38lb)

I have a confession to make. I've been buying bridal magazines!

It started not long after Gareth's gig, when I realized that staying together would probably mean an enormous leap of faith, and that leap meant marriage.

I've grown rather fond of the idea.

It's a bit like binge eating. *I'll just buy one*, I told myself. But soon I was hooked on the flavour, and now when Gareth comes over I have to hide the big pile of magazines in the back of the cupboard, just like I used to do with chocolate wrappers.

I haven't raised the topic since that day in the pub, because I refuse to nag my way to a proposal. I'd like to think I have more dignity than that! So aside from strewing my desk with printouts from the Home Office website with the pertinent passages highlighted, I'm playing it cool. In the meantime I'm daydreaming of low-budget weddings and frocks that disguise meaty arms.

It's not the idea of a wedding that I'm getting excited about, but the thought of us becoming Doctor and Missus Gareth Reid. It's crazy how something that terrified me a few months ago now seems quite delicious. I am filling whole notebook pages with my potential new signature. *Shauna Lee Reid*. Don't you just love it? It sounds like a tragic country and western singer.

WEEK 204
9 December 2004
14st 6lb (91.8kg, 202lb)
10st 9lb lost (67.7kg, 149lb) – 2st 9lb to go (16.8kg, 37lb)

Rhiannon is leaving me!

The treacherous wench found a proper job with a work permit so she's moving to London. Damn her and her impressive résumé and employability!

We told everyone it feels like a divorce. I've seen the rolling eyes; I know they think we're being melodramatic. But you have to understand I'll no longer be near someone who finishes my sentences and instinctively knows when to buy pizza on the way home. She's my best friend.

Just like retired old farts in a caravan, we had routines and we treasured them dearly. I chopped the veggies for dinner while she wielded the wok. I booked our gym classes, she ordered in restaurants. I picked up the Thai takeaway while she got the cutlery and queued up the DVD player. Whenever I farted, she'd say 'Shall I reply?' and let one rip too.

Grocery shopping was one of our favourite rituals, and Monday night was the last one. We dawdled in the car park, talking about jeans and how the ones with the 'pre-faded' stripes down the front make your thighs look fat, when suddenly our bus barrelled round the corner.

'Shauna!' Rhiannon screamed: 'Stop the bus!'

I panicked, spinning the shopping trolley round in small, helpless circles. I am useless when asked to make a sudden movement. 'Stop the bus? *You* stop the bus!'

Rhiannon bravely leapt out on to the street with outstretched arms, 'SSSTOOPPP!'

Do you know how hard it is to find someone who'll stop a bus for you?

But I am happy for her. While she's enjoyed Edinburgh she's been craving more excitement, and I know there's plenty of adventures awaiting her in the big city.

Even so, I can't help but be jealous. Not only is her future secure, she's popping home to Australia for Christmas! She figured she'd be busy and broke once she moves to London so she wanted to visit everyone while she had the chance. She'll be back in Edinburgh for a few days in January so we can wage a bitter custody battle over the frying pan and hairdryer, then that will be it.

Today I did a dress rehearsal Solo Shop and it was very traumatic. The checkout chick was merciless, flinging bananas and soup tins and expecting me to keep up. For the past four years, on two different continents, Rhiannon packed the heavy goods while I took fruit and veg. Then she'd do the bread and loo paper and magazines while I handed over the cash. We had a *system*. How can you have a system with just one person?

My life has changed dramatically these past four years and I owe so much of it to my little sister. When Rhiannon moved in I was barely treading water. Without her I doubt I'd have found the spark to tackle my weight or move to the other side of the planet. Our friendship has become even stronger here in Scotland, now that I feel capable in my own right instead of leaning on her so much. Without her coaxing I wonder if I'd ever have mustered the courage to change.

'How am I supposed to go on?' I wailed when she broke the news.

She replied with a withering smile, 'I have nothing left to teach you.'

Sometimes you can just feel change in the air. It's as heavy and inevitable as the yeasty fug that spews from the Fountain Brewery. Change is a bit like a brewery, don't you think? It makes a lot of scary noise and it stinks like hell, but the end product is delicious and good for you.

WEEK 205
13 December 2004

One happy result from Rhiannon's impending departure is that she's been cleaning out her wardrobe and giving me her cast-offs. I fitted into her old size 14 suit!

I nearly cried as I zipped up the trousers. OK, they were snug and by no means ready to be worn in public, but I never thought my flesh would ever be arranged into a garment of such small dimensions.

Then again, Australian sizes can be generous. Last week I kicked the mirror at H&M because I could only fit into a size 20! Rhiannon tried to reassure me that H&M's clothes seem to be cut with gazelle-like Europeans in mind, but I raged anyway, convinced that the United Kingdom was united purely by a sadistic need to make me feel like a whale.

It's not just the trousers making me emotional. My sister and I are breaking up, dammit. Everything is changing. *Her* future is sorted but mine is still dangling. And I don't want to mention it again to Gareth because not only does he have a massive work deadline, but his thesis corrections are due before Christmas. Naturally I am trying to be supportive and fetch cups of tea, but what I really want to do is scream, 'WE ARE RUNNING OUT OF TIME! WHAT THE HELL ARE WE GOING TO DO? I NEED ANSWERS!'

For once in my life, the only thing going well is the food and the exercise.

Week 206
21 December 2004

I must apologize for the lack of weight loss heroism in this year's diary. It seems Dietgirl has lost her superpowers, as I'm basically the same weight I was at the start of the year. I blame chocolate, which has always been my kryptonite.

Considering the amount of gourmet travelling I did, I

suppose I should be grateful I'm not right back where I started. But I'm still cranky because it's the first time in four years that I haven't shed a few sizes.

But one thing I've shed is the old 'I'm Too Fat' excuse: 2004 has been the busiest, most exciting year of my life and for the most part I put the flabby thoughts on the back burner. I backpacked in strange countries, I talked to strangers and I took my clothes off in front of a bloke, many, many, times.

Of course I still bitch about my blubber sometimes but I'm so much happier in my own skin. If 2001 was the year of Obsessing about Fat, then 2004 was the year of Obsessing about Me. I've scoffed new experiences with the enthusiasm I used to reserve for scoffing ice-cream straight from the tub. It was like the carefree college days that I was too miserable to have at the time.

Next year is going to be a cracker. Are you voting for the hasty wedding or the tearful deportation? Speculation is rife amongst my colleagues. The diehard romantics are gunning for a wedding and have offered everything from dresses, garters and cake decorations to their back gardens for a venue. The cynics say he'll never propose and come March I'll be on the plane back to Australia.

I feel almost calm about the whole thing. If I've learned one thing from my weight loss adventures it's that life tends to get more interesting when you stop trying to control the outcome. Somehow I just know that everything will work out. Besides, there's still ten days left in this leap year – I can always pop the question myself!

'It's here, it's here!' Gareth leapt out of bed at the sound of the doorbell. 'Your present is here!'

I sat bolt upright. 'Oh my God!'

My stomach grumbled. I couldn't decide if it was nervous anticipation or unbridled gluttony. I'd been staying at Gareth's place for the lazy days between Christmas and New Year and I'd done nothing but eat and panic.

He'd told me there'd be a slight delay in the delivery of my gift, which I assumed had to be the Ring! Everyone predicted he would propose over Christmas. He'd been so incredibly sweet and tender over the past few days, even more so than usual; so he must be up to something! I've never heard of an engagement ring coming by courier, but the boy does like his online shopping.

I fluffed up the pillows and fluffed up my hair and tried to look as alluring as possible as he came back into the bedroom.

'Here you go!' He presented me with a large heavy box.

'What's this?'

'It's for you!'

'Oh I see,' I smiled. He's trying to be funny. He's buried the ring in that giant box just to throw me off the scent. I tore it open, scattering polystyrene bubbles over the bed. I reached in and pulled out a large plastic blob.

'Speakers!' I gasped.

'Yeah!' grinned Gareth. 'They're for your laptop. You've been bitching for ages that you missed your stereo back in Australia!'

291

'Oh! You're right,' I said. 'I *have* been bitching about that!'

'There's a sub-woofer too! You just plug it into your laptop and you're ready to rock! You're going to be blown away at the sound these little things pump out. I know how much you love your music.'

'Yes!' I beamed, 'I *do* love my music! Thank you, baby!'

He looked so happy and proud of himself that I wanted to cry. I cooed over my lovely speakers while discreetly pawing through the box, just in case I'd missed anything.

'What are you looking for?'

'Oh! Nothing. Thanks so much Doc, I love 'em. You're a legend.'

He went and fetched my computer and hooked up the speakers. We snuggled up close as the room filled with Radiohead.

I felt like a royal goose. How could I have been so presumptuous? Maybe he's not ready to ask me yet. Or maybe, somehow, he doesn't quite realize the urgency of our deadline.

Or maybe he just doesn't want to marry me at all?

YEAR FIVE
2005

Rhiannon came back to Edinburgh today bearing a slight tan and an enormous stash of Australian confectionery. I perched on the bed, my mouth shiny with Pavlovian drool, until she finally tossed me a mini Cherry Ripe bar. 'Oh yes,' I moaned, gnashing on the coconut cherry goodness. 'Tastes like sunshine.'

She smiled. 'Now I've got you somewhat sedated, how about an update on the greatest romance of the century?'

'Urgh. If you insist.'

I managed to keep quiet for three whole days after the Speaker Incident before I exploded from anxiety and/or sugar insanity caused by excess consumption of Cadbury's Roses. When we woke up on New Year's Day Gareth casually said, 'So. What do you fancy doing today?'

I stared at him, breathing heavily.

'Are you all right?' he asked.

'Are *you* all right?' I blurted.

'What?'

295

'Do you not realize we are *running out of time*?'

'Running out of time?'

'My visa, Gareth, my *visa*!' I shrieked. 'It expires in less than three months! I'll have to go back to Australia if we don't decide something soon.'

He looked mystified. 'Why would you have to go?'

'Are you kidding me?'

'Your visa runs out at the end of March, doesn't it? I thought we could get one of those Fiancée visa things?'

'The Fiancée visa?' I punched a pillow. 'Don't you remember when we looked at the Home Office website? I explained that it wasn't a good option because it's expensive and I'd not be allowed to work. I'd have to quit my job just for the sake of six months' grace, and then of course we'd have to fork out even more money for the Marriage visa!'

'Oh.'

'Besides, even if we wanted the Fiancée visa it takes months to come through. And *months* are something we don't have a lot of.'

'Oh,' said Gareth. I watched his face move from confusion to shock, the colour draining from his cheeks. 'Oh.'

Rhiannon was trying not to smile.

'Can you believe it?' I squeaked. 'That's all he could say. *Oh.*'

'Oh,' said Rhiannon.

'He was completely stunned. He just hadn't realized the urgency of the situation. I thought I'd said enough by showing him the website and explaining the options but clearly I was too subtle!'

Rhiannon started laughing.

'What's so bloody funny?'

'Because! It's classic Doctor G. It's just the sort of innocent yet catastrophic mistake he'd make.'

'I know!'

'You know what he's like, Shauna. Sometimes he's a little vague on details. He's the guy who carted a plastic bag around France for two weeks. His brain must have been ready to explode with a thesis, a job and a visa crisis all at the same time.'

'Yeah. That's what makes it so bloody frustrating!' I sighed. 'And three days later he hasn't mentioned it again. He's barely been in touch.'

'He's probably still in shock. Remember how long it took him to ask you out in the first place. He's not a fast mover.'

'I guess. Did you know at work today, five different people came up to me, picked up my left hand then sighed when they saw it was empty? And my boss gave me a bottle of champagne! He said, *I thought you'd be needing this by now!*'

'Don't worry,' Rhiannon said and handed me another Cherry Ripe. 'He just needs more time. He loves you and he'll come through. I know he will.'

I ripped into the chocolate and munched away mournfully. If I truly believed her, surely I'd be starting my wedding dress diet instead of stuffing my face?

'What the hell happened to you?'

Gareth stood on my doorstep after work with a wild scraggly beard and bloodshot eyes.

'Umm, just having a little trouble sleeping,' he mumbled. 'There was a really good documentary on at four o'clock this morning. The history of combine harvesters.'

'Well come in and I'll make you a coffee.'

By the time the brews were ready he was fast asleep. Nothing could rouse him – not coffee nor shortbread nor the batter and clang of *Ready Steady Cook*. Finally at eleven o'clock I gave up and drifted off myself.

I woke up suddenly at 2.02 a.m. with the moonlight sneaking through the blinds. Gareth was propped up on his elbow, looking at me thoughtfully in the half-dark.

I reached out and patted his furry face. 'Hey there, Doc. Still can't sleep?'

He smiled, brushed my hair out of my eyes and said quietly, 'Will you marry me, Shauna?'

'Are you SERIOUS!?'

Now that really annoyed me because, if/when the moment ever happened, I'd planned to respond with something witty and memorable like, 'Depends . . . will you wear a kilt?' But instead I said, 'Are you SERIOUS!?' in a painfully broad Aussie accent, like I was Steve Irwin and I'd just spotted a rare sabre-toothed kookaburra or something.

Gareth said that he was serious.

'Am I awake?'

He said that I was indeed awake.

'Well then . . . YES! Of course!'

Proposing to someone in bed at 2.02 a.m. was a little different, but it was perfect. I'll never forget the tenderness of his voice and his smile when I said yes. I was so stunned and shocked that it was actually happening that I kept saying, 'I'm so stunned and shocked!'

'You shouldn't be,' he said. 'This is what you get for being so good to someone. For being loving and encouraging and making them feel they can just be who they really are.'

'Whoa,' I blushed and grinned. 'I love you.'

'I love you too.'

'Hee-hee! I'm so excited I could *spew*!'

'I'm sorry I've been so rubbish,' he said. 'I needed to think about things. I've never doubted us, you know. I just had to get my head around the whole marriage thing.'

'It's OK. It took me a while to get used to the idea too.'

'But you're cool with it now?'

'Yeah. You had one more week before I planned to go totally batshit crazy on you.'

'Speaking of batshit crazy, what time is it in Australia? Should we start spreading the news?'

The next two hours were a blur of phone calls, emails and text messaging until my thumbs went numb. We laughed and cried and everyone was happy for us. Finally we went back to bed and Gareth curled up behind me with his arm draped over my waist like he always does. I slept peacefully, knowing he'll be doing that for good.

10 January 2005
15st 1lb (95.9kg, 211lb)
10st lost (63.6kg, 140lb) – 3st 4lb to go (20.9kg, 46lb)

I got back on the scales today: 15 stone 1 pound. I've gained NINE POUNDS in five weeks!

It all fell apart the week before Christmas with that box of Celebrations. Some kind soul put them out on the Cake Table at work and I vowed to ignore them. But they kept calling to me with their shiny, miniature voices. *We won't hurt you! We're so tiny and cute! What harm could there be in a Milky Way the size of your fingernail?*

But with that first sickly sweet bite the beast was unleashed. I abandoned all forethought and didn't stop eating for the entire festive season.

Here's a sample of my feeble excuses:

- Rhiannon is leaving! We'll never go out to *[insert name of yet another favourite restaurant]* together again, so what the hell!
- Poor me working at Geriatric Rescue on Christmas Day, surely I deserve another handful of sweeties for my noble deeds? They're *free*, after all.
- I'll make Gareth this huge Heart Attack in a Bowl Butterscotch and Banana Trifle for our Belated Christmas dinner even though it's designed to serve eight and contains two pints of double cream!
- It's Christmas and it's cold outside so I'll have another glass of port (and so on until I'd emptied the entire bottle over a four-day period)!

- Gareth is in the next room so I'll sneak yet another handful of Cadbury's Roses from the giant tin his mum gave him even though I hate Cadbury's Roses, but he hasn't proposed and I'm stressed!
- My future is so horribly uncertain that I may as well have cheese on toast for dinner and a bar of chocolate for dessert!
- I just got engaged so I'll bring in cakes for my colleagues and eat three pieces of Caramel Shortcake because I'm so overjoyed!

The diet books always tell you to pinpoint your triggers, to figure out the reasons for your poor choices. But I covered all the classics: loneliness, boredom, frustration, anger, extreme anxiety and happiness. There's been secret eating, drunken eating, bathtub eating. I'm very versatile!

By New Year's Eve I could barely zip up my jeans, my skin was grey and spotty, my head was throbbing and I couldn't bear for Gareth to snuggle behind me as we slept because his arm felt like a log draped over my tortured, bloated stomach. Yet I kept shovelling in the food, mindlessly and endlessly, perhaps convinced the indigestion would distract me from all the doubts and fears.

It was a classic battle of the Old and New Shaunas. The Old Shauna didn't quite believe that Gareth would propose, because who'd want to commit to her lardy arse for all eternity? So why not bury her face in a trifle? But the New Shauna knew deep down that love would conquer all. Old Shauna may have triumphed over Christmas, but now the New Shauna wants to slap the Old around the chops and scream, 'We've got six weeks to look hot in a wedding frock. Look at the mess you've put us in!'

WEEK 210
17 January 2005
14st 8.5lb (93kg, 204.5lb)
10st 6.5lb lost (66.5kg, 146.5lb) – 2st 11.5lb to go
(18kg, 39.5lb)

Saturday marked the fourth anniversary of my epic lard-busting adventure. Four years is an Olympiad, or a whole term in the Oval Office. But please don't vote me out just yet. I am determined to deliver!

Nothing quite brings your weight loss efforts into focus more than the thought of walking down the aisle. And my anniversary was a timely reminder that I *can* do this. It just takes planning and focus, rather than sitting on the couch with a bottle of port wondering why I feel so bad. So I've put the festive feast behind me and I've channelled the Dietgirl of 2001 – determined, methodical and single-minded.

But without the obsession. The Old Shauna would be frantically calculating how many pounds she could shed before the Big Day, but I'm so happy that there's even going to *be* a Big Day that I'm not going to do anything radical. I'm just determined to look and feel as healthy as possible so I'll be glowing with endorphins.

So it's back to sensible eating and my trusty online food diary. I also drew up a gym schedule full of my favourite classes and have been moving my butt every day. In a month's time I'll be moving into Chez Gareth in the remote wilds of Dunfermline, so I may as well enjoy the Fancy Gym while I still can.

After just one week I feel focused and sane and I've already lost six pounds! I thought I'd be lonely doing the shopping, cooking and gymming without Rhiannon but I'm enjoying all this time alone with my thoughts, processing everything that's happened. It feels wonderful but it still doesn't feel quite real.

WEEK 211
24 January 2005
14st 7.5lb (92.5kg, 203.5lb)
10st 7.5lb lost (67kg, 147.5lb) – 2st 10.5lb to go (17.5kg, 38.5lb)

Today I spent three hours looking through all my bridal magazines. It was like a glossy, thousand-page reminder that I have no money, time or style.

Wedding Day magazine had a story on how to plan a wedding on four different budgets: £1,000, £10,000, £100,000 or ONE MILLION POUNDS! For £1 million they suggested buying your own Mediterranean island and icing your wedding cake with solid gold. I was more interested in the £1,000 job. They told me to save money by purchasing a vintage dress. Who actually finds vintage clothing unless they're a titless size 2? Vintage for me would involve going to a charity shop and asking, 'Have you had any donations in white polyester? Puffed sleeves? Pit-stains not too prominent?'

303

You and Your Wedding sounded like a friendly enough title, making the event sound comfy and manageable. They probably also do *You and Your Cocker Spaniel* and *You and Your Tracksuit*. I pondered the article, 'Are You a Summer Bride or Winter Bride?' Pollen-choked daisies or whisky shots by a roaring fire? I don't bloody know. Where is the option for Overweight Threat of Deportation Bride? Surely that's a niche market, I can't be the only Scot-loving Antipodean who likes to leave things to the last minute.

There's no scope in these magazines for people in a hurry. Apparently twelve months ago we should have met with our priest or rabbi and finalized the guest list. We should have picked the rings at Christmas and the Going Away Outfit should have been hanging in my wardrobe since October. What the hell is a Going Away Outfit?

Most damning of all, I was supposed to have started a fitness and weight loss regime over a year ago. Whoops. And my skin, hair and nail regime should have been established at the same time. My current regime consists of me idly thinking at midnight, *I should get up and wash this mascara off. And moisturize. And perhaps take off my stinky gym clothes.* Furthermore, the bags under my eyes are so dark and fat that it looks like I've glued on a pair of slugs. My sleep has been rubbish since Engagement Day because I keep waking up laughing in the middle of the night, still giddy with the news that Gareth wants to marry me. Sucker! And as for my talons, I've never had a manicure in my life, unless you count pushing my cuticles back with the front door key.

I suppose we should really be focusing on the basics, like picking a date and a venue. And a continent.

Week 212
31 January 2005
14st 6lb (91.8kg, 202lb)
10st 9lb lost (67.7kg, 149lb) – 2st 9lb to go (16.8kg, 37lb)

I've had three weight losses in a row! How long has it been? It's incredible what a dangling carrot in the shape of a wedding dress can do. Although I still have no idea what shape that dress will be, as I'm still in Wedding Planning Denial.

Instead I'm throwing my energy into my lard busting. In the first few days after my festive feast I thought I'd lost my mojo for good, so I borrowed half a dozen diet books from the library. They were all sensible tomes about nutrition and exercise, not sensational crap like *The Glass of Air Diet* or *Fart Yourself Thin*, but it still smacked of desperation. I thought I no longer knew what was best for me so surely someone else would. I pored over these books and waited for the moment of enlightenment. I took all the quizzes, scoured the menu plans, then it finally hit me – *I already know all this crap.*

There was nothing they were telling me – no diet tip or exercise or food combination or Jedi mind trick – that I hadn't already learned for myself over the past four years. I need to remember that the weight loss industry exists to make money, whether it's a diet book or Weight Watchers

305

or *Slimming* magazine or Crazy Bob's Blubber Bustin' Pills. They could all help me lose weight, but none of them is a substitute for thinking for myself.

And that has been a liberating revelation. Standing at the bus stop this morning I wondered why I wasn't in Bridezilla mode, worrying how I will fit into a wedding dress I haven't bought for a wedding I haven't planned. But I knew I had things under control. I was looking forward to eating my yoghurt and muesli breakfast at my desk. I'd go to my BodyPump class after work then eat my veggie chilli for dinner. After the madness of the past few months, now is not the time to panic. I can finally admit that I'm the one who knows what works best for me. I don't need my hand held any more.

WEEK 212.5
3 February 2005

Have you ever tried to organize a wedding in six weeks? It's a nightmare, especially with half the guests stuck on the wrong side of the globe and the Home Office breathing down your neck. After days of scouting venues and contemplating a registry office quickie, Gareth and I were nearing meltdown. Wasn't this meant to be exciting? Wasn't this meant to be a celebration of our wacky little relationship? No matter what ideas we came up with, it was going to be rushed and shoddy with one side of the family going bankrupt from air fares.

'This is madness!' said Gareth. He was taking on that bearded, bloodshot caveman look again.

'I know,' I wailed from behind my copy of *Scottish Wedding Directory*. 'There's just not enough time to do this properly. I haven't even found a dress yet!'

'It just doesn't feel like it's about you and me.'

'And I'll die of guilt if Nanny has to sell her china cat collection to pay for a flight.'

'Hey,' Gareth said suddenly, 'we should just go away somewhere.'

I put down my magazine. 'What? You mean like . . . elope?'

'Yes! Why don't we nick off to Vegas?'

'Vegas?'

'Yes, Vegas!'

'Are you serious?'

'I am deadly serious.'

'Well,' I smiled, 'I suppose if we have to do something as ridiculous as get married in a hurry, we may as well do it in the most ridiculous place on earth.'

'Exactly!'

After a brief poke about on the internet and a flurry of emails and credit card transactions, we had formulated our cunning plan. KLM had a New Year sale on flights to San Francisco, a city we've both always wanted to see. So we'll fly there for a couple of days while we shake off the jet lag. Then we'll nip down to Las Vegas to do the formal bit in a dinky chapel, just the two of us. After a brief excursion to the Grand Canyon, we'll return to San Francisco and stay in a charming boutique hotel for our honeymoon, giving us plenty of time to laze around and get used to the idea of being hitched.

And how to keep our families happy? We'll have a wee

party in the summer for the Scottish contingent and then, since I'm overdue a visit home, we'll head Down Under in October for a shindig with my Australian kin. This way we'll get to celebrate with *all* of our family and friends and each mother will get her own Event to fuss over.

Thankfully everyone agreed that Las Vegas, while insane on paper, is actually a very sensible solution.

'It's a bit . . . unusual,' said Gareth's mother Mary.

'It's a bit . . . different,' said the Mothership.

'But you're OK with it?'

'Darling daughter, if you two are happy then I'm happy.'

We are happy. It finally feels like our wedding belongs to us. I can hardly wait for our big day(s).

WEEK 213
7 February 2005
14st 3.5lb (90.7kg, 199.5lb)
10st 11.5lb lost (68.8kg, 151.5lb) – 2st 6.5lb to go
(15.7kg, 34.5lb)

I'm off to London this weekend to continue my dreary wedding frock hunt. I can't put it off any longer, I think Mary is worried that I'll marry her son in my jeans!

So far it's been a fruitless search. I'm not even looking for a proper wedding dress, just something vaguely stylish that you might wear to a fancy party. I'm too scared to try anything on because it's all dainty spaghetti straps or no straps at all. Designers just don't cater to the pale, wobbly-armed, dumpy-legged market. At this stage I'm resigned to being a vision of frumpiness, perhaps in some sort of formal caftan. I'll just burn the wedding photos if I have to.

In happier news, I zapped another two and a half pounds this week, bringing me to over 150 pounds lost! That just sounds so impressive all of a sudden.

Everything is purring along in the weight loss department, no doubt fuelled by vanity. Of all our weddings it's Part III: Return to the Motherland I'm really looking forward to. After two and half years all my Aussie family and friends will be gathered in one spot, giving me eight months to achieve maximum foxiness. Never mind showing off the new husband, I want to show off *me*! Short of landing on a red carpet in a helicopter, the most spectacular entrance I can think of is just to look confident and sexy as hell, instead of the joke-cracking wallflower they remember.

Meanwhile my social life is hectic. This week alone I've had farewell drinks at Geriatric Rescue (Yes! I'm down to one job!), dinner with my almost-in-laws, lunch with Jane and Rory and a 'Stag Do' with the blokes from the House of Sport. It's been food and booze galore! But instead of panicking, I planned. I kept my meals simple and bumped up the exercise so I didn't have to sit with a lettuce leaf and a glass of water while everyone else had fun.

I am trying to find that delicate balance, my friends. You'd think with three weeks to go I'd be chugging Slim Fast and nibbling on seaweed, but I want to be properly fuelled for this matrimonial circus. I am *busting* to get to the altar, and the size of my frock seems a secondary concern. I can't wait to be Gareth's wife. I know we'll have a blast together. I'm still prone to spontaneous tears of joy and relief that he wants to do this; that he thinks we're worth all this trouble.

WEEK 213.5
12 February 2005

The very first dress in the very first shop. Surely this was a Guinness Book of Bridal Records moment? But it was all in a day's work for Rhiannon, the High Priestess of the High Street.

My sister thinks of everything. She'd done a reconnaissance mission on Oxford Street and found what she thought was the ideal frock. Then she tracked it down to a small boutique in Kensington so I wouldn't get overwhelmed by the Saturday crowds and give up far too easily.

We arose at the crack of dawn and arrived just as the shop opened. No hovering salesladies, dressing room queues or abandoned husbands cluttering up the aisles. Rhiannon simply strolled in, plucked a dress from a rack and declared, 'Here it is!'

I looked at the little puddle of cloth. 'A skirt?'

'No!' She laughed and held up the hanger. 'It's a dress, see?'

I tried to picture my Boeing 747 arms and chunky ankles stuffed into that scrap and felt the stirrings of a full-scale Fat Girl Freak Out.

'No, no, no!' I said, 'it's too slinky, it's sleeveless and there's no way my elephant legs will wedge into that!'

Rhiannon rolled her eyes and said in crisp Mothership tones, 'How about we try it on and *then* decide what it looks like?'

Retail Fat Girl Freak Outs are always the worst. They start with a pounding heart and a burning throat. Then tears sting your eyes as your Fat Sense detects pending humiliation and bludgeoning of self-esteem.

'Can't we just go?' I begged as Rhiannon led me to the changing rooms. 'What's wrong with getting married in jeans anyway? Anything goes in Vegas. It worked for Britney Spears!'

'Come on!'

'No!' I dug my heels into the carpet like a toddler. '*You* try it on. Just so we can test the sizes.' The biggest size was a 16, and it didn't look like any 16 I'd ever seen.

'All right then!'

Of course it was too big for Rhiannon. It swished around her hips like a 1920s flapper dress.

'Now it's your turn,' she said firmly. 'There's no harm in trying!'

I instructed her to patrol outside the cubicle and shoot intruders on sight.

I stripped off my jeans and stepped into the dress. It slid up over my hips . . . then my gut . . . then my boobs!

'Shit, I think this might work,' I whispered.

'I knew it!' Rhiannon threw back the curtain triumphantly. 'Oh please, take off your *socks*, Shauna!'

'Hang on, false alarm. There's a zipper.'

'Don't panic, we'll get it closed.'

311

It took ten minutes with much heavy breathing and grunting. It was a figure-hugging dress for starters, but on my voluptuous form it was bordering on figure-strangling.

'It's too small!'

'Nonsense,' said Rhiannon. 'You're just used to wearing slobwear from three sizes ago. Dresses are meant to show off your shape.'

The frock was a flattering gold colour, made of heavy lace. It wasn't a purpose-built wedding dress but it looked sufficiently glamorous.

'Nice and sparkly for Vegas,' said Rhiannon, handing me the matching beaded chiffon wrap. The wrap was sheer so it looked part of the outfit, rather than obvious fat girl camouflage.

I hadn't looked at my body that closely over the long winter, and now I could see it had been busy transforming. My waist was smaller and my shoulders were shapelier.

'Hey, my arms are not as ham-like as I thought,' I mused.

'Shauna, I will tell you one last time,' said Rhiannon. 'Get over your fucking arms!'

'Yes, ma'am.' I gave her a quick hug. 'Thank you for all your hard work. There's no way I'd have dared picked this up from the rack.'

She smiled serenely like the cat that had swallowed a thousand canaries. She'd delivered the project on time and within budget. 'No worries. You look fab. Gareth is going to love it.'

'And it's a size six*teen*!' I squealed, 'From a Normal Shop!'

312

'Of course it's from a Normal Shop!'

I think when you find your wedding dress there's meant to be a touching moment when you look in the mirror and cry prettily at the sight of your bride-to-be reflection. But I just said, 'Quick! Get this thing off me! We've gotta buy it before it changes its mind about fitting!'

'Right,' said Rhiannon as we stepped back out into the London sunshine. 'We need serious undergarments.'

There are two types of women in this world. There are chicks that can toss any scrap of fabric over their head and waltz out on to the street without needing serious hydraulics under the surface. Then there are we mortals who require smoothing and lifting and flattening.

We walked into the Shapewear section of the M&S lingerie department and Rhiannon said, 'Looks like we have choice of light control or firm control.'

'Are they the only levels? What if your flesh is out of control? Why don't they have "You're Not Going Anywhere Little Lady" Control?'

I tried on a beige bodysuit, a garment so vast and hideous it made Bridget Jones's knickers look like the tiniest whisper of a thong. I didn't really look at it closely before putting it on; I assumed you just stepped in like a swimsuit. But things got dicey around mid-thigh when I couldn't pull up the bra bit any higher. My knees were fused together by the crippling power of Lycra so all I could do was slide helplessly to the floor. I poked my head beneath the curtain and bleated, 'Rhiannon. Please. Help!'

She stepped over my body and snorted with laughter. 'I

think you were meant to put it over your head then pull it down. Did you undo the crotch snaps?'

'What crotch snaps? Oh.'

It was an elegant picture. I was hunched over, hands braced against the wall with Rhiannon positioned behind me trying to haul the fabric over my hips.

'It won't fit!' I gasped. 'It's just too tight!'

'Just stay *still*!'

Finally I was strapped in. Somehow I'd managed to find underwear even less attractive than my old size 26 Cottontails. But once we added the wedding frock I could see my unruly flesh had been somewhat tamed.

'Whoa,' I said. 'I'll have to be careful about what I eat until the wedding. One false move and the seams will explode!'

'Yeah,' Rhiannon admitted. 'But you're a veteran. You can do it!'

It took another ten minutes of wrestling to remove the bodysuit. How on earth am I going to do that on my own in Las Vegas?

Rhiannon waited with me at Piccadilly station for the tube to Heathrow. All weekend I'd been so proud and happy for her, the way she strutted around the big city like she'd lived there for ever. Yet I still felt a bittersweet ache at how our lives were pulling off in different directions.

She sighed suddenly. 'Well . . .'

'Well indeed.'

The two of us started bawling like babies, hugging and sobbing all over the ticket barriers.

'Bloody weddings!' sniffed Rhiannon. 'They bring out all the emotions!'

But I do suspect she was crying from the trauma of seeing me tangled up in a Lycra bodysuit. And perhaps I cried because instead of Wedding Night Action™, I'll be too busy having the damn thing surgically removed.

WEEK 214
14 February 2005
14st 1lb (89.5kg, 197lb)
11st lost (70kg, 154lb) – 2st 4lb to go (14.5kg, 32lb)

It's Metric Milestone Day! Today I weighed in at 14 stone 1 pound, which is 89.5 kilograms. I'm finally an Eighties Girl! I hadn't seen a number beginning with 8 since 1994. I've lost eleven years of lard!

Meanwhile I'm anxiously monitoring my intake and noting what foods give my belly the slightest amount of puffiness. So far lentils, alcohol, beans and pasta have been declared my mortal enemies until after 3 March. I assure you this isn't bridal hysteria; I'm truly walking a fine line between squeezing into and exploding out of that dress!

WEEK 214.5
17 February 2005

I experienced a mild Fat Bride Freak Out today. I called the Mothership and whined that I was genetically predisposed to be crap at marriage, since my parents are such prolific divorcees. But she assured me that you don't have

315

to let your genes dictate your path in life. Which I suppose is true. Joe Stalin had kids, and as far as I know they weren't genocidal tyrants. Likewise there are no reports of Apple Paltrow-Martin writing dull but heartfelt songs. YET. So I am cautiously optimistic.

In other news, our American itinerary is taking shape. My lovely internet friend Jillian offered to host us in San Francisco for our pre-honeymoon. We've been email buddies ever since she started reading my diet blatherings three years ago, so I can't wait to meet her.

All I have to do is figure out how to explain this to Gareth. So far Jillian is Just this Chick I Know from the Internet. I still haven't told him about my journal, in fact I still haven't told anyone, not even Rhiannon or the Mothership. I've kept it secret for so long that it would be embarrassing to mention it now. Jillian says she'll go along with whatever I decide. In the meantime she says that her husband Greg is coaching her to call me Shauna and not Dietgirl!

WEEK 215
21 February 2005
13st 13lb (88.6kg, 195lb)
11st 2lb lost (70.9kg, 156lb) – 2st 2lb to go (13.6kg, 30lb)

I've just had my final weigh-in as a single woman. Two pounds lost. More than eleven stone lost overall! And would you believe after 215 weeks of lard busting, the

Body Mass Index chart says I am no longer obese. I'm just plain old fat now. How generous of them.

Tomorrow night I'm moving out of my flat and over to Dunfermline. It would have been a quick and easy process if I weren't so sentimental. I came to Scotland with just one wee suitcase, but now I have the same wee suitcase plus eleven boxes of 'mementoes'. I like to sift through my magpie's nest and let random objects trigger memories, rather than having to remember things with my actual brain.

So in lieu of packing, I've spent two days blubbering over two years of Scottish detritus. The wrapper from my first Tunnock's TeaCake. A tiny lump of Icelandic volcano. Twenty-two boarding passes from our travels. A condom wrapper from a particularly good shag. A hand-written sign, SHAUNA AND RHIANNON'S FOOD CUPBOARD, KEEP OUT!

It amazes me I've lived overseas long enough to have accumulated nostalgia.

And what a crying shame to be parting company with my treasured flatmates, with their mouldy yoghurts in the fridge and penchant for playing *The Best of Elton John* at midnight. I woke up this morning and thought, *This is the last day on my own. Tomorrow I'm off to what will soon be the marital home. Soon I'm going to be MARRIED!*

What would you do if you had just twenty-four hours left as a single person? Take yourself out for lunch? Go clubbing? Bungee jump? Furiously masturbate, all day long?

I chose to go to the gym, scramble some eggs then arrange my boarding pass collection in chronological order. I was a thrill-seeking singleton right to the end.

I finally made my confession in Amsterdam airport while we waited for our connection to San Francisco. We'd been up since 3 a.m. so we were dishevelled and barely coherent. The timing was perfect!

'Hey Gareth,' I said nervously, 'there's something I have to tell you.'

He turned paler than his already pale Scottish complexion. 'Oh?'

'Yeah. It's about how I met Jillian. There's this website.'

'Oh?'

'It's a diary, really. My diary. It's about losing weight and stuff. I've been losing weight and writing about it for years. And lots of people read it.'

'You're kidding me?'

'That's actually how I met Erin and got involved with the book stuff.'

'Oh!'

I babbled on apologetically for ten minutes but he just sighed and said, 'Jeez, you had me worried! I thought you were going to call off the wedding. I mean, how many times does someone say there's something they have to tell you and it's not awful news?'

'So it's not awful?'

'Of course it's not awful!' he smiled. 'I think it's rather cool. I don't know why you'd think otherwise.'

Bloody hell. I've been such a goose.

Twelve hours later we sat in Jillian's big American kitchen.

I gazed in an adoring, jet-lagged stupor at her big American fridge with the big American gallon bottles of milk and her big American pantry with the big American cereal boxes in it.

'So before Gareth comes downstairs,' Jillian whispered as she ladled out home-made vegetable soup. 'Does he know the score?'

'Yes.' I grinned. 'I'm out of the closet!'

I loved Jillian the moment I saw her jumping up and down and waving at the airport. Not only was she kind, funny and totally not a serial killer or stamp collector, she'd made soup and salad to help keep me sweet inside my wedding dress.

Over dinner with her husband Greg, she told Gareth how she'd started reading my site after a woman mentioned it at her Weight Watchers meeting. I almost choked on the tiny alphabet pasta to hear that somebody had been talking about my silly website, halfway around the world.

'I'm so proud of Shauna,' she went on. 'It's been amazing to see her transform!'

Gareth smiled as Jillian talked about how she'd 'watched' me go from large and depressed to significantly smaller and happier. I always forget that I'm not just talking to myself when I send my tortured text into the ether. There are real people like Jillian, reading away over a morning coffee. And now I was in her house eating her soup! Could life get any more wonderful and bizarre?

Later, as I was drifting off to sleep at the jetlagged time of 7.30 p.m., Gareth snuggled up and said, 'I'm proud of you. It was dead cool to hear Jillian talk about how you've inspired people.'

I squirmed and blushed, too mortified to speak. Dietgirl had only lived in my head for four years, so it felt strange to have her come to life.

'Steady there, tiger,' I finally said, 'I'm not like Mother Teresa or anything.'

I told him that there are hundreds of other people around the world writing about their fat and they make me feel I'm not alone. Every day, without fail, I'll read something that inspires me to think or cry or giggle. Blogging has been my favourite lard-busting tool. We share our ups and downs and we're fallible, unlike those magazine success stories where they say, 'I walked the dog and ate fun-size Mars Bars and lost a steady two pounds a week!'

I don't think it was until I heard Jillian talking about it to my almost-husband, out loud and so far from home, that I truly appreciated that it's a living, breathing incredible thing.

WEEK 216
3 March 2005

On Wedding Day I woke up cucumber cool and keen to get down the aisle. Gareth, on the other hand, stared out the window of our Luxor hotel room, looking handsome but bewildered in his kilt.

'Don't jump, sexy legs,' I said, 'I promise you it won't be that bad!'

I was too busy being vain and obnoxious to be nervous. Ladies, if you've ever thought of eloping, consider a few things. Are you capable of dressing yourself? Will you remember to break in your shoes *before* the day of the wedding? Can you do up your own frock, or do you need to coat your body in margarine to have any hope of closing the zipper?

If not, you should go the traditional route, i.e. with bridesmaids and mothers and make-up artists and hairdressers – also known as personal slaves. These people will remind you to unpick that wedgie or powder your shiny nose before the photos. They will give you Something Blue so you don't have to settle for writing the word BLUE on your foot with a pen. They provide the brains on the big day, so you don't have to climb on to a hotel room sink and batter your head against the mirror like a moth, shrieking as you try to apply eyeshadow under a fluorescent strip, 'My eyes! My eyes! I can't see my *damn eyes* in this *damn light*!'

After spending the past two weeks hiding my dress from Gareth, the surprise was ruined because I couldn't zip it up myself. His strongest memory of the frock will be me slumped over the bathroom sink wheezing, 'Just pull . . . a little . . . harder!'

I'm also sure that if the Mothership or Rhiannon had been present I wouldn't have got married with only one earring. I lost one somewhere on the journey from our room to the Inclinator (the Luxor Hotel is shaped like a pyramid, with lifts that run on a diagonal down the side of it). It was only £4 worth of earring, but they were long and dangly and foxy, dammit! Gareth and I crawled around on the pharaoh-patterned carpet for ten minutes to no avail.

Cue Fat Bride Freak Out.

'Great!' I moaned. 'The one day of my life I need to be classy. Why not just *one day*?'

'Just wear the one earring,' said Gareth calmly. 'You'll be totally punk, like Cyndi Lauper or something.'

'Bah. By the way, why didn't you tell me to wear shorter heels? I feel like Lurch standing next to you.' With my fancy new shoes I thought I'd finally crossed off item number 3 on my 'Things To Do When I'm Skinny' list, but losing eleven stone hadn't made my feet any more delicate.

I finally ceased grumbling when we got into a taxi and headed down the Strip. We zoomed past our fake Pyramid, the fake Statue of Liberty, the fake Eiffel Tower and the fake Venice. With every tacky landmark my grin grew bigger. I was about to marry the love of my life in the most bizarre town on earth. Woohoo!

The wedding chapel was in downtown Vegas, conveniently located between a seedy motel and an establishment that promised HOT NAKED CHICKS!

The foyer was decorated with photos of the veritable galaxy of previously wed stars. Jon Bon Jovi, Jay Leno, Billy Ray Cyrus and some guy that used to be on *The Young and the Restless*. I gazed up at them as the receptionist handed me a bouquet of white flowers. 'You're here for the 11.30?'

'We're the eleven.'

'Oh right! Groom's name is . . . Garth? Garrett?'

'Gareth!'

'Oh, how unusual! Okey-dokey then. You guys ready to get married?'

The photographer herded us into the chapel and arranged us into a dozen different poses in three minutes. Bride stand here, groom stand there. His arm here, her feet there. Hand up, chin down. Kiss here, grope there.

'Now, will you be exchanging rings? We need to get the bling shot.'

Gareth and I grimaced. 'Umm, sorta.'

I pulled two rings off my hand. 'We didn't get round to buying them so we're just going to use these ones and turn them upside down so they look like wedding bands.'

The photographer pointed at one of them. 'What is *that*?'

'It's jade! Well . . . pretend jade. Got it from a market in Moscow for 20 roubles.'

He raised his eyebrow at Gareth, 'Big spender, aren't ya, buddy?'

Next we were introduced to the Reverend who'd be doing the officials. She was cute and round like Dawn French in *The Vicar of Dibley*.

'So it's Shauna and . . . Gar-eth?' She pronounced his name like it rhymed with 'caress', with an added lisp.

'Gareth!'

'Shauna and Gary, OK. Now, Gary, you come with me down the aisle and we'll shut those french doors so the bride can make her dramatic entrance. I'll say a few poignant words, then we do the vows, and then you'll be married!'

Even as the Bridal March cranked up, I still couldn't grasp that this was our wedding. I just smiled at the cheesy photos on the wall and adjusted my dress for the hundredth time. Despite abstaining from carbs for the past week, it still choked my flesh like a sausage casing.

Suddenly the doors opened and I strolled down the aisle in a daze, vaguely thinking, *Oh, there's Gareth in his kilt*, but mostly *Woohoo! I can walk in these heels!* I half listened as the Reverend said a prayer and some words about love and two lives coming together.

But as soon as she started the vows – *pow!* I was finally in the moment.

We didn't know beforehand how the vows would be phrased, but they turned out to be simple and eloquent. Gareth held my hands, absently brushing his thumbs back and forth over my wrists like he always does. That gesture usually makes me feel calm and reassured, but this time it was electric. Until that moment this whole Vegas caper had just felt like a really elaborate vacation. But now we looked at each other with a mixture of nerves and tenderness and Holy Fucking Shit Batman, We're Getting Married!

'Now repeat after me,' said the Reverend. ' "Jared, I love you." '

'GARETH!' I corrected, 'I love you!'

And I'd never meant it so much as right then. My eyes prickled with tears and my heart pounded like a Bon Jovi power ballad.

We promised to love and cherish, but there were no lines about obeying, darnit. Then we exchanged our shoddy pretend wedding rings.

The Reverend smiled. 'Now you may seal your marriage with a big kiss!'

And then we were hitched.

We headed to the counter to collect our certificate and pay the bill. A lady in a red sequinned minidress and her tight-denim fella were next in the queue for the aisle.

'So you guys are all done,' smiled the receptionist, handing me a receipt.

'Cool!' I gawked at the wedding certificate in disbelief. 'Oh! I almost forgot. Do we get the DVD now or will you post it to us later?'

'You ordered the DVD? I don't think there's a DVD included with your package.'

'True, but I called back a few weeks ago to add it.'

She flipped through the book. 'Oh yes. Here it is. So you did. OH. Right.' She looked pale. 'Umm. Let me go check with the photographer.'

A few minutes later the photographer rushed in, clutching his forehead, 'Oh . . . shoot!'

'You didn't film their wedding?'

'OH . . . SHOOT!'

They were aghast and apologetic; perhaps they thought I'd go all Litigation Bride on them!

'We are so sorry,' said the lady. 'Our photographer didn't see that we'd added a note about the DVD. I can refund you right away?'

'It's OK, really,' I said. 'But the only problem is that my mother was very insistent we get the DVD, so I don't dare go home without it.'

'OK,' she said. 'We'll just have to reshoot.'

'Reshoot? Do the wedding again?'

'If you guys don't mind. It's the least we can do!'

Gareth and I were in stitches. Two weddings in ten

325

minutes? Classy! If we stuck around another hour we could beat Elizabeth Taylor's record.

'I'll tell you what, how about we throw in Elvis, too? Since you're being so good about this. He's right here and ready to go!'

'Well . . .' I'd seen the Elvis impersonators on the Chapel website. One was a strapping specimen; lean, leather-suited and in his prime. The other represented the King's declining years, when he'd discovered the fried peanut butter sandwiches. Was it wrong of me not to want the Fat Elvis? Was I betraying my own kind? I felt a guilty rush of relief when Elvis the Slender swaggered in. The photographer briefed him on the situation and he grinned and gave the thumbs-up.

Gareth took his place by the altar and they closed the french doors again. I caught my reflection in the window. My dress, so snug around my hips, had twisted around so the zipper was at the side instead of over my butt. I prayed I'd get through my fake wedding without splitting the seams.

The doors opened again.

It was then I recalled the Mothership's reaction when I told her we were running away to Vegas. There'd been a long pause on the line before she asked, 'Are you sure you're taking this marriage thing seriously?'

'We're taking the marriage seriously, Mother,' I explained. 'Just not the wedding!'

And there was Elvis waiting for me, strumming his guitar and crooning 'Love Me Tender'. I hooked my arm through his and willed myself not to laugh for the next five minutes. I could hear the tripod screech every time the video camera changed position. This was going to be a highly sophisticated production.

'Who gives away this woman today?' the Reverend asked as we reached the end of the runway.

'On behalf of her friends and family,' drawled Elvis, 'I do! Elvis, the King of Rock and Roll!' He winked at Gareth, 'She's all yours, buddy.'

'Thank you,' Gareth drawled. 'Thank you very much!'

The Reverend ploughed through the vows again. For the benefit of the camera we tried to recreate the sincerity and sentiment of our first marriage. I tried to get my voice to waver on the vows, so people wouldn't know this was my second time. I managed to kiss the groom with the same enthusiasm I had all those minutes before.

As we unlocked lips the photographer hit the Play button on the portable tape deck. Muzak dribbled forth as Elvis burst back into the chapel. The Reverend gestured with her eyebrows for us to take a pew and be serenaded. We grinned into the cameras as the King sang 'Can't Help Falling in Love'.

It's cool to be on your second marriage without encountering lawyers, bitter arguments or property settlements. Best of all they gave us each a free XXXL T-shirt with the slogan, I RENEWED MY VOWS AT GRACELAND WEDDING CHAPEL!

Back at the Luxor, we paused in the casino to put two dollars through a slot machine but then I couldn't stand it any longer. We went back to our room and unzipped my dress and my squashed-up flesh screamed with relief. Once in our usual jeans and T-shirt uniforms we went

down to the Pharaoh's Pheast buffet, where I dove into the all-you-can-eat American goodness. Then it was back to the room to watch *Judge Judy* and a take quick nap. Finally we headed over to the MGM Grand and watched Tom Jones live in concert, holding hands and feeling ridiculously in love.

'*It's not unusual,*' he told us.

And that was the happiest day of my life, right there.

WEEK 218
14 March 2005
14st 0.5lb(89.3kg, 196.5lb)
11st 0.5lb lost (70.2kg, 154.5lb) – 2st 3.5lb to go
(14.3kg, 31.5lb)

I left my heart and stomach in San Francisco. We've been back in Britain for a week and still I can't stop thinking about all the yummy things I ate in the States.

I was so restrained before the wedding, convinced that an extra lettuce leaf would cause the sequins to blast off my dress. But once I was safely down the aisle I got acquainted with the local delights. Giant breakfasts with homefries and bacon. Fat burritos bursting with beans and cheese. Fresh, affordable sushi. And all those American candies that I'd only known from television shows – Junior Mints, Peanut Butter Cups, York Mint Patties and Three Musketeers. Oh my.

But while my candy wrapper collection expanded, miraculously I only gained a pound and a half in the three-week trip. It helped that we shared a lot of dishes and walked up dozens of steep San Francisco streets. Maybe I'm learning the fine art of moderation, or maybe I just didn't want to be a pig in front of my new husband?

On our last day I was anxious and annoyed because I hadn't tried all the foods I'd wanted to try. What if we never came back to America again?

'I want ice-cream!' I declared as we walked through Golden Gate Park. 'I must have ice-cream.'

Gareth look conflicted. 'You told me to tell you that you didn't need stuff like ice-cream.'

'That was pre-wedding angst. This is supposed to be a holiday and I haven't eaten anything *good*.'

'But what about all the restaurants?'

'We didn't have *dessert* in any of those.' I rolled my eyes. 'Dessert is good. Dinner stuff is just dinner. It doesn't count unless there's something sweet at the end of it.'

'Didn't you have dessert when we went to Greens with Greg and Jillian?'

'We *shared* a dessert between *four* people and I only had two bites.'

'Only two?'

'Three, tops.' I sulked. 'I just want something SWEET!'

'Oh.'

'And I really wanted to go to Ghirardelli for the apparently famous Hot Fudge Sundae but we didn't get there and I'm still spewing. I haven't had my treat quota!'

'But we shared that bar of chocolate earlier . . .'

'That was *dark* chocolate with nuts and raisins. All those antioxidants, that's practically health food!'

'What about the chocolates we ate on the bus to the Grand Canyon?'

'I ate those because the only other thing available was a blackened banana that cost one whole dollar. Plus tax. And it was crap chocolate. It wasn't something I was *busting* to have.'

'So . . . ?'

'So it doesn't count. It's only a treat if it's something you really, really wanted. Can't you see the difference? Jeez.'

Gareth smiled, but I'm sure he was wondering just what he'd signed up to.

But I can't dwell on food-related disappointments. I've got work to do. I've signed up for a running race!

Well it's not really a race *per se*. It's the Race for Life, a 5K charity event. You could walk or scoot along backwards on your arse if you preferred, but I'm going to run.

My friend Julia, a Dietgirl reader in Italy, is a running coach and late last year she volunteered to virtually teach me how to run. With three sessions a week for ten weeks she promised I'd transform from breathless slob to Chariot of Fire. I was too full of angst to take up her offer at the time, but now I've got no excuse. The commitment scares me more than marriage but now that the initial Wedding Dress Fear has passed, I need a new challenge to keep me on the straight and narrow.

I got my race pack in the mail today. There was a piece of paper with a number on it that I am supposed to pin on my shirt then run five kilometres. I know thousands of people can run five kilometres with their eyes closed but it's my idea of hell. Why would I want to take my lard to the streets? It's bad enough lurking up the back row of BodyPump!

But then I remembered my 'Things To Do When I'm Skinny' list. 'Run' was item number 4, so I'm contractually obliged to give it a stab. I managed to learn how to *walk* again a few years ago, so let's see if we can take it up a gear.

WEEK 219
21 March 2005
14st 1.5lb (89.8kg, 197.5lb)
10st 13.5lb lost (69.7kg, 153.5lb) – 2st 4.5lb to go
(14.8kg, 32.5lb)

Today I bought a set of scales for the marital home and stepped on to discover I've gained a pound. I've only been married three weeks, it's far too soon to be letting myself go! Besides, how can I let go when I never got hold of myself in the first place?

I'm struggling to come to grips with life on the other side of the Forth Bridge. I was so spoiled living in the centre of Edinburgh, close to shops, cinemas and the Fancy Gym with a dozen buses whizzing by to take me to even more exciting places. Out here in Dunfermline it's a twenty-minute trek to the train station, and the trains are always late or full of drunks. The nearest decent supermarket is a thirty-minute walk away, and the return leg with the grocery bags is uphill.

I miss my old Edinburgh routine. I've been too busy sulking to establish a Dunfermline routine. My commute sucks. I hate washing my hair in the bath with a teacup

331

since Gareth doesn't have a shower. And he doesn't have an organizer tray in his cutlery drawer! All the knives and forks are just tossed in one big metallic pile. I asked him how he could possibly live with such chaos and he just shrugged, 'It makes mealtimes an adventure.'

I had a brief moment of resolve on Saturday and joined the local gym. But afterwards I stopped at the mini supermarket in search of olives and peppers for our pasta dinner. There were no peppers and only a tiny jar of anaemic olives for £1.89. I glared at the jar, simmering with bitterness, for those olives were a metaphor for the crapness of my new existence. I prowled the cramped aisles looking for something to calm me down and finally arrived at the freezer.

'Aha!' I thought, 'a freezer! And in the freezer is *ice-cream*, that stuff that I really wanted in San Francisco but didn't get. Now it shall be mine!'

I bought one of those Mars Bar ice-creams. Then I got an original Mars Bar too, just in case I wasn't satisfied with the frozen one.

I was halfway home when I remembered Gareth was there with his band mates. So I quickly unwrapped the ice-cream and wolfed it down, lurking behind a tree, putting it down every time a car went by so people wouldn't think I was a Greedy Fat Chick. I was so jittery that I barely registered the taste.

I squinted into the window of a parked car to make sure I hadn't left any chocolate evidence on my mouth. When I got home I said hello to the lads then hid in the bedroom for the rest of the evening. I read my *Running Made Easy* book while breaking off sly chunks of non-frozen Mars Bar.

What the hell was I doing? Was this how I wanted my married life to be? Clandestine chocolate bars and stuffing foil wrappers in my underwear drawer? Just like Mum used to do when she was married to my stepfather. Just like I used to do too. But I am not my mother nor am I a child any more. I have nothing to be afraid of. Gareth doesn't care if I eat a Mars Bar.

Don't get me wrong: I'm overjoyed to be married. But leaving Edinburgh was harder than I'd anticipated. I didn't expect to feel so resentful. I was so relieved that I wouldn't have to get deported and leave Gareth that I didn't think about how my daily life would change. I hate having to come up with new ways of doing things. Every time I get a rhythm going, life gets in the way!

WEEK 220
28 March 2005
13st 13lb (88.6kg, 195lb)
11st 2lb lost (70.9kg, 156lb) – 2st 2lb to go (13.6kg, 30lb)

Last night I sat on the kitchen floor in front of the washing machine, mesmerized by my socks thrashing around in Gareth's washing machine. Well, *our* washing machine now. That beast will be washing my socks until death do us part.

It felt like the first time I'd really sat still since I left Australia. I thought about the random, crazy way it had all unfolded. I'd just thought I'd do a little travel, eat a bit of haggis and then two years later go back to Canberra

333

and slip back into my old life. But I'm still in Scotland and I've got a husband that I've married twice. I smiled and watched his boxers and my knickers mingling in the suds, letting it all sink in.

This week has been the Official 'Stop Moping, Start Coping' Week. A cheesy, rhyming slogan always boosts my motivation.

Sunday kicked off with a domestic overhaul. I introduced Gareth to the joys of planning a weekly menu rather than opening the cupboards and hoping for inspiration. Then we ordered groceries online to avoid that uphill trudge home from the supermarket. Then I reorganized the pantry in a more logical fashion, and it warmed my heart to see my quinoa and Brazil nuts nestled beside Gareth's Branston Pickle and spaghetti hoops.

'You don't mind all these reforms, do you?' I asked timidly, once I'd sorted the dreaded cutlery drawer.

'Of course not, it's great,' Gareth said as he surveyed our handiwork, 'I never knew I had so many teaspoons!'

I smiled. That man makes me believe that marriage really can be about compromise and communication, not flying crockery.

My lard busting is back on track with a two and a half-pound loss. I've also done two BodyCombat classes at my new Non-Fancy Gym and tomorrow I start Mistress Julia's running programme. I know I'll get there if I keep doing all these positive things. Weight loss isn't about willpower or motivation; it's just the cumulative effect of tiny actions over time. Putting down the chocolate bars, putting on the running shoes. You just have to keep picking yourself up when you fall, over and over again, for however long it takes.

WEEK 221
4 April 2005

It's only been a week but I can tell you I officially hate running.

It doesn't help when my earliest memories of the sport are being chased around the athletics track by plovers, giant Australian birds with spurred feet, while the teachers stood around laughing. And then there's the bitter sting of high school PE classes, where I couldn't trot more than 50 metres without coughing up a lung. By far the slowest in my class, I was always picked last for teams. One by one my chosen classmates would line up behind their captains, until only I remained in all my red-haired red-cheeked crapness.

CAPTAIN A: Ummmm. I pick that tree.
CAPTAIN B: I pick that stray cat over there.
CAPTAIN A: I pick that abandoned crisp packet.
CAPTAIN B: Damn! *All right* then, I pick Shauna!

I must confess, I actually bought my running shoes six months ago but I've been too afraid to use them. It took three attempts just to get inside the door of the running store! The first time I let my bus sail right past, too nervous to press the Stop bell. The second time I stood on the opposite side of the street in a blur of tears. I was convinced the sporty salespeople would laugh me right out of the shop, because why the hell would such a fatty fat guts need running shoes? After all the lard I'd lost, I still couldn't shake the idea that there are things I'm not allowed to do and places I shouldn't go because of my weight.

All this was despite reassurance and encouragement from Rhiannon, Gareth and Mistress Julia, who all insisted running was for everyone. They said the shop folk would be happy to help, and my fat money would be just as welcome as some withered marathon dude's money. Everyone has to start somewhere!

Annoyed into action by such logic, I made my third trip to the store. I hid behind a rack of very tiny shorts while the saleswoman sold some socks to an athletic gentleman. Sadly the other people were only browsing, so I was spotted before I could escape.

'Can I help you?'

'I'm looking for some running shoes,' I said meekly.

'Excellent!'

'I'm just starting out,' I said in a rush. 'Well, obviously!'

I still can't suppress the urge to justify my presence to skinny people. *Yep, I'm fat! I know. Beat ya to it!*

But the woman just focused on the task at hand. She asked me to take off my shoes and walk up and down the shop. She instantly spotted my over-pronating right foot and fetched a mighty stack of shoes for me to try.

All that attention on my body made me squirm. I'm so used to being anonymous with exercise, hiding at the back of the class and muddling my way through. It was strange to be taken seriously.

'OK, just have a wee run up and down the shop so I can see if your feet like those shoes.'

I froze. 'Run? Me?'

She smiled. 'Don't worry, no one's looking at you.'

'Oh man.'

'I'll just be looking at your feet, not analysing your technique.'

'I have no technique.'

I squirmed for another thirty seconds before doing a half-hearted little trot. My face was burning red, but at least it was just from embarrassment and not exertion.

I must have tried a dozen different pairs. I kept blurting, 'These are OK! I think these will do!' Anything to get her to stop paying so much attention. Finally after half an hour she was satisfied with my choice and I made my escape.

Perhaps I thought I didn't need to use the running shoes, since the act of buying them was such a remarkable achievement in itself. But I've signed up to a charity race and Mistress Julia's programme so I'm out of excuses. And now Gareth is doing the training with me! When he offered to come along for moral support I said I'd be delighted, but now I'm cursing my politeness. Not only is he humiliatingly fitter than me, it means I'll actually have to do some running. I can't just sit under a tree for half an hour, splash my face with water then go home and say, 'Dude! Tough workout!'

The first session this afternoon was hell. I thought I'd built up a reasonable level of fitness with all my gym classes, but running is a different beast. There's no instructor to tell me what to do. There's no machine to slump on when I get tired. It's just me, my body and the open road.

When you've avoided running your whole life, it feels bizarre to arrange your body in a running-type configuration. Julia's instructions were customized for the absolute beginner, so I alternated walking with one-minute bursts of running. Or rather, one-minute bursts of slightly swifter shuffling. My lungs! My poor lungs! Where had all the air gone? Why was my face on fire?

I'd never felt so inept in my life. I looked at the ground the whole time, hoping it would render me invisible to all the real runners in the park. I should have resurrected the old Vampire Method!

Gareth on the other hand loped along effortlessly, throwing punches and singing the theme from *Rocky*, 'Shauna's training! Getting strong now! Won't be long now!'

When we finally finished, my face was so red it melded seamlessly with my hair and eyebrows. Gareth hadn't even broken sweat. The bastard.

How will I ever last five kilometres?

WEEK 222
11 April 2005

There was a girl beside me on the train platform this afternoon who appeared to be about the same size I was at my largest. She looked nervous as the train pulled in, shuffling from foot to foot. I wondered what was wrong. Sometimes I look nervous when the train arrives too, because I'm always trying to guess where the carriage doors will be when it stops. I've been very lucky lately; the doors have landed right in front of my nose so I can get right on board with a good chance of getting a seat. It's a beautiful thing!

The Door Gods smiled on me again today, and I was about to jump on when I noticed the girl looked even more flustered. Suddenly I recognized that agitated expression. I stepped back and let her get on first.

She didn't venture into the carriage proper, where most of the seats are; but instead hung round in the open space at the end where the bike rack and toilets are. There's just one seat that folds down from the wall, and she swooped on it immediately. That space is always hot and noisy, but since everyone else was busy fighting over the seats in the air-conditioned bit, she had it all to herself.

I didn't feel pity; it was simply a moment of recognition and empathy. I've almost forgotten how my days used to be an endless series of logistical operations. Trying to manoeuvre my body down narrow shop aisles without knocking over merchandise. Praying that I'd fit in the cape at the hairdresser's. Making plans with friends then wondering if I should put anti-chafing powder on my thighs in case they wanted to walk anywhere. Rushing on to trains to find a seat so I wouldn't have to squeeze past anyone. Always trying to anticipate danger.

The Fat Girl Logistics Department has been retired for quite some time. I don't have to worry about non-retracting seat belts or breaking chairs in restaurants any more. But today I remembered how exhausting it was, physically and mentally, just getting around. All the dread and fatigue flooded back, and I kept patting the empty space around my seat to make sure I really did fit.

WEEK 224
27 April 2005

Gareth still hasn't read a word of this journal. I didn't ask him to stay away; he just said he didn't want to intrude on my private space. If the situation was reversed I'm not sure I'd be so polite. If he told me he used to be really fat and depressed and I could read all the filthy details, there's no way I could resist!

Part of me wants him to visit and slog his way through the archives. I want him to see the hard evidence of how different I used to be. Not to show off my lard-busting prowess, but to give him the full background. I've only made vague references to my pudgy past, so if he read about it maybe he'd understand why I can still be such a nutter about my body.

On Sunday we commenced Week Four of our running regime. Well, Gareth was running, I was still gasping and turning redder than my hair. I had that blind, white-hot pre-menstrual rage coursing through my veins. It was just too bloody hard, and there was still another twenty-five minutes to go.

I glared sideways at Gareth. I hated him for barely breaking sweat while my own heart clobbered against my ribs. Didn't he realize how traumatic this was for me?

Didn't he realize that I used to be so unfit that I might as well have been comatose?

'Hey,' I wheezed, 'do you want to know why I hate this so much? [*Puff puff puff*] Do you want to know why I'm so bloody cranky and find this so bloody difficult? Well! I used to weigh twice as much as you do now. [*Pant*] Yeah that's right, TWICE as much! I couldn't *walk* around the block let alone run! So just try and imagine that, buddy. Two of YOU stapled together!'

That's him told, I thought. At last he knows the awful truth!

'It doesn't matter what you used to weigh,' he said, handing me a bottle of water. 'What matters is that you found the guts to change your life. Learning to run is just your next adventure.'

What? He was supposed to say, 'Wow, you were huge! How remarkable, then, that you jogged for thirty seconds today when before you couldn't tie up your own shoelaces. Let's go home and I'll make you a cup of tea to celebrate!'

I just don't know what to make of myself or my body these days. Am I still a helpless blob that deserves patronizing applause for making the effort to waddle to the fridge? Or am I just as Gareth sees me, a normal, healthy chick taking up a new fitness challenge?

Last week I was hanging out with Maghie and Vicki, two friends of Gareth's who are fast becoming friends of mine. We're all madly into healthy living so we got together to drink herbal tea and talk about tofu and yoga. Part of me was in seventh heaven to find such like-minded souls, but part of me wondered if they were thinking, *Who's this big lump, thinking she knows all about health and fitness?* I felt like a fraud.

Eventually curiosity got the better of Gareth. He asked me as we were drifting off to sleep, 'Did you really weigh 25 stone?'

'Yes.'

'Life must have been a lot different back then?'

He was warm and understanding, just like he would have been if I'd been honest right from the start. But instead of being relieved I got defensive and refused to talk. I started crying there in the dark, feeling ashamed, as if all those extra pounds had suddenly reattached to my body. I imagined floating above the bed, looking down at the two of us – a huge blubbery pile of me with slender Gareth curled up behind.

I don't quite know who I want to be lately. I feel so desperate to escape from the Old Shauna but part of me doesn't want to let her go. Maybe I'm just too scared to find out if the new one is for real.

WEEK 227
16 May 2005
13st 9lb (86.8kg, 191lb)
11st 6lb lost (72.7kg, 160lb) – 1st 12lb to go (11.8kg, 26lb)

I'm happy to have lost four pounds over the past seven weeks but all this running makes me ravenous. I can't stop thinking about food! I was walking home from the train station today when I caught sight of a sign above a shop on the high street. Half of it was obscured as I went around the corner, so I could only see:

N T A L

E R Y

Oh yes! My stomach purred with excitement. Continental Bakery! Bring on the pies and pastries!

Imagine my heartbreak when I got closer and saw the full picture:

D E N T A L

S U R G E R Y

WEEK 228
23 May 2004

Today I came out of the fat-blogging closet!

Well, partially. *Tales from the Scale* was finally released in America this month, so in a bold move I sent copies to Rhiannon and the Mothership.

Mum sent me a text message last night, *Nice book, thank u!*

I wrote back, mimicking her nagging tones, *DID YOU LOOK at the contributor biographies in the back of the book?*

OMG! came the reply.

It's so exciting to be in print! At first I played it cool, thinking I shouldn't get too smug about having a few pages in someone else's book. But then the glee won out and I had to jump up and down and scream. This is something I've dreamed of my whole life. When I was a kid all my friends wanted to be teachers or models, but I'd always say, 'I want to be an author'. I don't know where I heard the word but I liked the way it sounded. Try and imagine my tiny Aussie accent: OR-THA!

Now all my nearest and dearest not only know I'm an Ortha, but they know I've spent the past four years babbling about my blubber on the internet. It's been such a relief to come clean. Rhiannon was excited and seemed to understand why I needed my little sanctuary, which helped ease my guilt. The Mothership was over the moon too. 'I'm very proud of you, Miss Dietgirl!' she said on the phone tonight. 'Would you mind if I took a peek at your internet hideout?'

'Umm, if you like.'

'I might pick up a few more tips from you. Not that I need them, I'm melting away!'

'Are you?'

'Oh yes! I started with the walking just like you said, and six months later, well! I don't think you'll recognize me by the time you come over.'

'That's great, Ma. I'll look forward to it.'

'You know I showed your chapters to my neighbour,' she went on. 'She's a big lady too. She just *cried* because she couldn't believe how much she related to your story. It's amazing, don't you think? How we're all fat and going through the same thing?'

'It's true, dear Mothership. We're all well-padded people in a universal padded cell.'

There's only one week until race day! I'm trying to remember to breathe. I know I've improved, but I'm still going to be overtaken by leathery grandmas, so much fitter than me despite living on tins of cat food.

What we need here is a Rocky-esque montage of my progress over the past ten weeks. We wouldn't even need to make it in slow motion, because my motion is slow enough already. Cue soft focus and stirring orchestration!

Imagine if you will:

- Pathetic pre-run arguments:
  SHAUNA: I can't believe you're making me do this again!
  GARETH: I'm making you do it?
  SHAUNA: Yes, you!
  GARETH: You'll be fine.
  SHAUNA: But we only did this two days ago! Shouldn't that be enough? Until the end of time?
- A dramatic collapse on the grass at the end of Week Three, Session Two followed by a dramatic declaration, 'I will never walk again!'
- The ongoing saga of The Reddest Face in the World:
  CONCERNED FATHER-IN-LAW: Did you get a wee bit sunburned today?
  SHAUNA: No, I am still recovering from my run three hours ago.
- The Hill Sprints of Week Six: Gareth racing up stairs and pumping a triumphant fist in air *à la* Rocky; Shauna arriving some two minutes later.

- Great moments of fatigue and delirium, when Shauna is so slow that Gareth must literally run on the spot to match her pace:

  SHAUNA: My body won't work! I can't run any more!

  GARETH: It's not running if you don't lift *lift your feet* off the ground!

- Revenge of the Vegetable Chilli: In which Shauna farts uncontrollably when running up hills.

- Tears and icepacks in Week Eight as our athlete spends a week sidelined by a knee injury. Experts recommend increasing your mileage by no more than 10 per cent per week, but some bright spark wrote down Julia's instructions incorrectly and accidentally increased it by 25 per cent!

- The touching finale. After Sunday's gruelling run, once again collapsed on the grass, our athlete experiences her first endorphin rush:

  GARETH: You look as though you enjoyed that.

  SHAUNA: No I didn't.

  GARETH: You did so.

  SHAUNA: Perhaps, briefly. On some level.

After ten weeks, I still hate running. I commence bitching and moaning two hours before each session and do not let up until we're finished. Then I feel all smug and virtuous for about twenty-four hours before I start fretting about the next run. Every step has been a constant battle between my increasingly adventurous body and my lazy, sabotaging brain.

But running has been such a positive experience. In terms of the lard busting, there hasn't been much change on the scale but my clothes are fitting better and my legs look much slimmer.

Most dazzling is what's going on in my head. Running has given me a newfound respect for my body. I'm focusing on what it can *do* instead of what it looks like. I'm in awe of its incredible ability to adapt to every challenge I throw at it. Five kilometres is hardly a marathon, but I can honestly say learning to run is one of the hardest things I've ever done. I'm so proud that I completed every training session and didn't give up. Most of the time it's sweat and torture and yappy dogs getting under my feet, but it's worth it for those brief, thrilling moments when my limbs move like liquid and my mind floats happily above.

WEEK 230
6 June 2005

Signs your running event may be in Scotland:

1. It's raining so hard that worms have been washed up from underground.
2. There's a burger van.
3. The chick beside you at the starting line is eating a burger from said van AND smoking a fag at the same time.

The atmosphere at the Race for Life was electric, with 7,000 women of all ages, shapes and sizes limbering up in the rain. Some had little pink signs on their backs with the names of loved ones they'd lost. Some folk were in fancy costume. Some were just content to gulp down their pre-race cigarette and let the irony of smoking at a cancer charity event waft over their head.

I'd had to staple my race number to my T-shirt since there were no safety pins in our house. Who the hell has safety pins? The Mothership, Nanny, my supremely organized sister; *they* would have had safety pins. It took Gareth and me around half an hour to attach the stupid number without getting it crooked and/or piercing my boobs but I was happy with the end result. They say safety pins are punk rock but I say staples are even more so.

Finally it was time to line up. There were two different starting points, one for runners and one for walkers. This sparked a minor existential debate/ Fat Girl Freak Out.

'You haven't been just *walking* these past ten weeks, have you?' Gareth reasoned.

'But I'm not exactly a runner, am I? I can't run for longer than five minutes without feeling like I'm going to cark it!'

'Go and line up with the runners! And good luck, baby!'

I gave him a kiss on his wet nose and scampered off. By then it was so crowded I got shoved in with the walkers, beside a girl dressed in a Batman suit. I was so dazed by the crowd and the rain that I didn't think to be nervous, I just had a faint inkling that something exciting was about to happen.

Somewhere in the distance the starting horn went off. It took five minutes to inch my way to the line, then finally I could hit the Start button on my stopwatch. Go go go!

My trance broke and I panicked, *What the hell? What am I doing here?!*

Everywhere I looked there were legs and arms and numbers and puddles. Mistress Julia had advised me to start out slow so I wouldn't fade at the end, so I did a leisurely jog, ducking around walkers and water. Then the course headed up a hill beneath Arthur's Seat. Bloody hills. Better not waste energy weaving around people. I alternated fast walking with slow jogging. When I finally got to the top I was confronted by a second, steeper hill. Shit!

Stupid hill and stupid slow legs and stupid thousands of runners cluttering up the road, I grumbled as I made my painfully slow ascent. *What's so great about this running lark? Why do people rave about it like it's so damn special?*

My friend Meg had written to me about her first race. 'You will love it,' she declared. She said it changed the way she thought about herself for ever. WELL YOU LIE, MEG! I DO NOT LOVE IT! I was never going to get to the top of that stinking hill, and furthermore I hadn't seen any mile markers so I had no idea how far I had to go.

Finally the course evened out and after a minute's walk, I picked up the pace and began to relax. I acknowledged the spectacular panoramic views of Edinburgh. Then some guy shouted from the sidelines, 'You're just passed halfway, girls!'

Only halfway?!

I looked at my watch and wasn't impressed with my time. Julia had told me not to worry about that, and just focus on finishing the damn thing, but I was dejected.

I gave myself a wee pep talk. Why are we here, Shauna?

- Because my excellent sponsors coughed up £300 for cancer research and they deserve value for money.
- Because Gareth trained with me and endured my whining so I want to make him proud.
- Because Mistress Julia has helped me so much and I want to impress her and make her proud.
- Because I worked hard and I want to impress ME and make ME proud, dammit!

And I wouldn't be satisfied with half-heartedly puffing over the line either. I wanted to finish as strongly as possible. I'd worked for ten weeks to get to this point, and it would never be My First Race ever again. I'd done some pretty half-assed runs in those ten weeks, so now I was going to stop the bitching. Just GO FOR GOLD!

I kicked up to a nice steady run. I told the slothful part of my brain that I could walk any time, but since the first half of the race had been relatively slow I had plenty of energy left. I found a steady rhythm and my breathing was measured instead of the usual desperate gasps. I relished the feeling of my legs striding out and my feet springing off the ground, as though it was perfectly natural and right for my body to be running.

The rained stopped as I headed down the hill. *Just run one more minute then you can walk if you need to.* But I kept on running and running and it felt amazing.

Finally there was a sign – 500M TO GO. Holy crap! 500 metres!

How far is 500 metres? Ten laps of an Olympic pool.

That sounded like an eternity. Half a kilometre? That sounded like ages too. OK then. How about one-and-a-bit laps of an athletics track. Hey, that wasn't so bad. I could handle that!

I have no idea where the energy came from but I'd never run so fast before. I broke into a grin as I approached the finishing line. I almost laughed but I didn't have enough breath left.

When I finally crossed, a big sob sneaked up to my throat. I glanced at my watch – 35:15. I was euphoric. Ten weeks ago I could barely run for one minute, yet I'd just run over half the course non-stop. I, Shauna Reid, formerly of the Whole Pints of Ice-Cream in One Sitting, formerly of the 2.5 Miles per Hour on the Treadmill, had finished a 5K race.

I collected my goodie bag and wandered through the crowd with trembling legs, searching for Gareth. It was the strangest mix of emotions I'd ever known. I made weird gulping noises, like a chicken being strangled, as my body struggled to cry and catch breath at the same time.

When I finally found Gareth I flopped into his arms and began to sob uncontrollably. The poor lad looked confused. Blame my hormones, blame relief and surprise and intense personal satisfaction, but I was crying for Scotland!

Later on I was embarrassed by my hysterics. After all it was Just a 5K Race, and a charity one at that. People run marathons all the time, hell, they run across continents or sail around the world blindfolded with one arm chopped off! I was all ready to downplay the whole day and dismiss it as a freak incident. But as I've reminded myself countless times during my journey, you can't compare your achievements to anyone else's. All you can do is compare where you've been and where you are now, and what you chose to do in between.

I remember a day when I stood at the bottom of the stairs in my Canberra flat, tearfully trying to summon the energy to walk up to my bedroom. It had felt like an impossible task. Now five years later I stood at the bottom of a nasty big hill and thought running to the top was just as impossible. So today I'm bursting with pride at how far I've come. There is no better feeling in the world than to take your mind and body to a place you thought it couldn't go; a place you thought it didn't belong. You should all try it some time.

WEEK 231
13 June 2005
13st 8lb (86.4kg, 190lb)
11st 7lb lost (73.1kg, 161lb) – 1st 11lb to go (11.4kg, 25lb)

My runner's high came to an abrupt halt at the physiotherapist's office last Friday. The niggling knee pain of Week Eight got worse so I called in the pros, who diagnosed a nasty case of runner's knee. Just when I was contemplating jogging back to Australia in September to save on air fares, they told me I've got to stop.

I was almost apologetic when I showed up for my appointment. After all I was just a fat chick flirting with exercise, not a legitimate athletic person. How could a lump like me have a real injury? But just like when I bought my running shoes, he took me seriously and didn't scream, 'Get out of here, fattycakes!'

He explained that my knee will take a few months to heal and I need to strengthen my hamstrings and glute muscles. By the time he'd taken me through my exercises I'd stopped feeling like an impostor. In fact I was almost proud that I'd actually done enough sport to have a sports injury!

The physiotherapist suggested I try cycling as a gentler form of cardio, so I've taken up RPM classes, which is similar to spinning. I'd always thought it was out of my league, especially when all the participants have sculpted thighs and wear those tiny bike shorts. But then I told myself, 'Dude! You just learned to *RUN* so now you can learn to pedal. Get in there!'

So I did. And instead of hiding at the back I marched up to the instructor and introduced myself. She helped me adjust the bike seat and handlebars and soon we were off.

Holy crap, I loved it! I never thought a stationary bike could be fun. My heart thumped in time with the techno as the instructor talked us through hill climbs and brutal sprints. The forty-five minutes flew by and I was amazed to find I could keep up with the nubile regulars. Why did I waste all these years hating my body when I could have been appreciating that it's an amazing *machine*?

At the end of the class I felt high, like I'd wrung every last drop of energy from my limbs.

'You did great,' said the instructor. 'You've obviously worked hard!'

I grinned at my beetroot face in the mirror, 'Obviously! Thank you.'

I remembered that day when my BodyPump instructor in Canberra told me my squats were good. That compliment kept me floating for days. But this time I'd already known I'd done great, I didn't need to hear it from anyone else to believe it.

My motivations are transforming. For the past four and a bit years I've worshipped the scale and ached to reach that elusive 11 stone 11 pounds, but the numbers just don't fire me up like they used to.

The closer I get to a healthy weight, the more I'm looking beyond that dreaded contraption. When I weighed over 25 stone, the scale was the only way I could gauge my progress, since it took so long to see visible physical changes. But now the scale results are far less dramatic because I no longer have a dramatic amount of weight to lose.

Training for the 5K showed me the value of having non-scale goals. It had all the structure and accountability that I crave, but my motivations were pure and positive. It wasn't about fat, nor was I obsessive or desperate to impress anyone. I was just chipping away at a long-term personal goal, feeling my body get faster and stronger each week. That was far more sane and satisfying than fretting about the scale.

Not only did it make me feel balanced and wholesome, it got results. I've only dropped two and a half pounds in the past six weeks but my body is shrinking. I went jeans shopping today and fitted into size 16s in five different Skinny Shops! I nearly bought all five pairs because of the sheer novelty of having *choice*, instead of having to settle for the only thing that fitted.

From now on I'm focusing on getting fitter and stronger. I don't loathe my body any more, I'm intensely proud of it. Over the past four years we've progressed from couch potato to Vampire walking to weight lifting to running, and I'm desperate to find out what else we can do. I want to be a woman of action and sweat my way to a slinkier body.

WEEK 232
20 June 2005

Tales from the Scale has been released in the UK!

I hadn't considered this possibility. I thought I'd get the smug satisfaction of being a published writer without any-one having to know about my secret fat life, since the book would be safely tucked away on American shelves.

But then I got a call from a publicist from the UK publisher. Not only had the book crossed the Atlantic, *Grazia* magazine wanted to publish an extract of my chapters.

I've been swinging between gleeful and horrified ever since. Part of me loathes the idea of Dietgirl going into print. I'm not ashamed of myself or what I've written, but my innermost thoughts are something I've preferred to keep to myself. And a thousand kind strangers on the internet.

But the wannabe writer inside is quite chuffed. It will be the first time I've made headlines since my groundbreaking piece as an intern at the local rag: *Pensioners Welcome New Motorized Shopping Carts at Supermarket.*

What's been most terrifying is the photo shoot. The publicist told me that magazine wanted full-length 'After' photos, and I wasn't allowed to hide behind a pillow or a pony.

I went into denial. A lardy dork like me in a glossy women's magazine? It would never happen! Surely I'd get bumped by a Paris Hilton scoop or plastic surgery exposé? So when the Picture Desk called last Monday to arrange a shoot for Saturday, I curled up into a ball and howled.

The photographer asked to me to wear (a) something I felt comfortable in, (b) something that showed off my figure and (c) something that wasn't black. That ruled out approximately 100 per cent of my wardrobe.

I paced the streets of Edinburgh in a panic. Everything was too small, too black or too sleeveless. I tell you, wedding dress shopping has nothing on the trauma of photo shoot shopping. At least if your wedding dress is rubbish you can hide your photos in a drawer, as opposed to displaying them next to a picture of Kate Moss for all the world to see!

Why wasn't I rich with a crack team of personal shoppers? And how selfish of my sister to move away in January instead of foreseeing that I'd need her sartorial sense in June!

Finally on Friday night I resorted to a pair of jeans and simple wrap top. I cursed my laziness and lack of interest in fashion. Why had I left this to the last minute when I'd known for weeks this was on the cards? Why hadn't I bought new clothes as I'd shrunk? Why didn't I have a bra that held my boobs up? Why had I eaten all those cakes?

Before Las Vegas, Rhiannon and I had brainstormed How to Look as Skinny as Possible in the wedding photos. Shoulders back but relaxed. Sucked-in tummy. Arms held slightly away from your sides so the flab doesn't splodge in an unbecoming fashion. Body turned ever so slightly with hip and leg forward. The Vegas photographer barked orders and I moved easily through the poses. The photos turned out great, considering how I was crammed into that frock like haggis into a sheep's stomach.

I'd naïvely hoped the *Grazia* photo shoot would be just as brisk, but it took three hours. Firstly because they weren't a Vegas wedding factory, and secondly because they wanted to try all sorts of poses.

The shoot took place in a posh hotel room, which intimidated me right from the start. Once the hair and make-up were done, I leaned against the couch while they did some test shots. I slyly positioned my body according to my sister's advice. The photographer started shooting and I grinned or smiled or looked 'mysterious' or 'knowing' or 'flirtatious' as requested. I doubt my expression actually varied but she said I was doing great.

But then she made me get on the bed.

It was a vast four-poster with a luxurious satin cover. Anyone with a bit of extra flesh knows there is a very limited number of ways you can arrange your body in a flattering light. Standing upright is one. Actually that's about it. Once you're seated or prone, you have no control over how your flesh will flip and flop around.

'I'm not sure this will be a flattering angle!' I squeaked. The photographer told me not to worry. She told me to take a break and got the make-up artist to try out the pose while she set up the lighting. The make-up artist, gorgeously slim and elegant, jumped on to the bed and landed delicately on her side, leaning on her elbow. Perfect.

Then it was my turn. The bed groaned as I clambered on.

Now I know why models are so skinny. Because it's just easier when there's less flesh to arrange. I tried to stretch out all languid and feline, but my stomach flopped on the quilt, no matter how hard I sucked in. My jeans, which I now realized had been on the £20 bargain rack for a reason, were baggy in the crotch so the fabric bulged. And my smile was tortured from straining to hold my breath.

'Just relax, Shauna,' said the photographer in soothing tones. 'Why don't you tell us about your *Grazia* story?'

'Umm,' I cringed. 'Well. I lost a bunch of weight and wrote about it for a book.'

'Wow, that's fab!'

'Obviously I still have a few stone to go!'

By the time we move to the next move, the Come Hither on the Chaise-Longue, I was fighting back a full-scale Fat Girl Freak Out. I felt ridiculous posing for a story about weight loss when you could tape these two chicks together and I'd still be wider. The fact that they were so kind and friendly made it worse. They complimented my skin and my hair and my ability to smile on cue, but I felt like a fraud. Why can't I be proud of myself? What happened to that confident woman who ran the 5K? I thought I'd turned things around. I thought I liked myself more than this.

Afterwards as I washed off all the war paint, I felt a brief flicker of pleasure at the sight of my fancy hair and make-up. I was shocked by how much my face had slimmed down. But then I pictured my blobby body in the magazine, plonked beside those skinny stars. It just seems too ridiculous to contemplate.

And now comes an agonizing three-week wait to see how it all comes out.

WEEK 235
13 July 2005
13st 8lb (86.4kg, 190lb)
11st 7lb lost (73.1kg, 161lb) – 1st 11lb to go (11.4kg, 25lb)

We interrupt this angst to inform you that this weekend I finally learned that there are more important things in life than my lard. Like friends, family, love . . . and cake.

Saturday was Wedding Part II: Scottish Edition. Gareth's mother Mary had organized a wonderfully laid-back affair, with a ceilidh dance followed by a buffet.

I was more nervous about the party than the original wedding. All these people giving up their Saturday night because of us? Wasn't there something better on the telly? Some people relish being the centre of attention but it turns my stomach to ice. What if no one had a good time? What if they thought the ceilidh was naff? What if people whispered, 'Couldn't Gareth have found a bride with smaller arms?'

Luckily this time I had Rhiannon on board to calm me down and help me into my dress. It was a less strenuous wrestle than in Vegas. I've lost less than half a stone since March, but my exercising has whittled me down enough to allow unassisted breathing in the frock. I no longer feared my boobs were about to jump out and slap somebody.

'You look lovely!' gushed Mary when I made my entrance. 'And your dress is sitting so much better now!'

'Oh really?'

A look of horror dawned on her face. 'I mean, not that it didn't look good the first time!'

'It's OK!' I laughed.

So I felt foxy, but I couldn't help fretting about my upper arms. I tried to disguise them with the chiffon wrap as I romped around the dance floor.

The ceilidh was a brilliant icebreaker. We trampled on toes and swapped partners while the band fiddled and a bossy lady told us what to do. It was a scorching evening by Scottish standards and soon our guests were red and glazed like Christmas hams. I handed out all the cards from our wedding gifts so the ladies could fan themselves between dances. Finally it was just too hot for the wrap so I tossed it aside and let my wobbly arms say hello to the world.

And then I didn't think about them for the rest of the night.

I mean, really. Who gives a shit about my arms? Our guests were here to celebrate our marriage. And get drunk and dance. They were too busy having fun to be bothered with my arms. Why the hell was I bothered? Wasn't I there to have fun too?

So I did. Perhaps a little too much fun, as demonstrated by my drunken speech.

Cutting the cake was the only Official Wedding Thing that Gareth and I thought we'd have to do. We stabbed the slab, posed for pictures then poised to flee. But people started hollering, 'Speech! Speech!'

'Ummm,' gulped Gareth. He briefly thanked our friends and family then we attempted to scurry away, but the guests were still looking at us expectantly. Rhiannon bellowed from the back row, 'How about we hear from the *bride*?'

The gin had impaired the part of my brain that makes one think before speaking. 'Yeah!' I blurted. 'Thanks, David and Mary, for putting on a great party. Especially Mary, who ran round organizing the whole thing while David played golf and me and Gareth sat on our arses!'

Silence fell and a dozen snowy-haired Friends of the In-Laws pondered, 'How did nice young Gareth end up with this uncouth flabby-armed Australian?'

But my joy was more than just alcohol talking. On Saturday night, surrounded by friends and family and semi-strangers, it finally really felt like we were married. As much fun as cloping had been, celebrating with a room full of sweaty folk was extra special. There were Gareth's school buddies catching up over a smoke. There were aunties and cousins and golfing buddies. There were small children who quite literally crapped their pants from excitement. There were Jane and Rory, without whom I'd never have met Gareth. There were my kind and generous in-laws. There was my wonderful, delirious sister gulping down the helium from all the balloons and asking, 'Does my voice sound funny? Does it? Does it?'

As our guests trickled home I grabbed my husband and we had our belated First Dance on the abandoned dance floor. I'd never felt so happy and hopeful. And now I see that this lard-busting journey hasn't been so much about busting the lard as about busting the fears and insecurities and learning to like myself . . . learning to like *life*, really.

Two weddings down, one to go.

WEEK 237
25 July 2005

I bought my copy of *Grazia* first thing Tuesday morning but couldn't bear to open it. The potential for public awfulness was just too much!

But curiosity got the better of me around five o'clock. I sat on my Reebok step waiting for BodyPump to start, flipping through the pages and muttering, 'Oh no! Oh yes! How awful! How cool!'

There it was on page 36, the story of my amazing weight loss, followed by a feature on ultra skinny jeans that I wouldn't even get my ankle into.

It was like reading about a stranger. How could this be me? Had I really been all those different shapes and sizes?

The photographs were a visual history of my attempts to disguise my blubber over the past decade. Hiding behind the wedding bouquet in Las Vegas. Hiding behind the cake at my twenty-first birthday party. Hiding behind a brick wall at university. I'm still trying to hide in the latest photo, with my dark jeans and ultra-forgiving wrap top. But at least now

I only need clothes for camouflage, not brick walls.

It's been an emotionally turbulent week. I can best describe it using the Seven Stages of Finding Your Face in a Glossy Magazine:

1. *Relief* upon discovering the picture didn't turn out too bad after all. In fact I thought I looked rather pretty and slim. They'd chosen the Standing Up Pose that I'd done right at the start. See, I know how to best position my bulk!
2. *Professional Glee* at seeing my words printed in a magazine!
3. *Shameless Showing Off.* I presented Rhiannon and Gareth with autographed copies. I posted three to the Mothership and emailed a scanned version in case the wait would be too much for her. Or me.
4. *Bashful Pride* when the Mothership sent a text upon reading the article: U R 1 FOXY LADY!
5. *Over-analysis.* Once the novelty factor had worn off and I'd read the copy 1,000 times, all that remained was to stare at my photo and play Spot the Flaw. Necklace crooked. Arms wobbly. Bra grossly unsupportive. When you're a few pages away from Sienna bloody Miller you can't help compare and contrast.

   There was also a story about some *Grazia* readers who'd won tickets to an exclusive party attended by famous racing drivers. They were all tanned and slender with flimsy little dresses that folk with stomach rolls and jelly arms can only dream about. They were meant to be Real Readers. And so was I!

How could we belong in the same pages? Naturally, this sent me spiralling into . . .

6. *Mortification*. What if somebody I knew read the story? What would they think of my secret lardy past? What if they read all my self-indulgent rantings on the internet? What would they think of me then? Thankfully, by then Tuesday had rolled around again, so it was on to . . .

7. *Acceptance*. The next issue of *Grazia* will come out tomorrow without me in it. I'll soon be wrapping fish and chips and being crapped on by budgies across Britain.

WEEK 237.5
28 July 2005

I've totally gotten away with that *Grazia* episode! If anyone saw it they've been kind enough not to say anything. So I think it's safe to carry on sending my ramblings into the void.

I had a moment of clarity in my RPM class today. I was trying to ignore how the bike seat was bruising my girly bits so my thoughts drifted to my shiny red mug in the magazine. Why didn't I want anyone to see that article? Why am I still afraid to talk about my weight loss and my writing?

It seems that despite all this weight I've lost, I still have my head buried in a big greasy bucket of Fat Girl beliefs. Some examples:

- I am inferior to anyone thinner than me.
- Any success I have is undeserved, or at best a really big fluke.
- No matter how much weight I lose, I'll still look like a Big Girl to most people.
- Nobody wants to hear about my weight loss success. They'll just think, 'Why'd you get so bloody fat in the first place?'
- And if I was to celebrate my achievements, people might think I'm a raging egomaniac.
- And therefore would no longer like me.
- Therefore it is better to keep quiet and be mediocre.

I'm beginning to realize that this is pure bullshit. It's like saying to the world, 'Here, folks! Let me save you the energy of making assumptions about me, I've already done it for you!' It's also arrogant to assume that my perfectly intelligent and compassionate friends and acquaintances would think that way.

The reality is, the only person making these assumptions is me. Why do I still insist on viewing the world through the eyes of the Fat Girl? I know there is more to me than my weight, but I'm reluctant to let go of my favourite excuse. When I blame my fat, I don't feel rejection or failure or disappointment. I don't let unpleasant feelings get right through to the core, they just bounce off the blubber.

During the shoot I felt so envious of the photographer and the make-up artist; how they were so confident and comfortable in their own skin. The make-up artist was relaxed and chatty as she dabbed away at my mug, knowing exactly what colours she wanted to use and how to fix my hair. The photographer loped casually around the room, arranging the lighting and peering through viewfinders.

What's their secret? I thought. Where do I get me some of that?

But looking at my photograph I can see it in my eyes and smile, lurking just below the surface. Happiness. Confidence. Ambition. I just need to find the balls to admit that it's there and decide what to do with it.

WEEK 238
1 August 2005

'So do you want beans in a tin, haggis in a tin, or beef tongue in a tin?'

We were at the supermarket getting camping provisions. Gareth has been obsessed with the great out-doors lately. First he said he needed a new sleeping bag because his old one smelt like 'Man Fumes'. But he ended up buying two. And a tent. And a camp stove. Before I knew it I'd agreed to spend a night with the mountains and midges at Glen Etive.

It wasn't until we were at the supermarket that I began to get excited about our expedition. I wanted to buy one of those dinky disposable barbecues so we could grill vegetarian sausages into charcoaled stumps. I wanted to toast marshmallows over a roaring fire. I wanted to roast potatoes in the coals. Food food food. Food makes every-thing more interesting!

Only a few days earlier I'd been thinking, *There's*

absolutely nothing happening this week. No magazine shoots, no weddings; just a Perfect Empty Week. I'll be able to achieve seven days of Perfect Eating. Woohoo! But this was instantly forgotten when the camping trip came up, and now I was giddy with its feasting potential.

I had another epiphany right there in the supermarket aisle – there is really no such thing as a Perfectly Empty Week. For the past four and a half years I've been holding on to a misguided hope that there would come a day when I'd finally triumph and achieve perfection. But unless I revert to my old hermit life there will always be something getting in the way, whether it's a spontaneous camping trip, workplace cakes or a quick drink with friends.

That horrible phrase Lifestyle Change is really true. This is not going to end when I get to my goal weight. I will have to keep reading labels. I will have to keep thinking about what I eat. I will have to assess each situation individually and try to make the healthiest choice. All these little events that crop up will keep on cropping up. They're just life happening, not opportunities for wild, abandoned eating.

We ended up in the canned food aisle, deciding on a Tin of Something since we were only away overnight. Good Lord, you can buy some awful shit in a tin. Gareth chose a vegetable balti curry. I almost went for the Weight Watchers Ravioli, but what self-respecting ravioli would be seen in a tin? After reading some labels and tossing aside the trans-fatty candidates, I settled on a hearty beef stew. Then we bought apples, tea and shortbread.

My beef stew looked a lot like dog food and didn't taste much better. But I felt good about my choices as we sat under the stars in front of our campfire. I'll never be perfect, but I don't have to be out of control either. I'm going to find that middle ground.

There are a number of ways you can be awoken on a Sunday morning. With a nice cup of tea. Or a bacon roll. Or a leisurely shag. Or seeing your big mug inside Scotland's biggest tabloid newspaper.

There's me and my long-suffering husband on page 22 of today's *Sunday Mail* with the headline NET LOSS. They printed a gigantic wedding photo and went for the *Fat Chick Loses Lard Then Finds Love* angle. At least Gareth can share in the joy of seeing your pixillated face hogging half a page.

The paper saw the *Grazia* story and wanted to do its own piece. It seemed like a reasonable idea at the time but now I'm running around our flat in a grand panic, wondering if anyone I know reads the *Sunday Mail*. I am hoping they're more *Herald* or *Observer* people, so no one comes up to me in the kitchen tomorrow saying, 'So! You were pretty lardy, eh?'

Meanwhile, Gareth is still cackling over the Before photo in the article. Not at me directly, just the bizarre way they chopped me out from the background of the original photograph from my twenty-first birthday party then wrapped the text around my bulbous, disembodied form. So I just hover on the page, Jabba the Hut style.

They chopped the birthday cake out of the picture too, except for the flaming sparklers on top, so it looks like my guts have exploded.

It is utterly mortifying to see yourself floating in a national newspaper, yet the more I stare at it the funnier it becomes. But I'm going to punch Gareth if he doesn't stop laughing soon.

WEEK 240
15 August 2005

Apologies for the lengthy silence around here, I've been busy hiding in a dark room, rocking back and forth and speaking in tongues. It's been an interesting week, to say the least.

It finally happened, people. The mask is off. Dietgirl has been OUTED to all and sundry!

I admit that I'm a moron when it comes to all things arithmetical and statistical, so perhaps that's why I'd convinced myself that even though the *Sunday Mail* sells millions of copies, none of my acquaintances would be among its readers. I mean, surely they'd go for something a wee bit more highbrow?

Even so, I tiptoed into the office extra early on Monday morning, determined to keep a low profile. But right away a colleague ambushed me in the foyer.

'Morning.'

'Why hello!' she grinned. 'And how are *you*?'

Uh-oh.

'I opened the paper yesterday morning and I thought,

369

that looks like Shauna. And it was! I got the shock of my life!'

'Oh!'

And so it went all week. There were smiles, gasps, and heads shaken in disbelief. There were jokes, sideways looks and hush-hush conversations. Some people even brought in the clipping and passed it round their department.

But everyone has been lovely. Surprised, but lovely. They had no idea that I was larger before I came to Scotland, so I suppose it's understandable that they were shocked to have their Sunday morning cornflakes interrupted by my pudgy floating head.

The attention made me squirm, because despite my amazing NET LOSS! I am still bigger than 95 per cent of my colleagues. I wanted to get a T-shirt that says *I'm not done yet*. Now every time someone so much glances at me I'm worried they're trying to picture me twice as wide.

The most infuriating moment was when I got cornered waiting for the lift. That'll teach me not to take the stairs!

'I heard about your . . . *article*,' my colleague said in a stage whisper. 'It's amazing. But I just can't picture you being so . . . so . . . you know. Big!'

'Oh?'

'I mean, 25 stone!' Her face wrinkled up with mild distaste as though she'd said, 'I mean, two vaginas!' or 'Sleeping with horses!'

My body crackled with irritation. I'm extremely protective of my larger former self. I'm still the same person I was back then, just with slightly better eating and exercise habits! Sometimes I think I should have been an alcoholic;

it seems a more socially acceptable character kink. Obesity just isn't glamorous.

Yesterday Grant came up to me and leaned on my desk. 'So,' he said. 'I've got a sprawling beer belly, eh?'

'What?'

'I was reading your website last night.'

'Oh?'

'Does August 2004 ring any bells? You were describing someone very familiar!'

Shit shit shit! I'd written about him! And his former sprawling beer belly! I believed I'd described him as having an assortment of chins.

'I'm sorry!' I blurted. 'I was just jealous of you, flaunting your baggy trousers around the office!'

'Don't worry,' he grinned. 'I showed it to my wife too. It's not every day you find someone talking about your trousers on the internet.'

Oh God. How horrifying to hear your own words coming back at you from a real live person! For all these years I've been secretly typing away and thinking only imaginary cyber folk were reading. I've been so careful to use pseudonyms and not write anything that could weed me out in a Google search, but now my hysterically guarded anonymity has been destroyed!

There is no escape. Here are a few choice vignettes from the past week.

Scene 1: The vending machine at work.

SHAUNA: Bugger! It's out of Snickers. I really wanted a
    Snickers.

371

COLLEAGUE: Should you even be anywhere near that machine, *Dietgirl*?

Scene 2: At the train station.
[*My friend Richard spots me and runs over.*]
RICHARD: Hey! I saw you in the paper!
SHAUNA: Shit!
RICHARD: What a surprise, eh? You're the Diet Lady! Hello Diet Lady! Hey, don't look embarrassed; it's so cool. BE PROUD, DIET LADY! . . . it is Diet Lady, isn't it?

Poor Gareth has been copping it too. His friend Steve said, 'Mate, when you get married people usually put a photo in the local rag, not the *Sunday Mail*!' Then a client left a message: 'Nice to see you've found yourself a little wife on the internet.'

I've spent a few days in mourning. Dietgirl has been my outlet during this epic expedition and I naïvely failed to consider how the article might change that. For someone who used to regularly take refuge in the bottom of a cupboard, I feel exposed knowing my last hideaway is gone.

But I'm trying to look at this experience in a positive light. How many people can say they were tabloid news?

More importantly, I know it's time to stop hiding. Back when I was twice as big, I felt like half the person I wanted to be. I hid myself away from the world and made as little fuss as possible. Since I took up so much physical space, I tried to make my personality small. So my virtual space was where I could freely express myself and talk about my weight, something I was too ashamed to do in person.

But now everybody knows and it turns out it's not a big deal after all. I always worried that people would look at me differently if they knew about my past. But instead they've just said they were proud of me, even inspired.

I'm going to be proud too. I look back at my early writing and it's shocking to see how my words were full of venom and self-loathing. I'm torn between wanting to hug my old self or kick her arse. But I'm not ashamed or contemptuous any more. I'm proud of myself for surviving those darker days just as much as I'm proud of losing the weight.

So no more virtual double-life. I don't need a secret place to be my real self, because I'm being my real self all the time now, both online and out there in the big bad world. Now that I'm out I'm going to be proud. I'm tired of worrying about what people think when they're probably not thinking anything at all.

Week 241
22 August 2005

I've discovered the ultimate weight loss secret: Become a fussy eater!

There was a time when the right time for food was *any time* and the right food was *any food*. But now I've cultivated a certain snobbishness, and it has to be the right food, at the best time of day or week, consumed in the perfect locale with the planets in correct alignment.

373

The best example is chocolate. Green & Black's is now my preferred brand. I don't like to eat it on a Sunday night, because I've got work the next day. The middle of the week is no good either, because I'm always busy exercising or washing my hair with a teacup. Ideally I save it for a Friday night, when I know the working week is behind me and there's nothing else I should be thinking about. Then the next morning I can wake up and think fondly, *How about that great chocolate I ate last night?*

In the old days I'd buy half a kilo of cooking chocolate, hide in my room and cram it into my mouth in a frenzy. Now I get one of those tiny 35-gram bars and eat it on the couch with Gareth sitting beside me. He's usually reading or on the laptop so I'll close my eyes, savouring both my delicious treat and the marital harmony.

These days it's all about mindful consumption. I get annoyed if I succumb to a crappy bar from the vending machine or chomp M&Ms in the dark at the movies. If I can only have a tiny wee portion of chocolate then I should pay attention to the moment! If I eat chocolate in the dark, how do I know I really ate it? Did it really happen?

I'm finally making my peace with food. Sometimes it's just everyday fuel for my athletic endeavours but sometimes it's a moment to treasure. I don't punish myself for eating something indulgent, and nor do I go overboard when I fancy a treat.

Example of progress:

2000 – ATE: 2-litre tub of ice-cream. REACTION: Complete meltdown and minimum seven-day banishment to the Self Loathing Pit.

2005 – ATE: Mars Bar. REACTION: 'Oh well, I'll eat less tomorrow.'

It's getting better all the time. I'm not as obsessed with food as I used to be. I've managed to tame it into unbridled enthusiasm!

WEEK 244
12 September 2005
13st 7lb (85.9kg, 189lb)
11st 8lb lost (73.6kg, 162lb) – 1st 10lb to go (10.9kg, 24lb)

I've been so busy being a media tart that I almost forgot there's only two weeks until we go to Australia for Wedding Part III!

I can't wait to get back home. I've been glued to *Neighbours* and swooning at the sound of Aussie voices. I got tearful at my BodyPump class this morning when the Shoulder track was an AC/DC tune. I keep poring over our itinerary, my budget spreadshcct and my folder full of tickets and hotel confirmations. I've even made a list of my lists:

- Gifts to Purchase!
- Tours to Organize!
- Fake Wedding Vows to Write!
- People to See after a 2.5 Year Absence!
- Things to Pack!
- Things I Want to Eat!

The one item that will remain unchecked is Get to Goal. I was 15 stone 11 pounds and size 22 when I left and I'm 13 stone 7 pounds and a size 16 now. That doesn't sound as impressive as I'd imagined earlier this year, but somehow it doesn't seem to matter now. Overall I've still lost a whole Gareth!

What matters is that I feel completely new. I look in the mirror and purr at my reflection instead of wanting to destroy it. I'm fascinated by how my body is gradually revealing its shape after hiding behind those extra layers. I used to worry I'd end up with floppy excess skin but the leisurely pace of my weight loss has given things time to adjust. Every day there's something new to admire. I've got broad shoulders and a pretty collarbone. My waist is shrinking and sadly my chest is too. I've got curvy hips and chunky thighs. I've got pillowy upper arms that lead to slender wrists and hands with long fingers. I even have ankles now, thanks to all those RPM classes. My body is a mass of contradictions – muscle and curves, stretch marks and strength – but I'm starting to embrace it all.

So when I go back to Australia, for the first time I want to see people and I want them to see me. I'm feeling foxy and I'm ready for my close-up!

WEEK 247
3 October 2005

Australia looked exactly how I'd left it. The same empty blue skies, sinewy gum trees and sun so bright my eyes watered. So much has happened to me since I left, I thought maybe the landscape would have undergone a parallel transformation.

But with Gareth beside me it was like seeing the country for the first time. He pressed his nose against the window as I drove along the sprawling avenues of Canberra.

'Whoa! Look at that big pink *parrot*!'

'Ahh,' I laughed. 'That's a galah.'

'But it's just sitting there beside the road. It's huge! And . . . there's white ones too!'

'They're cockatoos.'

'We've only been here ten minutes and there's crazy wildlife everywhere! When do we get to see some killer snakes?'

The most spectacular creature of all was the Mothership. We pulled up at her house in Goulburn to find her hopping from one foot to the other, looking three stone lighter and twenty years younger.

'Hello, Daughter! Hello, Son-in-Law!'

'Mothership! You've shrunk!'

'Haven't I just?' She grinned proudly and did a little twirl. 'These are your fat old jeans that you gave me in Edinburgh. Size 18!'

'You look amazing. Is it all that walking?'

'The gym too,' she said, 'I'm into weights and all that.'

'Wow!'

'You inspired me. I said to myself, if Shauna can do it, why the bloody hell can't I?'

'Why not, indeed.'

'It's different this time, I can just feel it. I'm finally doing it for the right reasons. I don't do diets any more. I just want to live to a ripe old age and make the most of my life, you know?'

'Yep!'

'I'm a new woman, Shauna. I don't even tape *Oprah* every day now. I just don't need to,' she said breezily. 'I only tape it if the episode is going to be particularly relevant to me.'

'Well! You have truly reformed.'

'Thank you, darling!'

'But you know all this means you're no longer Too Fat to make the tea. Get that kettle on!'

After we'd been watered the Mothership said, 'We'll need to do a quick trip to Coles. But I promise I only need a few things!'

Fort the first time I didn't want to wait in the car. I dragged Gareth up and down every aisle of the supermarket, showing him the culinary delights of my fair nation, all the new things and all the old friends I'd missed. The tropical fruits unencumbered by plastic packaging and air miles. The piles of affordable seafood. The superior Australian varieties of Cadbury's Dairy Milk.

'And here we have the biscuit aisle,' I indicated with a sweeping gesture.

Gareth nodded with suitable reverence.

'Wow, look at all these different kinds of Tim Tams!' I spluttered. 'They didn't have all those before I left. Look at them, Gareth. Look at them!'

'I'm looking!'

I fought the urge to gather them all up in my tender

arms. People always seem amazed that I've managed to lose weight in Scotland, land of tablet, Irn Bru and deep-fried everything. But it's much worse in Australia, where everything is delicious.

WEEK 247.5
7 October 2005

Today I pawed through boxes of childhood stuff, showing Gareth my photos and prizes and mementoes. It was strange seeing him sitting in my mother's house, leafing through a pile of CDs and laughing at my questionable teenage taste. Until now my Australian years and Scottish years felt like two different lifetimes, but having Gareth on my home turf seemed to bring it all together.

And then I found what I'd been looking for, nestled alongside a dozen Sweet Valley High books. My size 26 jeans. I'd given them to Mum because she'd had a wacky idea of making a patchwork quilt out of my old fat clothes.

I shook them out and held them up against my body.

'Whoa!' said Gareth. 'Were they yours?'

'Yep. My biggest pair.'

'You've got to put them on!'

I stepped inside. I could lift the waistband up to my chin. As soon as I let go they fell to the floor in a blue puddle.

'Whoa!' Gareth said again.

I pulled them back up, stretched out the waistband and

379

peered down into the empty space. It was shocking to get a true sense of the Before and After.

The Mothership peeked in. 'Oh my God! I'm getting the camera.'

'Aww, Ma!'

'Come outside in the sunshine. This is going to be gold!'

So I stood in the backyard striking poses. I held the waistband out in the traditional Where Did My Belly Go? position then climbed into one leg for the requisite Half the Woman I Used To Be shot.

'Right Gareth,' Mum directed. 'You hop into the other leg.'

It was an awkward squeeze but we managed to do it: my husband and I both inside the jeans that I once couldn't fit into on my own.

Afterwards we gathered round the camera to review the shots.

'Here's Gareth getting into your pants,' said Mum. 'And right in front of his mother-in-law!'

'Jeez, my arse looks kinda big in those jeans.'

'Shauna,' Gareth laughed, 'you're standing in *one leg* of them!'

'Oh yeah! You've got a point there.'

Mum was shaking her head. 'Can you believe you used to wear these?'

'Not really.'

The memory is distant and fuzzy. It just seems impossible that I'd ever filled all that space.

I've just spent two weeks eating my way around Australia. It started in Cowra, where Nanny wooed her new grandson-in-law with vast amounts of home baking. I had intended to show restraint to maximize my svelteness for Wedding Part III, but I was seduced by Nanny's sweet treats and flattering words.

'Shauna,' she said. 'You are looking very slim.'

'Do you think so? Really?'

'Oh yes.'

'Why, thank you!'

'Do you fancy some of my passion fruit cheesecake?'

'Don't mind if I do!'

Really, it would have been rude not to, especially as she'd been baking all night despite her painful arthritis. That's why I also had a lamington and two pieces of caramel slice to show that I truly appreciated her efforts.

I'd made a pact with myself only to eat the things I really wanted on this trip – all the things I'd truly missed while living in the UK. The only problem was it turned out I truly missed a lot of things. When the tour rolled on to Canberra, I dived into al fresco café breakfasts, luscious non-greasy pizzas, giant smoothies and a good old Aussie hamburger with the works, including fried egg, bacon and beetroot.

In Melbourne I rediscovered decadent hot chocolates, Turkish banquets, sweet potato fries, chocolate thick-shakes in old-fashioned metal cups, papaya salad and elaborate pastries from the bakeries in St Kilda. In

Queensland, on the Sunshine Coast, we feasted on fresh pineapple and strawberries from a roadside stall.

What can I say? I love good food, and Australia is a well-stocked nation. I'd forgotten the joys of eating outdoors with the sun gently toasting your skin. I'd missed lazy hours in cafés and restaurants that don't cripple your bank balance. Which brings us to Sydney and those $20 sushi platters.

Despite all that eating, I feel calm. For the first time I'm not neurotic about calorie contents or fighting the urge to overeat or wondering if people think I'm fatter than last time they saw me. I just feel like a normal person, savouring the company of old friends, both human and edible. The sensible salads and soup will be right there waiting for me back in Scotland.

And of course it was my duty as an Australian to introduce my Scottish husband to as many local delights as possible. He's now seen the Sydney Harbour Bridge and the Great Ocean Road, but somehow it meant more to me to watch him scoff his first fresh oyster, his first steaming bowl of Vietnamese pho and his first juicy kangaroo steak. It's nice to feel stuffed with happy memories, instead of stuffed with remorse.

WEEK 250
24 October 2005

I stood at the top of the makeshift aisle, clutching a bouquet of irises from Nanny's garden. I'd only needed about ten minutes to get ready for Wedding Part III as I

382

finally had the routine off pat. Hair, make-up, squishy undies. And magically, the frock fitted perfectly. I could even zip it up all by myself!

We'd decided to conduct a mock wedding ceremony to give things a sense of occasion, kind of like those dramatic reconstructions on *Crimewatch*. Mum had found a lovely café for the party with a great courtyard and garden, perfect for a pretend wedding.

I was overcome by mushiness as I surveyed the scene. The Mothership was about to pretend to give me away, looking dazzling in her new size 16 suit. Gareth looked handsome and golden after three weeks under the Australian sun. Beside him was my friend Belinda, looking stunning in her role as Gareth's Best Girl. The finishing touch was my friend Matt playing the part of Minister.

Jenny took her role as imaginary bridesmaid very seriously. She spontaneously bellowed the Wedding March as she led the way down the aisle, 'DUN DUN DUN-DUUUUN!'

I followed her as daintily as I could manage in my flimsy gold flip-flops. I surveyed the guests – my aunties with their golf-ball perms, my gorgeous friends with their assortment of partners and babies. I'd vowed to look dignified and classy because we'd hired a photographer but I couldn't stop grinning.

The Mothership took my hand and squeezed it tight. Matt cleared his throat and pulled a priest's collar out of his pocket and plopped it over his head.

'We are gathered here today to celebrate the marriage of Shauna and Gareth. Marriage is a sacred institution, one that is not to be entered into lightly. Therefore, as today is Shauna and Gareth's fourth wedding this year, we can all be safe in the knowledge that they are pretty serious about it by now.

'So, who takes this woman away from this man, and then gives her back again?'

'I do! I do!' said Mum.

'Excellent.' He turned to Gareth. 'Gareth David Reid, do you promise to keep on loving Shauna, in sickness and in health, for richer and for poorer; even though she always leaves bits of food on the plates when she does the dishes?'

'I do.'

'Excellent. Now Shauna Lee Reid, do you promise to keep on loving Gareth, in sickness and in health, for richer and for poorer; even though you still can't always understand his Scottish accent?'

'I do!'

'Do we have the wedding rings?'

Jenny and Belinda dutifully coughed up the bling.

'Gareth,' said Reverend Matt: 'Please take your wife's hand and repeat after me. With this ring, I re-wed.'

'With this ring, I re-wed.'

Matt smiled. 'Shauna, take that Scotsman by the hand and repeat after me. With this ring, I re-wed.'

'With this ring, I re-wed.'

'I now pronounce you, once again, husband and wife,' Matt said triumphantly. 'You may kiss the bride!'

I'd forgotten that some of the guests hadn't seen me for years. The reactions ranged from, 'Oh my God, look at

YOU! You're so SKINNY!' to simple demands to know my weight loss secrets.

'You're looking great, you know,' said one aunt. 'Really, really, really great!' Which perhaps was a polite way of saying: Holy CRAP you were fat before. I didn't want to say anything at the time but I was worried you might explode! So what a relief to see you somewhat deflated!

The afternoon passed in a glorious blur, fuelled by champagne and mild sunburn. I recall explaining to my aunties numerous times that no, Matthew wasn't a real priest, he was just pretending. Sometimes I just stood back for a while and watched, trying to soak up every detail. My old friends immersed in conversation, my aunty's startled expression as she took her first ever bite of sushi, the curious sight of Gareth in sunglasses, and the Mothership's slightly sozzled laughter. I never was one of those chicks who fantasized about their wedding day, but somehow this tri-continental spectacle turned out to be more incredible than anything I could have ever dreamed up.

Later on all the Cowra High School clan gathered at the bowling club for Steak Diane and chicken schnitzels. Gareth ordered fish and chips for the fifteenth time on our trip, vowing to resume his vegetarian lifestyle as soon as we got home.

It's been ten years since we left school. It was incredible to see the different paths my friends had taken while still retaining all the wit and charm that carried me through my high school days.

'So what have you been up to since I last saw you,

Shauna?' asked Sharon. 'Aside from all your weddings?'

Damn. I'd been dreading that question. 'I'm still a secretary,' I said with a self-deprecating laugh. 'Putting that journalism degree to great use!'

'Hang on,' Jenny piped up. 'What about your writing? Shauna was in a book!'

'Oh yeah,' I mumbled. 'That.'

'You were in a book? Wow!'

'Yeah.'

'So what was it about?'

And that was when I realized most of my friends still had no idea about my Incredible Transformation. I quietly slipped off the radar after the glut of 21st birthday parties, determined not to let them see me at my worst.

Gareth leaned over and whispered, 'Be proud, Diet Lady!'

I took a deep breath. 'Well . . . it's a bit complicated, really. Basically after we left school I got grossly over-weight and severely depressed. And then I lost a load of lard. I wrote about it on the internet and then I wrote about it for a book!'

So there it was, ten years in my life wrapped up in a sentence. 'Umm, that's about it, really.'

'Shauna, are you crazy?' said Jenny. 'That's bloody fantastic!'

'Yeah!' chimed in Sharon. 'I always loved your writing.'

'Ahh, thanks.'

'You should be proud. We're all proud!'

I stared down at my plate and counted the ridges in the crinkle-cut chips. Gareth gave my knee a squeeze under the table.

Is that what the past decade really boils down to? My fat? I spent the first five years accumulating ridiculous amounts of it; then the next five obsessed with making it go away. That's not something to really crow about. It only reminds me that as a pampered Westerner I had the luxury of being able to 'achieve' obesity in the first place.

But as I listened to the burble of chatter around the dinner table, I realized that while it might feel like the last ten years were all about my fat, other people don't see it that way. My friends asked about my writing and my travels and my love life. And when they told Gareth stories about our high school antics, not once did my size rate a mention.

I wanted to cry right there at the table, thinking of how I'd actively avoided these people for so many years, thinking I was unworthy of their friendship. I viewed my world through the fat goggles and assumed that's how they saw me too. I told so many lies and hid so many secrets. Who knows how different things could have been if I'd just reached out?

I'm longing for the day when I can look back at these long years of lard busting and it will simply be a throwaway sentence. Like 'I went to university' or 'I got married'. It will just be 'I was fat but then I wasn't'. It's still too raw right now, but I know one day it will become part of the landscape. Just another story to tell.

After dinner we took a nostalgic stroll down Cowra's steep main street. I pointed out my old haunts to Gareth – the KFC, the Chinese takeaway, the cinema where I ate all that free popcorn. But there were non-fat landmarks

387

too – the Motor Registry where I'd spectacularly failed my driving test, our mailbox at the Post Office, the Clints Crazy Bargains shop where the prices are just *crazy*.

We ended up at the Town House, usually a happening nightspot but dead on a Sunday night. We got turfed out before we had a chance to down our first drinks. So we called our parents to pick us up. Just like old times, except now we all had mobiles and didn't have to queue at the phone box.

We all stood there in the deserted street, watching the traffic lights flip lazily between red, yellow and green. It was surreal to be here again, just as we were ten years ago except with a collection of partners and husbands and experiences.

And for the first time I felt I belonged. I wasn't hiding anything. I'd always tried to compartmentalize the pieces of my life – keeping friends and family far away from my darker thoughts, separating first with emotional distance, then with physical distance. But as I stood there with my re-newly-wedded husband and my oldest friends, I finally felt it all come together. Big Shauna, Smaller Shauna, Old Shauna, New Shauna. It's all me. From now there's just going to be one Shauna for every occasion.

EPILOGUE

WEEK 333
28 May 2007
12st 7.5lb (79.8kg, 175.5lb)
12st 7.5lb lost (79.7kg, 175.5lb)

I'd always pictured the perfect ending. Just as I thought there'd be a grand epiphany for me to start losing weight, I thought there'd be an equally spectacular moment when I finished. Sunbeams would stream through the window as I stepped on the scale, and the magic number would appear just as the last sliver of excess fat fell from my body. I'd be presented with a bouquet and tiara and then I'd tearfully declare my mission complete.

I returned to Scotland after Wedding Part III all fired up to secure my happy ending. I'd gained four pounds on the trip, taking me back up to 13 stone 11 pounds, so I had a neat two stone left to lose.

I was consumed by the need to finish the job properly. I couldn't fight the flab for six long years only to let it just fizzle out. And what about the hundreds of people around the world who'd faithfully tuned into my adventures? Didn't I owe them all a grand finale?

The pounds came off painfully slowly. I was thoroughly fed up with calorie counting and weekly weigh-ins and longed for the day when I could hurl the scale off a cliff and just live like a normal healthy person. I daydreamed about being a grizzly bear in hibernation. I'd only need one winter! I'd live off my body fat, snooze away the last two stone then emerge from my cave in the springtime, all slender and complete.

By August 2006 I'd dropped 18 more pounds and finally reached the magical milestone of 12 stone 7 pounds lost. I'd shed half my body weight. My inner statistician rejoiced at the beautiful symmetry of it all, and when I took some progress photos in my new size 14 jeans I was proud of what I saw. I felt confident, sexy and content. I felt *done*.

But how could I possibly be done? I was still fat in the eyes of the Body Mass Index chart. Surely my successes didn't really count until I reached that number? I'd made a public commitment way back in 2001, so I couldn't give up so close to the end. I was Dietgirl, darn it. I was supposed to be a weight loss superhero!

For the next few months I was obsessed with reaching that mystical goal weight of 11 stone 11 pounds. But the harder I tried, the more the scale refused to budge and I began to see elevens in my sleep. They frolicked hand in hand through meadows, laughing at my inability to catch them. I grew panicky and impatient, and instead of keeping faith in my tried-and-true formula of sensible eating and exercise, I scoured my old diet books in the hope of finding a better way. In a fit of lunacy I even went back to Weight Watchers for a month, until I overheard a woman complaining she'd gained weight because she'd worn heavier socks than usual.

Finally in January 2007, on the sixth anniversary of my lard-busting adventures, I stopped and asked myself, *What the hell am I doing? Haven't I learned anything? Why am I torturing myself?*

For six years I'd battled to achieve a balanced approach but now I'd fallen back into my old, obsessive ways. And what for? I was fit and healthy. I liked my body. I liked being me. And that was what I'd wanted more than anything when I'd stood under the clothesline all those years ago. But all those positives were being trampled by my goal weight fixation.

I decided to try a radical experiment and just *stop*. No more number crunching, no more ritual weigh-ins and no deadlines. Obsessing was getting me nowhere, so I resolved to just let go and see where my instincts took me.

Why hadn't I tried this tactic before?

I'd always been slightly suspicious of my achievements. Despite losing a mighty twelve and a half stone it somehow felt like a hefty stroke of luck. Me, a success story? I worried that I was one bar of chocolate away from being 25 stone again. How could this person doing all the exercise be me? Am I really someone who chooses brown rice more often than cake?

Even though I hadn't followed a diet for years, I'd been clinging to the dieter's mindset, taking comfort from the rules and rituals and boundaries. What would I do if I weren't obsessing? Would my healthy habits come undone without the fear of a weekly weigh-in? What if it's all been a six-year fluke?

But letting go turned out to be liberating and empowering. Instead of worrying about weight loss, I simply did the things I'd do if I were already at my Happy Ending weight.

I focused on my fitness because getting sweaty had always made me feel sound and strong. I developed a thirst for new activities and each one indulged a different side of my personality, from the serenity of yoga and Pilates to the gruelling pleasures of canoeing and cycling. I explored my aggressive streak with kickboxing classes. I laced up my boxing gloves, thought of everyone who'd ever annoyed me and just let fly. After all those years of kicking thin air at BodyCombat it was thrilling to finally connect with something. I loved the sound of my foot smacking the pad, *pow pow pow!*

I also took up hill walking with Gareth. I grumbled with every step as I'd done on Mount Ainslie, but secretly revelled in the ache and burn of my leg muscles as we made our ascent. Every time I reached the top I thought of the Old Shauna hiding in the house with the blinds drawn, so disconnected from her body and surroundings. I longed to drag her into the wilderness so she could know this beautiful silence and feel the cold air on her skin.

I even tackled my lifelong fear of the pool and signed up for swimming lessons. I was nauseous with panic beforehand, so pale and wobbly in my new swimsuit. But my teacher led me into the water with the soothing, encouraging tones she normally reserved for hysterical toddlers. Soon she had me thrashing up and down the pool in a messy front crawl, too busy concentrating to be self-conscious. I felt strong as I pulled my body along, yet peaceful and serene as the water enveloped me. Afterwards I relished the chlorine sting in my eyes and proudly crossed item number 1 off my 'Things To Do When I'm Skinny' list.

Recently a friend and I were preening in front of the mirror, as we got ready for a night out on the town.

'God, I'm so fat,' she muttered. 'Look at my gut. It's huge!'

I frowned at my own reflection, trying to select a fault to contribute to the conversation.

In the old days I'd have blurted automatically, 'That's nothing, look at my hefty arse! And watch I don't slap you with my arm flab!' But now I realized I had nothing to say. I no longer saw my body as a collection of flaws. My body was something to savour and celebrate. I looked in the mirror and saw sparkling eyes and glossy lips curved into a confident smile. Instead of the old shapeless sacks, I'd poured myself into a figure-hugging dress that showcased my nippy waist and rounded hips. Every time I put on high heels and jewellery and lipstick and perfume it felt like I was singing to the world about the joy I'd found within.

So I had no desire to put myself down, not even in jest for sisterly solidarity. I realized that you have to be your own superhero. I'd always been desperate for approval and validation from others but now I know that the real pleasure comes from impressing yourself. Now after a lifetime of self-loathing you could drop me on a runway with a pack of supermodels and I'd still be happy. They've got their look and I've got mine.

Way back at the start of my journey I was in deep denial that I was seriously overweight. Now I know the situation has reversed – I've been in denial that I'm healthy and slim. But over the past few months, just as in the beginning, all the evidence has come at me in little bursts of awareness. How I'm optimistic by default. How I exercise purely for the joy of it, not to make my body more pleasant to the masses. How my eating is instinctive and balanced but with room for guilt-free indulgence. How they have no trouble finding a vein when I donate blood. How I can fit into size 12 skirts at H&M. How I can walk past a bakery without being restrained on a leash. How instead of thinking, 'These are things I must do to lose weight' I now truly believe, 'This is just how I live my life.'

I decided it was time to revisit my 'Things To Do When I'm Skinny' list. With a flourish and a red marker I ticked off each item, savouring the thick lines slashing through what I'd thought were impossible dreams. I felt a surge of pride, realizing that I hadn't waited for official Skinniness to achieve them.

And now there were only two things remaining.

5. Buy some sexy leather trousers.

What the hell was I thinking there? I must have been

going through some sort of Jim Morrison phase. I'm sure you'll forgive me for abandoning that one.

Then my heart leapt into my throat as I read the very last item.

6. Have a full body massage.

Rhiannon and I headed into the English countryside for a girly spa weekend. I'd booked my massage for the very last day, giving me plenty of time to work myself up into a traditional Fat Girl Freak Out. When my massage therapist finally collected me, I felt like a bathrobed lamb being led to the slaughter.

She told me to undress and make myself comfortable. I couldn't believe this was really happening. Back when I made my 'Skinny' list I was ashamed to hang my knickers on the clothesline, let alone parade them in front of a stranger. But here I was, six years later in a soft-lit room, completely naked except for my brand new size 12 knickers.

I lay down on the massage table and put my face over the hole. Her hands were warm and tender but my body was knotted tight. It felt strange and shocking to be touched with such firmness and purpose.

But soon I could feel myself letting go, as if I was melting into the table. I'd never felt so aware of my body, the space I filled and the shape I made. I imagined I was floating above, following the path of her touch. I felt her fingertips press into the strong curve of my shoulders, then down to my arms with their firm biceps and wobbly undersides. Then her palms were on my hips and waist tracing over the stretch marks that used to repulse me so much. Now they seemed like battle scars, tiny silver souvenirs. She moved on to my legs with their crazy blend of firm and dimpled flesh. She finished with my feet, once cracked and dried from supporting so much weight, but now soft and slender with painted toes.

I cried for the entire fifty-five minutes. My weight loss has been so slow – spread over two continents and six years – that I'd never quite grasped the enormity of the transformation. But today I finally felt the full scale of all this change. Six years ago I couldn't bear to look at myself in a mirror but now I felt proud. Every lump and bump of my body belonged to me and told the story of where I'd been. The emotions finally swam to the surface and poured out of my skin. So I cried, great honking sobs of joy and relief and release.

And that's when I knew I'd found my Perfect Ending. I actually found it a long time ago, but it's taken me a while to see it. I always thought I needed that number on the scale to prove that I'd earned this happiness, but from the moment I looked in the mirror and began to appreciate the view, I was already winning the prize.

I don't know where the scale will end up, but after 333 weeks and a lifetime of angst I'm not going to waste another minute worrying about it. My journey was never about what I weighed or the size of my jeans. The true reward is finding peace and acceptance and embracing my own skin, with all its quirks and charms.

So this is how it ends, my friends. There's no scale or tiara. It's just me here on the massage table, stripped down to my knickers and dripping tears and snot on to the floor.

It's time to make a new list. 'Things To Do Now I'm Happy'. It's time to find out what's next.

ACKNOWLEDGEMENTS

First and foremost, a million thank yous to the legendary Samone Bos for 'throwing a meddling paper plane in the right direction'.

Thank you to the lovely Sarah Emsley for all your insight and patience. Thanks also to Rebecca Jones, Emma Buckley, Miriam Rosenbloom and the good folks at Transworld.

Thanks to SJ Alexander, Sarfraz Ameerali, Maghie Connor, Jane Ewins, Rory Ewins, Jenny Hayes, Argyro Koutsou, Elaine McLaren, Peita Meadley, Cassie Penfold, Witold Riedel, Emma Robertson, Erin Shea, Vicki Spruce and Daniel Talsky for your friendship, encouragement and all-round grooviness.

Thank you to every single one of my wonderful blog friends and readers. I would have been lost and/or buried under a mountain of chocolate wrappers without your inspiration, support and humour over the years. Special thanks to Beth, Kek, Julia, Jillian, Meg, Row and Scott.

Cheers to my magnificent pals at Caledonia House for all the good times and great cakes.

I am indebted to my crack team of Crappy Draft Readers – Gareth, Rhiannon, Mum, Argyro, Vicki and Bronwyn Ingersole. Thank you for your eagle-eyed honesty.

A huge thank you to my family, especially Nanny, Hollie and James.

Love and gratitude to the Mothership for always being there, and never failing to be a Character.

Thank you Rhiannon for being my beloved best mate and the smartest dame on the planet. You're always teaching me something new, despite claiming you had nothing left to teach.

Finally to Gareth, fetcher of tea and Freddo Frogs. Thank you for your endless patience, support and good humour as I relived every moment and mood of the past six years while writing this book. I love you Doc, with all my heart. YOU RAWK!